THE CIRCUIT
OF FORCE

Occult Dynamics
of the Etheric Vehicle

THE CIRCUIT OF FORCE

Occult Dynamics of the Etheric Vehicle

by
DION FORTUNE
and
GARETH KNIGHT

THOTH PUBLICATIONS
Loughborough, Leicestershire.

Details of the "Work and Aims" of the
Society of the Inner Light, founded by Dion Fortune,
may be obtained by writing (with postage please) to the
Secretariat at 38 Steele's Road, London NW3 4RG

A CIP catalogue record for this book is
available from the British Library.

Cover design by Rebecca Mazonowicz

Published by Thoth Publications
64, Leopold Street, Loughborough, LE11 5DN
First published 1998

ISBN 978 1 870450 28 7

CONTENTS

INTRODUCTION

Between February 1939 and August 1940 Dion Fortune published a series of articles that she called *"The Circuit of Force"* in monthly instalments in *"The Inner Light Magazine"*. Fortunately the series was complete by the time the magazine ceased publication as a result of wartime paper rationing.

Her general theme was the recovery and practical application of what she called "the lost secrets of the West". She cast her net wide, from tantrik yoga to spiritualist development circles, from sexual conventions in current society to ceremonial magic.

In preparing this book for publication I have retained the sectional divisions of the original text and have given the date of the magazine issue in which each section appeared. As she almost certainly wrote most of the articles close to their time of publication, and probably in a great hurry, this dating throws an interesting light on her recent reading and writing and contemporary happenings, including the content of her weekly war letters, a selection of which I have edited under the title of Dion Fortune's *"The Magical Battle of Britain"*.

All I have done by way of editing is to correct one or two minor errors that escaped Dion Fortune's notice in the exigencies of the time; to provide section titles for her articles, and to break down some of the longer paragraphs into the shorter conventions of today. Although time has eroded some of the criticisms she had to make about contemporary moral attitudes, or conditions within her group, I have foregone the temptation to add expository footnotes as I feel neither Dion Fortune nor the intelligent reader needs any elbow jogging in this respect from me.

My accompanying text is in the form of five Commentaries on general background topics which will, I hope, give a broad background for the many hares that she has set running in the course of her stimulating series of articles. Together they should make up to a serious contribution to the informed and responsible use of the powers of the etheric vehicle.

GARETH KNIGHT

THE MYSTERIES OF EAST AND WEST

The Circuit of Force Part 1.1 [February 1939]
Dion Fortune

Part 1.1

It is not easy to convey Eastern thought to Western readers because the dictionary equivalent of the terms employed is very far from being their significance in mystical thought. It is well known to those who have penetrated beyond the Outer Court in these matters that there is a special use of language, a *double entendre* as it were, which is made use of whenever questions of practical procedure are under discussion, lest the once-born should discover the short cuts to the secret places of the soul. It is both right and necessary that this precaution should be used, and it will be observed in these pages; for these short cuts are effectual psychological devices, and can be made use of by the undedicated as well as the dedicated, and if they are employed by persons with unpurified and undisciplined minds can prove unfortunate for others as well as themselves. I would be the last to deny to an adult the right to burn his own fingers if he so desires. But I think it best to withhold from him the means of raising conflagrations in other folk.

Another difficulty in the way of conveying Eastern thought to Western readers lies in the fact that the attitude towards life of East and West is entirely different; it is strikingly illustrated by the sacred buildings in the two hemispheres. In the West, the central emblem commemorates suffering: in the East it commemorates joy. The men and women conditioned to these emblems naturally evaluate the experiences of life differently. As Kipling truly said: "The wildest dreams of Kew are the facts of Khatmandu, and the crimes of Clapham chaste in Martaban."

9

The best approach to Eastern thought is through a classical education. The Greek and the Hindu would have no difficulty in understanding each other; each has the same concept of Nature and the same regard for asceticism as a means to an end and not as an end in itself. Eastern thought, however, has penetrated far more deeply into natural religion than the Greeks had the capacity to do, and the Mysteries of Dionysos and Ceres are but pale shadows of their Eastern prototypes.

It may be not without value in this connection to examine what is known concerning the origin of the Greek Mysteries. It is believed, and for the grounds for this belief the reader may turn to the pages of *"Prolegomena to the study of Greek Religion"* by Jane Harrison, that when Greek national religion began to lose its hold on an increasingly enlightened people, an attempt was made, by no means unsuccessfully, to provide a rendering of it acceptable to thinking men by borrowing the method of the Egyptian Mysteries and expressing it in terms of the older earlier Greek Nature cults that preceded the highly poetised tradition of the bright Olympians. These old Nature cults still lingered in the out of the way parts of Greece, in the islands, and in the mountains, and the Mystery myths have shown clearly that their originators knew this fact, for in them the god comes down from the mountains or the goddess takes refuge in the island. It must be clearly recognised that these Mystery myths are not by any means primitive material, but very sophisticated material indeed, being the work of scholars and mystics of a highly civilised era seeking in the ancient traditional roots of Greek religion for untapped springs of inspiration. It was exactly as if a modern Englishman sought inspiration from Keltic or Norse folklore. No doubt the initiates of the Mysteries were regarded as pagans in their own day.

There is another fact, which, though known to specialists along this line of study, is unrealised by the majority of writers on mysticism, and consequently by the majority of their readers. It will no doubt be a surprise to many to learn that Indian initiates believe that the inspiration of their mysteries came originally from Egypt. The relevant data may be found in the works of Sir John Woodroffe (Arthur Avalon). See, in particular, the extract from Panchkori Bandyapadhyga on p.xxiv of Vol.II of that author's *"Principles of Tantra"*.

It follows, then, that those who have been initiated in the Western Esoteric Tradition, and have taken those grades that draw their inspiration from Greece and Egypt in addition to the better known alchemical grades, will have no difficulty in understanding much in Eastern thought that is obscure or even obscene to the ordinary student.

The practical applications of such teachings, valuable as they could be as a corrective to our insularity, are, however, far from easy to attain. It is frequently said that yoga as taught in the East is impractical in the West because the Western conditions of life are utterly unsuited to it, and the western attitude utterly unsympathetic. I can only repeat this standard advice yet again. The student should on no account attempt the practical work of advanced yoga unless he has the necessary conditions of mind, body and estate, for all these three play their part. Practical yoga should not be done in any makeshift manner, but with proper care and attention to all the material conditions that are necessary for its achievement. If these are not available, it is inadvisable to make the attempt with substitutes. Among these necessities are the necessary number of properly trained persons in a properly trained equipped and prepared place that is secure from profanation. Again, I emphasise that makeshifts are worse than useless. If you do yoga at all, do it under proper conditions or leave it alone.

But despite these provisos and warnings, I think it worth while to write on the subject of yoga because I feel that my training in the ancient Mysteries of the West has given me an insight into it that the average Christian does not possess. There have been a great many books written on the subject, their writers all frankly recognising that yoga in its original form is unsuited to the West, and one and all trying to present an adaptation of it that should be suitable; but one and all, so far as my experience goes, have thrown away the baby with the bath-water, and presented a version of that ancient science which is like a version of Hamlet edited by a rationalist who removed all reference to the supernatural. The result does not make sense.

The fact, however, remains that yoga as it stands, does not suit the West as it stands, and that if the mountain cannot go to Mahomet, Mahomet will have to go to the mountain if he wants to enjoy the delights of a high altitude. Our western culture has bestowed many benefits in the way of physical sanitation but the same cannot always be said of it in regard to mental sanitation, and a modification of its attitude is due, and overdue, as the psycho-analysts have long been pointing out.

YOGA AND
THE TREE OF LIFE

The Circuit of Force Parts 1.2 - 1.4 [March 1939]
Dion Fortune

Part 1.2

Having unburdened myself of these preliminary explanations, and made my position clear, if that is ever possible in dealing with the subject of yoga, I will now endeavour to show the manner in which the western initiate can link up his knowledge with the eastern methods and thereby enrich both his theory and practice.

The uninitiated have no means of achieving this unification because, even were the necessary keys given to them, the necessary trained and dedicated capacity is lacking. Having no wish to cause the unenlightened to blaspheme, I will pursue the traditional method of using the language of the Mysteries – clear to those who possess the keys; obscure to those who do not.

It must always be borne in mind that the clue to all these Mysteries is to be sought in the Tree of Life. Understand the significance of the Tree; arrange the symbols you are working with in the correct manner upon it, and all is clear and you can work out your sum. Equate the *danda* with the Central Pillar, and the Lotuses with the Sephiroth and the bisections of the Paths thereon, and you have the necessary bilingual dictionary at your disposal – if you know how to use it.

So much for the practical side of the matter – not for the philosophy. It must be realised that there are two broad types of yoga, the kind that leads on to *sadhana* – the higher states of consciousness, and the one that aims at conferring the *siddhis*, or magical powers. The kind that is exported to the west is the former; the more spiritual kind because it is the more acceptable to the ascetic Christian ideal; whereas the other, which is really nature worship naked and unashamed, though it would have appealed to the Greeks, would no doubt rouse the modern analogues of King Pentheus to fury.

The only place in the Western world where the *siddhis* are seen is in the Spiritualist movement, where the circle is the undeveloped analogue of the *chakra*. It is easy to see what happens in "the circle" - the component members pool their psychic forces and so provide the raw material for the phenomena.

No one quite knows what they are doing, nor why they are doing it; but they find that if they do certain things they get certain results, and if they neglect to do them they do not get results. They also know by experience that the phenomena of greater intensity occur in the presence of certain persons which are absent in their absence, the conclusion being reasonably drawn that some persons are more gifted by nature in these matters than others; but very little is known concerning the causation of this gift, which is either present or absent in a given individual, though the fact of its observation in every conceivable gradation, from the most powerful to the most feeble in different individuals, and its variation in strength in the same individual point to it being a thing which ought to respond to cultivation if we understood its nature. It has often been alleged that the marvels reported of Indian yogis are achieved by means of mass hypnosis; that the yogi does not really float in the air unsupported - he lies comfortably on the ground and by the power of his mind causes his audience to think they see him floating in the air. I am not in a position to argue this point, having no first-hand acquaintance with yogis. I know, however, that physical phenomena in the west are highly suspect; and I know that mediums who for long have been regarded as most convincing have with painful frequency been shown up in the end. It may be that all non-fraudulent psychic phenomena are of the hypnotic and auto-hypnotic order - I do not know and have no opinion on the subject, preferring to keep an open mind in the present state of my knowledge, but it is quite certain that much of the so-called supernormal is achieved by means of an applied psychology of which the west is utterly and entirely ignorant; and this to me is the most interesting part of it.

Part 1.3

The word *Yoga* itself gives us a clue to the nature of the activities it denominates. It is derived from the root *Yug*; and implies a joining, conjunction or union. The same root appears in the words *yoke* and *conjugal*. Thus it may be taken that yoga is a method of achieving union and so it is generally defined - but union with what? This is where we need to be careful and precise for we can easily go astray. It is taken for granted by the western students of yoga who have to accept what is given them at second and third hand in the popular books on the subject, that the union aimed at is union with God. This, I think, would be agreed by all the schools of yoga; but what the western student does not realise is that the Hindu recognises, not more than one God; but more than one aspect of God and more than one aspect of God's being. Thus the union aimed at by the devotee may be with God as the Great Unmanifest; or it may be with God made manifest in Nature. This latter aspect of the Godhead is indicated in eastern thought as the Goddess – the spouse of God, the *Shakti*, or female aspect of the Godhead. This idea is not as alien to western thought as the uninformed might think; for as McGregor Mathers points out in his introductory essay to his translation of *"The Kabbalah Unveiled"* the word *Elohim* is a feminine noun with a masculine plural termination. This teaching, at first sight crudely anthropomorphic, indicates, when understood in its deeper mystical sense, which is the only sense in which it can be understood, that the universe is strung between two poles of manifestation in the form of a magnetic field of interacting force.

Let it be remembered that the term *anthropomorphic* is a two-edged sword and that if God is conceived of under the symbol of man, it is only because man is made in the image and likeness of God. Moreover, and this is an important clue, it was the Elohim who are reported as responsible for the act of creation recorded in the first chapter of Genesis and created everything male and female, and ended the act by saying "Let us create man in Our image and likeness... male and female created He them." Here we see clearly indicated the primary esoteric idea that manifestation always takes place by means of the Pairs of Opposites, in this case

symbolised as male and female. In fact the prevalence of the use
of the sexual symbolism has bewildered many students who have
sought to go to the fountainhead in this field of study. Since it is
there, however, and unavoidable, we must accept it and make the
best of it, though not necessarily taking it at its face value. We
meet the same symbolism in the Greek, the Egyptian, the Norse
and the Celtic pantheons - in fact we meet with it wherever men
look upon Nature as the manifesting Godhead and as such hold it
holy, and also, by implication esteem the corresponding factors in
themselves to be holy. This is an attitude so different from that of
the average westerner, who is Christian in outlook even if not in
action, and who has been taught to worship God in His aspect of
the Unmanifest only, that he has no concept at all of what is meant
but at the same time disagrees with it utterly, believing that to be
sinful which the East believes to be sacred. If the East regarded
it as the West regards it, it would undoubtedly be sinful, but this
is exactly what the East does not do. It may be said, in brief, that
it is impossible for anyone who is at war with himself to practice
yoga. He must follow the example of the great Roman who said:
"I reckon nothing human alien to me."

Part 1.4

It is agreed by all who have practical experience in this field that
the things of the higher mysticism can only be conceived of by
means of symbols, a sort of algebra of the soul, and the processes
of yoga are no exception to this truth; by means of symbolism
they are conceived of and handled. The comprehensive glyph in
the East corresponding to the Tree of Life in the West is of a man
seated cross-legged in meditation with the seven Lotuses or chakras
displayed as seven disks placed one above the other up the central
line of the body, the basal one approximately corresponding with
the base of the spine, and the highest one situated immediately
over the head, thus entirely agreeing with the allocation of the
Central Pillar of the Tree of Life, providing the intersections of the
Paths are added to the Sephiroth.

That these lotuses or *chakras* and the nerves connecting
them actually exist anatomically, no initiated yogi believes, but

experience proves that there are centres and channels of magnetic energy in the etheric double that can be located by using the indicated points in the physical body as markers. The practitioner of this method visualises in his imagination, not his physical body but his etheric double, and where he concentrates his attention the magnetic force flows and concentrates itself. As these centres roughly correspond to the endocrine organs far-reaching physical implications may be surmised. Certainly there must be changes in the blood as one or another of the ductless glands is stimulated into pouring out its secretions. We probably have here the secret of rejuvenation.

These different *chakras* or centres are held to correspond to different levels of consciousness and the corresponding planes of manifestation. This is taught in the Qabalah, at any rate, and reasoning by analogy, I presume it to be the same in the East, and that if a given centre is awake and functioning, it will form a channel of ingress or egress onto the corresponding inner plane.

The *Muladhara* at the base of the spine is held to be the basal chakra of all, from whence the slumbering force of kundalini is called up, and that it is by that force, and that alone, that all the other chakras are vivified. With this the Qabalist would agree, equating the *Muladhara Lotus* with the Sephirah Malkuth, which, be it remembered, is not the physical earth, but the Sphere of the Elements, and therein is an important key to Qabalistic thought. Bearing in mind the fact that the microcosm is the mirror of the macrocosm, let us remember that there must be a Sphere of the Elements in man, and that it is not his physical body that is his Malkuth, but his etheric double. We must therefore look for four elemental factors in man - and I use the term generically to include woman also - these four factors being, like the elements, two of them active, a subtle and a dense - and two of them passive, also a subtle and a dense. From this fact we deduce the Law of Alternating Polarity both up the planes and in function. This equates with the eastern *Ida* and *Pingala*, the Sun and the Moon forces, and everything that is taught in yoga with regard to *Ida* and *Pingala* can be applied to the Law of Alternating Polarity. It has truly been said that the perfect marriage does not consist of the halves of a single whole, but of the four quarters.

THE OVERCROWDED MONKEY HOUSE

The Circuit of Force Part 1.5 - 1.7 [April 1939]
Dion Fortune

Part 1.5

For the further understanding of our subject we must remember that just as the physical body builds itself up out of the inert substances of the physical plane, so each of the subtler bodies renews its substance from the corresponding level of the subtler planes; there is a constant subtle psychic metabolism going on; a constant in-breathing and out-breathing on every plane. If this is impeded, the corresponding level of being becomes unhealthy. If it is entirely cut off, that level dies, and the levels below it are cut off from the central directing guidance. This no doubt accounts for certain forms of insanity.

This in-breathing and out-breathing appears to be readily susceptible to regulation by the mind; it is in fact normally controlled by the mental attitude. This unquestionably explains the forms of psycho-neurosis attributable to what Freud calls *repression*, but which might equally aptly be termed *constriction*, for a self-repressive mental attitude undoubtedly restricts the subtle bodies just as the old-fashioned, wasp-waisted corsets restricted all the vital activities of their proud victims and produced the vapours, fainting-fits and *green sickness* nowadays never seen owing to the acceptance by fashion of the natural waist-line. Could we be brought to accept the natural attitude of the mind towards nature and its processes, we should soon see the last of our mental and emotional anaemias, rickets and scurvy.

A well-known writer once stated that when he looked upon the monkeys at the zoo in their old cages he thought them the nastiest of created beings; but when he saw them after they had been transferred to their new home, on the open air terraces, he revised his opinion. The same might be said of the civilised man's subconscious mind, explored with such thoroughness by the psychoanalytical schools of thought. Dr. Trotter, in his epoch-making book on *"The Instincts of the Herd in Peace and War"* remarks that the Freudians seem altogether too ready to accept the present repressive conditions of emotional life as standard and unalterable, and to direct all their patients to the Procustes bed of custom and convention, and no one seems to be found bold enough to put on trial the conditions that give rise to so much mental and social misery and enquire whether they are inevitable and unalterable. One has only to wade through the case histories in the four stout volumes of Havelock Ellis' *"Psychology of Sex"* to realise that one is studying the natural history of an overcrowded monkey house.

Our purpose, however, is not at the moment to study the remedial possibilities offered by yoga to sick minds, though this is a very fruitful field awaiting exploration. I want here to consider the possibilities of yoga for the development of normal minds into super-minds, for just as Freud found that the study of pathological mental processes threw light on normal ones – as might be expected in our caged monkey-house of a civilisation – so we may find that the study of the methods of training that develop super-normal minds may throw light on the healing of abnormal ones.

Part 1.6

First and foremost it must be realised that just as an unnatural attitude towards life is the basic cause of the functional psycho-pathologies, so a similar attitude renders the development of the mind by yoga quite impossible, because the energies that are to produce the development are drawn from the Sephirah Malkuth – the Sphere of the Elements, the four petalled *Muladhara* Lotus. Inhibit life at this level by a repressive attitude, and the *kundalini* cannot rise; let life flow freely, and the way opens for the sublimation of *kundalini*.

Man, however, being essentially a social animal, incapable of existing alone and suffering severe discomfort from the disapproval of his fellows, it follows that direct action in the way of a return to nature is not always possible. Compromises have to be made;

alternative routes have to be found, because the cost of direct action is too high. Once "the clouds are off the soul", many forms of compromise become possible which make life liveable when otherwise it would be unbearable; it is possible to twist a rope, and quite a satisfactory rope, out of a number of short strands, and where all the factors necessary to a balanced diet do not exist in one dish, to avail oneself of the psychological equivalent of dietary supplements.

The most effective and practical alternative route for the by-passing of direct action is to be found in ritual performed with knowledge; wherein each member of the ritual team works with true magical power, knowing the meaning of the symbols employed, and that the personal forces of each officiant have to act syphon-like for the bringing through of the corresponding cosmic forces. This being achieved with genuine power and understanding by those working the ritual, the onlookers can participate each according to his or her need if they have the necessary knowledge; and even if, from force of circumstances this must be withheld, nevertheless they are not sent empty away, for the ritual, couched in terms of primordial symbolism, "speaks to their condition".

In the East, the home of yoga, in addition to the meditations on the chakras there are the rituals of the *chakras*. In the West these are represented by the Mystery rites of such centres as Eleusis and Memphis, and the same factors, unrecognised and imperfectly realised, come out in modern ballroom dancing. Were the psychology of these things understood, and their technique adapted to modern needs, we should have a most valuable contribution to the armamentarium of psycho-therapy as well as a callisthenics of the mind.

Part 1.7

From the practical point of view however, the matter is far from simple in Western countries, where such things receive neither acknowledgement nor sympathy. How then can the by-pass be built, when every field is plastered with notices announcing that trespassers will be persecuted, as the small boy so aptly paraphrased the notice?

Ritual, with its symbolic enactment of the cosmic drama, can go a long way but cannot go the whole way. It can provide dietary supplements that will enable the undernourished to keep alive, but it will not give the bounding energy of real health. As a means to an end the symbolic ritual is admirable; as an end in itself it is a compromise and a makeshift; better than nothing but not the genuine article.

It cannot, moreover, be worked satisfactorily by those who themselves are obliged to rely on substitutes for life in its fullness. Those who possess fullness of life can mediate to others by means of ritual; but if they themselves suffer from restriction or inhibition of life force, they can no more mediate the cosmic life to those for whose benefit they work a ritual than a starving mother can feed her baby.

It is necessary that those who work the rites should themselves know the full function of the Four Quarters, and I write for those who are so fortunately situated as to be able to achieve this, for they are the true priesthood of Nature.

I would say to them that the sacramental attitude is the key to life, a sacrament being the outward and visible sign of an inward and spiritual power. Ritual, we know, is action; and action becomes ritual when performed with intention.

As I have pointed out elsewhere in my writings on magic, the contacts with the cosmic forces are picked up mentally by means of the use of symbols on which the imagination dwells, thus building them on the astral. The mind has to be "conditioned" to any given abstract symbol before it can be influenced by it, and this conditioning is achieved by presenting the symbol to the mind under impressive ritualistic circumstances so that it is for ever after associated in the mind with the emotion of the moment, and will consequently call up the emotion whenever it is subsequently seen.

No abstract and artificial symbols, such as the Cross or the Crescent, can ever become so potent to stir the emotions, nor stir them to such an intensity, as the natural objects of feeling; it is for this reason that the Church superimposes the tortured figure of the Redeemer upon the bleak, abstract symbol of the Cross, and offers for our adoration the Mother nursing her child. It is probably for the same psychological reason, though reversed, that Mohammed forbade all representation of natural objects in art so that the faithful might never be led away from the strict monotheism he came to teach.

The great nature worshipping religions, however, avail themselves of the power of the natural emotion-stirring objects with a directness of appeal that is not appreciated by the sophisticated westerner accustomed to the viewpoint inculcated by an ascetic faith.

It is indisputable that there are drawbacks to the unrestricted use of powerful stimulants, and civilised countries have found it necessary to control their use, whether in the form of drugs and alcohol, or of psychological stimulants to the imagination. A stimulant is not a food; it is, on the contrary, simply a releaser of inhibitions, which enables reserves of energy to be made available. It is a very useful thing to be able to call upon one's reserves in an emergency, and may make all the difference between life and death, success and failure; but in order to be able to call upon one's reserves, one must have reserves to call upon, and this cannot be if one is constantly drawing upon them by the habitual use of stimulants.

For this reason in the West the sale of alcohol was restricted to certain hours and certain places, and psychological stimulants to the instincts were banned whenever recognised as such, though many passed unrecognised. Christianity by denying the right of life to the instincts and banning their stimulation, has undoubtedly made a vital contribution to culture by forcing a sublimation of primitive energies and interests into social channels. Unquestionably such a reform was due and overdue in the pagan world to which Our Lord came. But there is such a thing as too much of a good thing, and this our religious zealots are never able to realise, and no one who is in a position to form an opinion on the subject has any doubt whatever that we are suffering with our nerves today owing to the over-earnestness of St. Paul and St. Augustine some twenty centuries ago.

What India needs is a restriction in the hours and places for the display of psychological stimulants so that her people may have energy to spare for the tasks of civilisation, instead of draining themselves dry though the natural channels; and what Anglo-Saxon civilisation needs is a realisation that Prohibition is an unworkable substitute for public house reform. It must not be thought by this that I regard what has euphemistically been termed "the poor man's club" as any real substitute for the home. On the contrary, it is in the homes that reform should come, and if it comes there, it will not be needed elsewhere. That is the real solution of the problem of psychological Prohibition.

Commentary A

MYSTERY ORIGINS IN ANCIENT GREECE

Gareth Knight

"Examine what is known concerning the origin of the Greek Mysteries," writes Dion Fortune in her introduction to *"The Circuit of Force"*. In support of this she recommends Jane Harrison's *"Prolegomena to the Study of Greek Religion"*, an enthusiastic review of which appeared in the November 1938 issue of the *"Inner Light"* magazine, notwithstanding the fact that the book had been around for no less than thirty-five years! The appearance of this belated review suggests that it had only recently come to Dion Fortune's notice but had made a considerable impact.

There was a considerable burgeoning of interest in the ancient Mystery traditions within the Society at this time with regular magazine contributions from senior members such as S.F. Annett and Colonel C.R.F. Seymour (writing also as "F.P.D.") on the Egyptian and Celtic mysteries.

Jane Ellen Harrison, (1850-1928), the author of *"A Prelogemena to the Study of Greek Religion"*, gained an international reputation when her book first appeared in 1903. She was a remarkable scholar at a time when women academics were rare, who broke into what was then an essentially male preserve, of academic classical studies. A former student of Sir James Frazer of *"The Golden Bough"* fame, she employed the data of evolutionary anthropology as well as classical archaeology to challenge the scholarly consensus about how the ancient Greeks thought.

She based her research upon early ritual practices, long before the Olympian gods gained their ascendancy. This was an era of matriarchal religion when local earth goddesses were the power behind local heroes. This led her into a deep investigation of the cult of Dionysos with his wild rout of meneads and satyrs, and of Orpheus, the magical musician who could tame all wild things including the forces of the underworld.

As the *"Inner Light"* review points out, these two cults are of particular interest to students of the Mysteries, for they gave rise to a new impulse in ancient Greek religion.

The Cult of Dionysos

In the rites of Dionysos the ecstatic worshippers believed they were possessed by the god. This was completely foreign to the way the Greeks had previously thought about themselves and their gods. As may be seen in the epic poetry of Homer of the 9th century CE the Greeks saw the gods as separate from and superior to man. Anyone who presumed to "become like the gods" would have been blasted with divine fire by Zeus and cast into the underworld for presumptuous impiety.

The Dionysian religion came into northern Greece some time in the 8th century B.C. Originally Dionysos was the god of an isolated and unconquered mountain tribe whose reputation for brigandage and banditry lasted well into the Christian era. His rebel rout of satyrs, centaurs and meneads might well have been real wild men and women in the beginning rather than mythical beings. His mother, Semele, was a local earth goddess and, as bride of the local thunder god, was also known as "the thunder-smitten", as indeed the earth goddess of a mountainous region could very well have been.

A key to Dionysos' popularity was his association with the vine, the discovery of wine, and hence alcoholic intoxication, but although his original wild worshippers might have been excessive drinkers, as his influence spread over the Greek world there came a gradual shift from the physical to the spiritual aspects of inebriation.

As he had been fathered by a thunder god he was later proclaimed to be a son of Zeus, the universal thunderer, and eventually was elevated to the ranks of the gods of Olympus, where he replaced Hestia, the goddess of the hearth, as one of the major twelve. Hestia, it has been suggested, was not unduly put out by this, as she had a home in every family and city hearth throughout the land.

Under the local name of Iacchos, Dionysos also found a place within the Mysteries of Eleusis. The Eleusinian Mysteries were originally a simple harvest festival. As ancient local goddesses began to merge, so many became identified with a common Earth Mother, who with the development of agriculture also embraced the qualities of a Corn Mother.

In Jane Harrison's analysis, aspects of the goddess mirror the four conditions of a woman's life:

i)   the virgin maid or Kore, (as with Persephone),
ii) the nubile bride or Nymph, (as many ladies of the woods and
        waters),
iii) the mother or Meter (as in De-meter),
iv) the grandmother or Maia, (as, for example, Rhea).

In some respects they remain the same goddess, just as these four stages can be experienced by the same woman.

Thus, at Eleusis, Demeter and Persephone, mother and maid, were fundamentally one goddess but expressed under different aspects. However, in the course of time, Demeter became more and more identified with the physical corn and took to herself affairs of the upper world such as marriage and motherhood and Mother of the Harvest; while Persephone became more withdrawn into the world of the spirit, as ruler of the dead, and Queen of the Underworld.

Ancient goddesses form an important background to all Greek myth and religion. A local earth mother, who was mother of both the quick and the dead, and lady of wild things, played a role somewhere between that of mother and lover to any local hero, urging and inspiring him to great deeds. Eventually these tribal heroes became petty kings, and at Eleusis, when it was an independent city state, the king himself was a priest of the two goddesses, the *mater* and the *kore*, who became identified with Demeter and Persephone.

When Athens grew in power and status and annexed Eleusis, which was only fourteen miles away, it took over the Eleusinian worship as well, which it then began to transform. Athens made the Eleusinian festival one of the key points of the Attic year, with two main developments. They promoted the old king of Eleusis into a legendary culture hero, sent abroad by Demeter to sow seed and teach mankind the arts of agriculture; and they introduced Iacchos, a form of Dionysos as god of the underworld and its mysteries. He had a shrine at Athens, where his spring festival eventually became a focus for the drama, and at the autumn festival his image was paraded to Eleusis with great celebration.

These celebrations included fasting, elaborate purification rites, sacrificial offerings, a ceremonial partaking of the first fruits, a mystical marriage, and the processing and revelation of sacred objects. After a procession from Athens along the seashore, the devotees entered a large building, a hall of initiation. This was most unusual for Greek religious observance, which was generally conducted in the open. A temple was exclusively the house of a god into which only a priest might enter. At its peak the great hall at Eleusis could contain three thousand initiates.

The precise details of the Eleusinian ceremonies have never been revealed, but it is known that at some point the hierophant and the priestess would descend into a secret chamber for the celebration of a sacred marriage ceremony, which was probably enacted chastely and symbolically in this period. Then the hierophant came forth and, standing in a blaze of torchlight, cried aloud that the supreme mystery was accomplished: a holy child had been born of a virgin. The final act seems to have been connected with bringing forth a newly cut sheaf of corn and distributing ears of wheat to those present as an emblem of new life.

It seems there were no secrets given out in the terms of a creed of belief or revelation of ideas. Some have spoken of seeing the sun shine at midnight in the subterranean groves, which suggests that the Initiation was essentially an experience that transcends the intellect.

The Mysteries of Eleusis maintained an exemplary reputation, and it was generally believed that those who had received initiation had a significant advantage over those who had not, not only in this world but in the life after death. They were open to women as well as to men; and to slaves as well as to free citizens. The only bar to entry was to those who had committed murder, until at least they had undergone elaborate purification.

The spring festival at Athens, the Dionisia, where the dramatic competitions came to be held, became in effect the Lesser Mysteries. Only after acceptance into these was it possible to enter the Greater Mysteries at the autumn festival at Eleusis, eighteen months later.

These Lesser Mysteries lie at the root of theatre. What began as a procession with priest leader and initiate chorus, chanting hymns to Dionysos, developed into a form of dialogue and from thence into more complex dramatic forms. The priests gradually took on the role of actors, yet there remained a strong religious and magical element in Greek tragedy, for the masked actors, on their high boots under long robes, became vehicles for the gods and the legendary beings they portrayed. There is a thin dividing line between where ritual ends and drama begins.

The aim was to purge and purify the audience with the emotions of fear and of pity, and as the festivals developed it became part of the tradition to follow the tragedies with satirical comedy, also in its way a purgative, but after another manner. It is interesting to note that the word satire derives from the satyr play featuring the wilder followers of Dionysos in a less than respectful send-up of the gods of the day.

The Athenian drama, as we know it from the earliest manuscripts that have survived, flowered more than a hundred and fifty years after the first Dionysia, with the three great tragedians, Aeschylus (525-456), himself a citizen of Eleusis, Sophocles (495-405) and Euripides (480-405), and the comic dramatist Aristophanes (444-388).

Despite the comparatively late date we can learn much from Euripides' great Dionysian drama, *"The Bacchae"*, which was written in his last years and not performed until after his death. The occultist and psychotherapist Israel Regardie in an essay entitled *"A Greek Ritual of Magic"* claimed that it would be no difficult matter to recast the play into a magical ceremony, and one whose symbolism lies very close to psychoanalytic theory, with the entire mechanism of the Freudian scheme there, from repession and resistance through to the Oedipus complex. The rational consciousness of man, represented in the drama by King Pentheus, in overstepping the legitimate confines of its powers is torn to pieces by the repressed feminine powers as a consequence. The god himself represents the vital stream of spiritual energy, the totality of man's forces, to whose service the Meneads must be dedicated.

Even Aristophanes' *"The Frogs"* contains a chorus of the *mystae* of Iacchos and a hymn to Demeter as bearer of fruits, while *"The Clouds"* contains a satirical depiction of certain Orphic doctrines, wherein Socrates, (as stock comic character for an otherworldly philosopher,) dangles in a basket over the heads of the populace, offering to mediate between them and the higher powers represented by the clouds of metaphysical abstraction. It may be remembered in passing that the Elizabethan magus Dr John Dee had a great enthusiasm for this same playwright and got into a certain amount of trouble by inventing a flying Egyptian scarab for Aristophanes' *"Pax"* that was so realistic that it was thought to be propelled by sorcery.

The doctrines of Orpheus came to play an increasingly important role in the religious world of the Greeks from the seventh century B.C. onwards. Indeed Orpheus became virtually identified with Dionysos, in spite of the fact that in many ways they were polar opposites. The all-important thing they had in common was a knowledge of the Mysteries of the Underworld and the means of becoming identified with the gods.

Dionysos, as befits one who was to introduce the possibility of spiritual birth to man, was himself "twice born". His mother, Semele, once her earth goddess origins were forgotten, was said to have been the daughter of the King of Thebes, and courted by no less than Zeus, the king of the gods, who visited her in human form. This aroused the jealousy of Hera, Zeus' consort, who came to the palace in the guise of a nurse when the pregnant Semele was expecting Zeus' child. Hera persuaded Semele to insist that Zeus reveal himself to her in his true form as a god. This she did, by means of the old stratagem of holding him to his word on an open promise. Unfortunately for her, when Zeus appeared to her in all his divine glory she was struck down as if by lightning, her body was consumed in flames and her shade went down to the underworld.

Some say a shoot of ivy appeared miraculously to screen her unborn child, winding itself around the columns of the palace. All agree that Zeus then seized the babe and concealed it in his thigh, from whence it later came to birth. As a result of this double pregnancy Dionysos was known as *Dithyrambos*, the "twice born"; once from a premature human birth, and then from a divine birth.

This is an epithet which came to be applied to initiates, who had been born of the flesh and then of the spirit.

The child was entrusted by Zeus to Semele's sister, until Hera struck the foster parents with madness, when Zeus, with the help of Hermes, changed the child into the form of a kid or a ram and placed him in the keeping of the cave nymphs of Mount Nysa, who were rewarded by being placed in the stars as the Hyades, which make up the face of Taurus, the bull.

Mount Nysa has no precise location although there are many claims as to its physical site; it is the archetypal sacred mountain. Here the child was brought up attended by satyrs and other strange creatures, tutored by old Silenos, a wise and down to earth Falstaffian type of teacher, to whom Socrates later declared an affinity. Some said another of his attendants was Macris, a daughter of Aristaeus, or Pan, who fed him on honey.

As he grew older, Dionysos took to wandering the mountain woods, crowned with ivy and laurel, accompanied by the nymphs, making the glades ring with joyful cries and simple musical instruments of pipes and drums. In the course of time he discovered the vine and the art of making wine from it. This discovery led him into extensive travels, taking the vine stock with him and accompanied by his wild rout.

Their emblem was an ivy twined staff topped with a pinecone, called a thyrsus, an early form of the caduceus. They also carried swords and serpents and howling holed stones on strings known as bull roarers, and were aided on occasion by wild animals.

From the mainland of Greece he visited the islands of the Greek archipelago. He introduced the vine to Egypt and with the Amazon women successfully fought a war against the Titans. This was the first of many military victories including one over the King of Damascus, whom he flayed alive for barring his way across the Euphrates, over which he then built a bridge of ivy. He was helped by a tiger to cross the other great river, the Tigris, and eventually reached India, where he introduced the vine to the whole sub-continent, founded cities and established laws. We are talking of a time somewhat before Buddha, and the mythology may be identified with the spread of viticulture.

When he eventually returned to the west, Dionysos had undergone a certain change of appearance. In place of the bearded rustic god often depicted with horns he was seen more often in the guise of a graceful adolescent dressed in long robes in the Lydian fashion.

There was some reaction to his changed appearance. He was at first opposed by the Amazons, but he defeated them, helped in his battle with elephants that he had brought from India. He then invaded Thrace where his army was repulsed but he escaped by plunging into the sea. The ancient goddess Rhea helped the prisoners of war to escape and inflicted madness upon the victors, whereupon Dionysos travelled on to Boetia where he visited Thebes. Here, as depicted in the celebrated play by Euripides, he caused the patriarchal disciplinarian King Pentheus to go mad. When the king tried to imprison him he shackled a bull by mistake and then, dressed in women's clothes, went up into the mountains to spy upon the meneads and their mysteries. Here Dionysos secured him to the top of a fir tree, which the meneads uprooted, and led by his mother Agave, fell upon him and tore him to pieces, his mother returning to the palace brandishing his severed head.

At Orchomenus, three princesses refused to join his revels although he invited them to in the form of a girl. He then changed shape into a lion, a bull and a panther and drove them mad. They tore their brother apart and ran into the mountains where Hermes turned them into a bat, an owl and a crow.

In Argos, Dionysos was opposed by the hero Perseus. However, Dionysos drove all the women mad causing them to start to devour their children. A this, Perseus built a temple in Dionysos honour.

At some point in his travels, despite a warning from their helmsman who recognised his godhead, pirates tried to take him and sell him into slavery. No sooner was he secured when ivy and vine tendrils sprang from the deck and enveloped the sail and the mast, the bonds fell from Dionysos and he turned into a lion. Wine filled the sea all around the ship, and phantoms of wild beasts appeared within it to the sound of flutes. The terrified pirates jumped overboard and were turned into dolphins. Only the helmsman/pilot was spared and lived to tell the tale.

On the island of Naxos, Dionysos came upon the princess Ariadne, the daughter of King Minos of Crete, who had helped the hero Theseus to find his way through the labyrinth of the minotaur by means of a thread. Theseus had deserted her, but Dionysos consoled her, proving his status as a god by throwing her bridal diadem into the stars, where it remains as Corona Borealis, the Northern Crown. Some versions of the story say that the marriage took place after Ariadne's death, so that two ceremonies were later celebrated in her honour, one bewailing her death, and the other celebrating her subsequent divine marriage, a combination of rites that has distinct initiatory resonances.

Having established his worship throughout the world and been accepted into the Olympian heaven, where he sat at the right hand of Zeus as one of the Twelve Great Ones, Dionysos descended to the underworld. Here, with a gift of myrtle or a phallus made of fig wood, he induced Persephone to release his mother from the realm of the dead. Semele ascended with him to the temple of Artemis at Troezen where Dionysos changed her name to Thyone, which means "ecstatically raging", the condition of many of his menead followers. Having made her immortal he took her up with him to live with the gods. In this we have another initiatory sequence.

So much for the general body of Dionysian myth, some of it very wild indeed, that was taken over and adapted by the Orphic movement.

The Cult of Orpheus

Orpheus however was a man not a god. He was a magical musician who had the power to tame wild things including, it would seem, wild gods and their wild worshippers. He played a lyre, rather than the Pan pipes and the clashing cymbals of frenzied dancers, and became closely associated with Apollo, a higher and more rational form of the old sun god Helios. As poet, seer, musician, metaphysician, and religious reformer Orpheus transformed the savage Dionysian rites, rooted in blood sacrifice and orgy, and gave them a spiritual significance. So much so that some early Christians even saw him as a prototype of Christ.

Orpheus was said to be the son of the King of Thrace and the muse Calliope, as well as being the most famous poet and musician who ever lived. Apollo presented him with a lyre, and the muses taught him its use. Thus by his songs and his music he could charm wild beasts, and even cause trees and rocks to move and follow him, which is said to account for various circles of trees or stones. After visiting Egypt he joined the Argonauts, sailed to Colchis on their Quest of the Golden Fleece, and his music helped them over many difficulties on the way. On his return he married and settled among the savage tribes of Thrace with his bride Euridice.

One day Euridice was beset by Aristaeus, a form of Pan, who tried to force her. In her flight she trod on a serpent and died from its bite, but Orpheus boldly descended into the underworld to fetch her back. He charmed the ferryman Charon, the watchdog Cerberus, the three Judges of the Dead, and temporarily suspended the tortures of the damned. He so soothed the heart of Hades/Pluto that the god allowed Euridice to return from the dead, provided that Orpheus did not look back. Euridice followed Orpheus up the dark passages until, reaching the sunlight, perhaps through a trick, or perhaps through a lack of faith, he looked back to see if she were there, and lost her.

There was initially considerable conflict between Dionysos and Orpheus. When Dionysos invaded Thrace, Orpheus neglected to honour him and taught other sacred mysteries including the evil of sacrificial killing. Every morning he would greet the dawn on the summit of Mount Pangaeum, preaching that Helios, whom he named Apollo, was the greatest of all gods. In vexation, Dionysos set the meneads on him, at Deium in Macedonia, where Orpheus was serving as priest at the temple of Apollo. After murdering their husbands, they tore Orpheus limb from limb and threw his head in the river Hebrus, where it floated, still singing, down to the sea, until finally carried to the isle of Lesbos.

The muses collected his limbs and buried them at the foot of Mount Olympus where the nightingales are now said to sing sweeter than anywhere else in the world. Orpheus' head, after being attacked by a serpent, which Apollo at once turned into a stone, was laid to rest in a cave near Antissa, sacred to Dionysos, where it prophesied day and night until Apollo eventually silenced it, as it was causing the other oracles, including Delphi, to become neglected.

Orpheus' lyre also drifted to Lesbos and is sometimes depicted as having his head attached. It was laid up in the temple of Apollo until it was honoured by a place in the heavens as the constellation

Lyra, which contains Vega, one of the Earth's polar stars in the precession of equinoxes.

Other stories say that Orpheus was killed by Zeus with a thunderbolt for divulging divine secrets. He had indeed initiated the Mysteries of Apollo in Thrace, those of Hecate in Aegina, and those of Subterranean Demeter in Sparta.

The diversity and popularity of Dionysos had caused him to absorb various foreign gods, including Sabazius of Phrygia, (a supreme god and solar divinity), Bassareus of Lydia, (a conquering god), and Zagreus, (a Cretan equivalent of Zeus). This last particularly was elaborated by Orphic doctrine into a story of the early childhood of Dionysos and a creation myth of the human race.

The Orphic stories that are derived from Zagreus make Dionysos the son of Persephone, from whence he received the name Chthonios "the subterranean". In a late version of the tale, Demeter hid her daughter Persephone in a cave, setting two serpents to guard her. In the cave the maiden began weaving a great web or tapestry of wool which was a picture of the whole world. While she was thus engaged Zeus came to her in the form of a serpent and begat upon her the god who was to be his successor as divine ruler of the world. All this was carried out according to Demeter's will, who in some respects was identified with Persephone.

The child, who had horns, indicating him to be a child of Persephone, was enthroned in a ceremony by his grandmother Rhea and the Korybantes, armed maidens who danced around him. The child's toys were all symbols of initiatory significance - dice, a ball, a spinning top, a cone, knuckle bones, a mirror, golden apples, a bull roarer, a tuft of fleece.

Spurred on by the jealousy of the other gods, the Titans, their faces whitened with chalk, came like spirits of the dead from the underworld, and seizing the child, tore him into seven pieces and threw them into a cauldron standing on a tripod, where the flesh was boiled and then roasted on spits. A pomegranate tree sprang from where his blood flowed into the earth.

Zeus appeared and with his lightning hurled the Titans back to Tartarus. He gave the child god's limbs to Apollo, who took them to Mount Parnassus and set them beside his own oracular tripod at Delphi.

He was however reconstituted by his grandmother, Rhea. Persephone, to whom Zeus now entrusted the child, arranged for him to be brought up by a local king, in the women's quarters, disguised as a girl. From this point the story melds in with the mythology of the growing and adult Dionysos that we have already described.

The bodies of the Titans, still wet with the blood of their victim, were rendered to ashes by the lightning bolt from Zeus, and from these ashes the human race arose. This embodied the Orphic doctrine that human beings are part good and part evil, as they have both Titanic and Dionysian elements in their nature.

This mythical story was intended to reawaken in the human soul the remembrance of its divine origin and to help it to find its way back to the divine state. The Orphics taught that the soul was subject to a series of earthly incarnations, between which it resided in the underworld, subject to judgement and rewards and punishments according to the deeds of the last life on earth, until eventually it was liberated from the wheel of birth and death. This process could be accelerated however by purificatory disciplines and rites of the Orphic Mysteries, by living ascetically and abstaining from eating meat.

Along with the underworld emphasis introduced to the Mysteries of Eleusis by Iacchos and Persephone, and through the development of the myth of Orpheus descending into it to rescue Euridice, the Orphics plotted a geography of the underworld. This of course is the function of funerary and initiatory rites the world over; the Egyptian and Tibetan Books of the Dead, to name but two, do much the same thing.

The Orphic religion was welcomed and encouraged in Athens at the time of the tyrant Pisistratus (who ruled more or less from 561 to 527 BC) and his sons. A prominent courtier, Onomacritus, was a leading Orphic teacher, and composer of a poem, *"The Rites of Initiation"*. A new edition of Homer prepared at this time introduced the episode of Odysseus' visit to the world of shades.

In general terms, beyond the vestibule known as the Grove of Persephone, with its black poplar trees and sterile willows, lay the gates of the Kingdom of Hades. Hades, who had espoused Persephone, was the brother of Zeus, for both were sons of Rhea and Cronos. His name Hades meant literally "not visible" or "unseen".

He was also called Pluto on account of the treasures buried under the earth, or more importantly, for sending up the crops that gave wealth to the land.

At the gate was the monstrous watch dog Cerberus, usually depicted with three heads, although he could have as many as fifty, bristling with venomous serpents. His function was not only to guard the gates against intruders, but also to prevent those inside from escaping. Only Hercules ever defeated him by main force and then but to carry him up to earth for a bare moment as part of one of his twelve labours. There were, however, two symbolic weapons that could charm or control him. One was the caduceus of Hermes and the other the lyre of Orpheus.

Various rivers flowed within the underworld. The first, Acheron, had a ferryman, Charon, whom it was necessary to pay for a crossing, otherwise the soul would be doomed to wander along the deserted banks. For this reason the Greeks always put a coin in the mouth of the deceased. There was also the river Styx which ran in nine great loops, and Lethe, whose waters erased memory, and which marked the boundary between Tartarus, abode of the unjustified, and the Elysian Fields of the blessed.

The souls of the dead were but a pale reflection of the personalities that had existed upon earth, living in a kind of limbo as phantoms of what they once had been. Only those who had been outstandingly guilty suffered exemplary torment. In the course of time this dim place of shades began to be regarded more as a court of judgement, after which souls were allocated either to Tartarus or to the Elysian Fields. Tartarus was a sombre jail enclosed by a triple wall, in which was a diamond gate, and surrounded by the river Phlegethon. This was the place where Tantalus, Sisyphus, and Ixion, legendary sinners against the gods, suffered their punishments. In the Elysian Fields, on the other hand, neither snow nor rain fell, and sweet breezes ever blew. It was originally the abode for children of the gods but was later extended to include their friends, and eventually the souls of all the just.

The Orphic teachers also taught a new matriarchal theory of creation. In the beginning there was Nyx, or Old Night, a primeval goddess who was sometimes visualised as a great bird with black wings. She conceived by means of the Wind, and laid a silver egg, from which sprang the son of the rushing wind, Phanes, a god of light with golden wings, who was also known as Eros. That is to say he was the great primal Eros, a cosmic force of divine creative love, not the little cherubic figure of sexual infatuation later associated with Venus/Aphrodite, (although this figure plays an important role in certain Rosicrucian symbology, not least in *"The Chymical Marriage of Christian Rosencreutz."*) Eros was also called Protogonos, the first born of all the gods. He brought into the light everything that had been concealed in the silver egg, from the sky above to the earth below.

There are of course resonances here that are very familiar to modern Qabalists. The Old Night being the Ain Soph, otherwise known as Sophia, beyond Kether, and the Primal Wind being like the Holy Spirit moving upon the face of the Waters of the Unmanifest, as the Divine Breath. Kether itself is like the primal silver egg, from which the God of Love emerges to create all that lies below.

Beyond Athens the Orphic doctrines were to undergo a significant development when they were taken up by the famous mystical mathematician Pythagoras, who founded a community in Croton, in southern Italy, in 530 BC The Pythagoreans accepted women into their ranks, believed in the transmigration of souls and followed the rules of life of Orphic initiates.

This community developed a number of lines of practical esoteric philosophy which have had a profound influence upon the whole of western culture.

Key Ideas and Images of the Greek Mystery Rites

Having investigated the historical development and the nature of the rites of Dionysos and Orpheus, as Dion Fortune recommended, it remains for us to consider some of the elements within this teaching that might form part of what she calls "the lost secrets of the West". These comprise a number of key ideas and images.

i) Persephone is a goddess within the Earth with whom man needs to be in a creative respectful relationship.

The idea of a goddess whose realm is within the Earth has been gaining currency in modern times although its roots go back a long way. She is often referred to nowadays as Gaea, deriving from the very ancient earth goddess who in Jane Harrison's book and some of Dion Fortune's rituals is known as Ge.

The modern feminist movement is a part of this reappearance of the goddess, but only a part, for in its wider aspects it embraces the whole field of ecological responsibility for the environment and for the non-human species that inhabit the Earth along with the human race.

Even this is by no means the whole story for the Earth is not simply a randomly located ball of plasma with an organic shell in an alien physical universe. It has realms within it which have their correspondence with inner realms that extend throughout the greater universe. In this respect all the stars and planets are vehicles of consciousness of great beings of one kind or another. Some of them support complex forms of organic life within which spiritual beings can dwell, (such as the Earth under the stimulus of its parent the Sun); others produce the basic atomic material of the physical universe, (such as the thermo-nuclear furnaces of the stars). In this respect even space itself is an entity, a great being not entirely unlike the Nox of the Orphic creation mythology.

The inner side to the Earth, which has always been known to those who lived closest to it, is a realm from which our modern technological civilisation has become increasingly alienated. This inner world has been variously named by different cultures but is generally known today, to its initiates, as the Underworld or World of Faery. Vaguely sinister or whimsically sentimental connotations may have grown up around these terms but this ambivalence is probably inevitable, for no matter what names we chose to use, if we refuse to countenance a whole realm of reality we cast it into our own shadow side, peopling it with projections of our own disturbed and repressed fantasies. One sees much the same kind of mechanism in xenophobia and various forms of social and racial intolerance.

ii) The ancient goddess appeared at all locations to inspire the local hero and to represent the sovereignty of the land.

This local element is not a matter of petty provincialism but the individual expression of the goddess at a specific location on the face of the land, in relation to the particular flora and fauna, geophysical construction, and the human beings living upon it. Whoever lives off this tract of land becomes its subject and whoever seeks to tend and defend it becomes wedded to its sovereignty. The goddess therefore represents the sovereignty of the land and the local lord or chief becomes her consort.

In earliest times we see this associated with his sacrifice for the good of the people and the land, later replaced by an annual surrogate. These are the origins of belief in the divine right of kings, although by the seventeenth century of our era this had become largely a political issue. The inner dynamics still exist however, and in a democracy we are all kings or queens of our own field of living space and there is ample scope for each of us to make our own contact with the goddess power within the land.

There is an ancient tradition enshrined in ballad lore whereby such heroes as Thomas the Rhymer met the Faery Queen on Huntley Bank and entered the Eildon Hills with her. More recently the Reverend Robert Kirk, a seventeenth century Scottish divine, wrote a book upon the subject, *"Kirk's Secret Commonwealth of Elves"*, and is also said to have entered their kingdom.

This tradition can still be followed and guided visualisation can provide a controlled approach to these realms, which are by no means to be dismissed as "only imagination". With the imagination we have the embryonic organs of interior sense perception of whole worlds that exist beyond the surface appearances presented by brain consciousness.

We might also turn to the visualisations of the seventeenth century Rosicrucian Thomas Vaughan and his entry into Mount Abiegnus, or to many of the symbolic diagrams of spiritual alchemy. Alternative visions can also be found in the traditions of Celtic mythology, as of the Greek, both of which have had their heroes who entered the Underworld. Indeed the tradition is a worldwide one.

By means of *"The Underworld Initiation"* R.J. Stewart, in book and tape and workshop, has enabled many modern people to approach this inner world quite normally and safely. Its dark queen was known to initiates of the Eleusinian tradition as Persephone but she has many names and epiphanies. She is not merely Ruler of the Dead but is also the Spring maiden, she who regularly gives new life in the rhythm and polarity of the coming and going of the light in the world above.

In the world below there is a perpetual light, that which might be called *"Earth Light"* and a *"Power within the Land"*, which, by no means coincidentally, also happen to be titles of Stewart's more recent books. The whole experience may bring about a vision and realisation of "the stars within the Earth" which is by no means a great way from what the ancient initiates meant when they talked of "seeing the sun shine at midnight".

iii) Dionysos as the "twice born", the discoverer of the vine and of divine inebriation, represented the inner forces and divine potential of the human individual.

The forces of the unconscious and of the underworld when denied expression can lead to catastrophe. This is a lesson behind some of the more violent elements of Dionysian mythology. A dramatic example of this is to be found in Euripides play *"The Bacchae"*, which we have already mentioned in regard to its relevance to personal psychology and spirituality.

There is also a wider side to this question, with regard to its social implications. In *"The Circuit of Force"* we find Dion Fortune's oft-reiterated concern about the repressive moral attitudes of the day, which were then assumed to be the necessary price for maintaining a stable society. She was writing in the nineteen thirties when even the King of England was forced to abdicate rather than marry a divorcée. Since the nineteen sixties and the arrival of easy divorce, easy abortion, easy contraception, and a considerable erosion in traditions of family life, it might be argued that the pendulum has swung quite far the other way.

Be this as it may, it is difficult to think oneself back into the repressive moral climate that concerned not only Dion Fortune but many others of her generation. Thus we have her references, sometimes with inflated enthusiasm, to contemporary writers who seemed to be on the side of progress in this matter.

Charles Morgan's play *"The Flashing Stream"* and its accompanying essay, produced and published in 1938, is hardly the greatest play of all time, but was a commercially successful and perceptive treatment of socio-sexual dynamics, which assumed that extra-marital sexual intercourse need not be evil if it did no harm to others - an idea which would be regarded commonplace today but which was considered very advanced then. It also made the point however that physical sex was not the be-all and end-all of male/female relationships, and that sometimes restraint and chastity mattered, which may not be too welcome an attitude to more extreme libertines.

Dion Fortune's enthusiasm for Trotter's *"Instincts of the Herd in Peace and War"*, (in origin a text of 1908 which was an early treatment of the idea of a group mind), is, in this context, grounded largely on Trotter's criticisms of Freudian analysts for thinking they were curing people when they were simply reconciling them to the standards of a sick society – standards that she describes as being those of an overcrowded monkey house!

iv) A civic system of Mysteries was once open to all, providing a realisation of personal spirituality and access to the inner aspects of the Earth through sacred drama and rites of purification and dedication.

This public celebration of the Mysteries in ancient times demonstrates that the way of personal spiritual realisation or revelation does not have to be a cultish esoteric pursuit as it later came to be when driven underground by state religious interests. The Eleusinian Mysteries was a system open to all, and lasted for several hundred years.

In later times the Mysteries of Mithra largely followed the Roman armies, and the wall paintings and mosaics of Pompei bear witness to the celebration of the Mysteries of Isis and Osiris, which are also the subject of the great comic novel, Apuleius of Madaura's *"The Golden Ass"*. This is an initiatic ludibrium (an outwardly comic tale that is the vehicle for hidden wisdom) for which I have provided a fairly lengthy exegesis in *"The Rose Cross and the Goddess"* and its revised and expanded American edition *"Evoking the Goddess"*.

The great religions may provide a Noah's ark of belief and liturgy for their followers, the bulk of whom may evince no interest in anything but material concerns between the celebration of key personal events such as births, marriages and deaths. Through their very "establishment" as pillars of society, the great religions may not answer the spiritual needs of those who seek a deeper personal spiritual knowledge and experience than that which is provided by catechism, moral homily, and act of public worship. Thus it was in the days of the state religion of ancient Greece and so it is today.

What the official religion fails to provide will, if the need is there, be provided by agencies outside it. Although this may lead to a proliferation of sects, sometimes of doubtful spiritual and moral integrity, as has been demonstrated over the centuries, persecution of religious minorities is no solution to this problem. The ancient Mysteries, as they developed alongside the established religions of the day, provided a genuine and well-trodden way of individual spiritual realisation based upon a system of carefully graded experience.

Once the Christian church came to power however, through the patronage of the emperor Constantine, it became a savage persecutor of the remains of the Mystery tradition, whether in the paganised form of Mithra that had been popular in the Roman army, or in the Christianised form of the Gnosis. The assumption was that the Holy Spirit was confined in its action to being an inspirer of the elders of the church, and therefore any other apparent manifestations of it must be the work of the devil.

On the other hand, there has always been a certain unease between the established religious mainstream and seekers after individual spiritual wisdom. Orphic initiates were by no means universally popular in Athens. Regarded as dissenters from official religious belief and practice they could expect to be branded as superstitious, and considered as transcendental prigs too much concerned with the state of their own souls. They were criticised for incantations, wand wavings, enchantments and magic, noisy drumming and "filthy" purifications, so described because these sometimes involved daubing their bodies and faces with white mud. Their habit of self-examination was thought morbid, and a typical initiate was caricatured in popular imagination as sitting at home in clouds of incense, bespattered with holy mud, in the company of a crowd of old women. Plato in *"The Republic"* complains of Orphic priests hawking tracts from door to door, and of others selling "indulgences" and duping citizens with wild promises of the wonders to be gained from performing their rites.

Much the same might be said today of more bizarre sects and

religions but this does not detract from the fact that there is and always has been a perennial golden thread of the Mystery tradition throughout history, manifesting in different ages in different ways, sometimes driven underground by persecution, at other times working openly and subject only to mockery, even thriving as a wholesome contribution to society.

v) The thyrsus of Dionysos is an image of the serpent power of yoga practice, developing into the paradigm of the caduceus, an emblem of healing, and the pattern is also discernible in the Qabalistic Tree of Life.

We shall deal with the question of the arousal of the serpent power in yoga in Commentary B. For the moment it will suffice to show the similarity of the yoga system with the magical weapon of Dionysos, the thyrsus, a rod surmounted with a pine cone, around which wind ivy or vine tendrils.

This image naturally elaborates into the caduceus of Hermes, the messenger of the gods. We may also see how it has parallels in the Qabalistic diagram of the Tree of Life, which forms the backbone (in more senses than one) of the Western Esoteric Tradition. (See Figure A.1.)

vi) Orpheus developed the higher dynamics to be found in the Dionysian mysteries by the symbolism of the seven or eight stringed lyre.

The human cultural exemplar Orpheus finds the middle way, the harmonious pattern, between the forces of the natural world and the heavenly heights. In basic Dionysian myth there are many ancient and powerful symbols that come from the depths of human racial consciousness. They have their roots in blood sacrifice and orgy, head hunting, totem animals, and ancient burial rites, which are sublimated into the needs and aspirations of a later society by the Orphic tradition. In a similar way there are oracular heads, guardian serpents, wild beasts, bloody sacrifices which find an echo also in native Celtic mythology, much of which was rendered into the Arthurian legends with the efflorescence of feudal society in

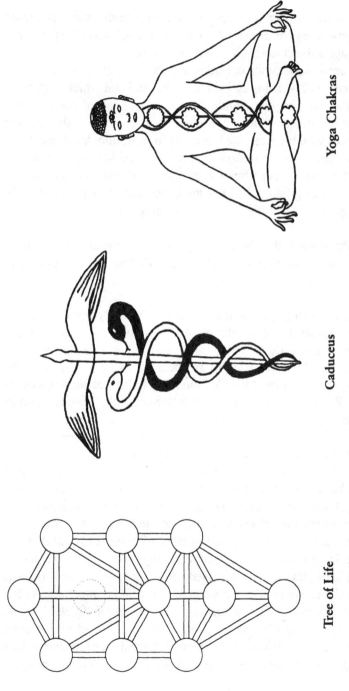

Tree of Life   Caduceus   Yoga Chakras

Fig. A.1. *Typical diagrams of yoga chakras and energy currents, Greek caduceus, and Qabalistic Tree of Life. Details will vary according to precise context of the teaching.*

twelfth and thirteenth century France. One might add that similar dynamics are to be discerned in Old Testament tales of the patriarchs although subject to much subsequent editing.

There is sometimes considered to be an archetypal opposition between that which is called Dionysian and that which is called Apollonian. The first stands for free expression of the instincts, the latter for conscious organisation and control. In this context Orpheus, with his lyre which is a gift from Apollo, his descent into and return from the underworld, and his seeking the company of wild beasts and his ability to tame their fierce natures, may be seen as a mediating figure. In Tarot imagery, he has an equivalent in the Trump called Strength, the maiden leading the lion.

vii) Pythagoras developed the lyre of Orpheus to reveal inner and outer harmonic structures, patterns in consciousness reflected in the outer world.

What the Pythagoreans discovered within the lyre was a system of harmonics based on the quality of whole numbers. This can be applied directly to mathematics, and in particular to geometry, and thence by application to architecture, as may be seen in the proportions of ancient temples and in ecclesiastical buildings of the High Renaissance deriving from followers of the Roman architect Vitruvius, whose work embodied Pythagorean principles.

The human perception of tone provides a unique meeting point where the spiritual perceptions of the human being meet the outer structures of the created world. The original and archetypal lyre may have had only three strings, emblematic of each element of a classic three tier universe, but for the full development of Pythagorean metaphysics we can see the number of strings as eight. This gives the required number of notes for a full diatonic scale in the western form of harmony, although the practical method of playing probably used a more complex system that was more than a simplistic allocation of one string to one note. As R.J Stewart points out in *"Music and the Elemental Psyche"* by the technique of lightly part-stopping a string a skilled player upon the lyre can produce a whole range of "partials" or high harmonics that give a considerable range and scope of tones and semitones after the manner of a modern pianoforte, especially if the eighth note is tuned to a half tone below the actual octave.

The Pythagorean system of harmonics is capable of very great complexity, its developments fill many a library shelf and any further analysis of it really belongs to a work on more general principles of Hermetic philosophy.

viii) The Lyre and Caduceus and "The Cosmic Doctrine".

It is interesting in this context to note that in *"The Cosmic Doctrine"*, Dion Fortune's early work of received inner plane communication in 1923, a combined glyph of the Lyre and the Caduceus plays quite an important part.

There was a certain ambivalent attitude towards this text and it remained a guarded secret until 1949 when a closely edited version was privately printed, since Dion Fortune's successor considered the original "a most dangerous book" – an epithet that has also been applied, as it happens, to *"The Circuit of Force"*.

In the edited version of 1949 the sections dealing with Lyre and Caduceus were largely omitted. This involves two chapters, one entitled *"The Law of Impactation"* and the other *"The Law of Polarity"* which in the original text had been respectively entitled *"The Law of Impactation, or the Transmission of Action from One Plane to Another"* and *"The Law of the Aspects of Force or Polarity"*.

These chapters have been restored and form part of the complete and original text in the 1995 edition of *"The Cosmic Doctrine"* that is now published by the Society of the Inner Light. It must be said that it is difficult to see just what was regarded as dangerous in these chapters. It is quite a difficult text requiring considerable intuitive powers to understand it and so is likely to try beyond endurance the patience of any less than worthy reader who seeks to penetrate its secrets.

One piece of advice that is given in these restored paragraphs is to superimpose one esoteric glyph upon another in order to elucidate and understand them, particularly if the principal application of each one is to a different plane. Thus it recommends that we try placing the Caduceus, that it calls *"the glyph of Mercury – otherwise*

Hermes, the Lord of the Mind" upon the Lyre, which is described as *"the glyph of Orpheus, Lord of the Elementals"*.

In this application the Lyre can be regarded as having its strings representing the seven planes of existence, which have of course been laid down by the primordial elemental powers. We must remember that the elemental powers are not just associated with the forces of physical nature but proceed right up the planes to form the Holy Living Creatures represented by Lion, Eagle, Bull and Man, that are the archetypal elemental powers at the highest spiritual level.

The Caduceus that we superimpose upon the Lyre may then be regarded as representing the intelligent forms of consciousness, that at their various levels express themselves upon the planes that have been laid down by the elemental forces.

C.T.Loveday, Dion Fortune's close collaborator at the time this material was received, took the trouble to make diagrams upon the lines described. These are reproduced in the 1995 complete edition of *"The Cosmic Doctrine"* and we provide a version here in Figure A.2.

Loveday's version of a lyre is somewhat unorthodox in strict musical terms in that in a real lyre the strings run the other way, that is to say, up and down rather than from side to side. However his version shows clearly enough what was no doubt intended by the communicator, and if a real lyre were being used it would simply be necessary to turn it on its side.

We can however usefully explore some of the ancillary symbolism that results from whichever way we diagrammatically construct the lyre. With the arms of the lyre conceived as being at each side, they take the symbolic place of the Pillars of Manifestation associated with the Qabalistic Tree of Life. That is to say, the planes are stretched between points of positive and negative expression.

If we were to take a more physically accurate representation of the actual musical instrument then the strings would be stretched from top to bottom, that is to say between the other great polarity of Spirit and Matter. However, in this instance we do not get such a clear representation of seven planes of elemental substance at various levels, one above the other.

As we shall see in Commentary B there has been some criticism of this way of depicting the planes on the part of followers of traditional yoga systems. They say that one plane piled upon the other in the form of a layer cake may have its uses as an elementary guide but is altogether too simplistic to represent a complex reality.

Rather than visualising layered planes in this fashion we should realise that they are all part of a uniform whole in which various vibrations or resonances can sound. That is to say, that spirit, intuition, mind, emotions, or atma, buddhi, manas – whatever planar

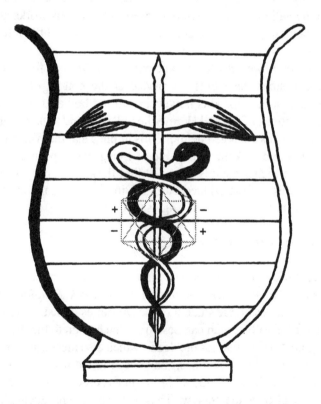

Fig. A.2. Lyre and caduceus diagram (after C.T.Loveday in 'The Cosmic Doctrine' with ancillery impactation symbolism).

distinctions we choose to make - exist altogether in one totality. We ourselves are not layered in the way that simple diagrams suggest but respond within ourselves to different wavelengths or frequencies of expression.

In this respect a "plane" is more like a sounding string that passes from heaven to earth, rather than as the gap in-between steps of a wire ladder. This may of course be a more accurate representation of the truth, but is not quite so helpful to the beginner.

Another more "advanced" way of looking at things applies to the Caduceus, where in modern symbolic usage it is always represented as having its wings just below the serpents' heads. This has a symbolic validity that is plainly expressed in various works and is not difficult to justify from simple observation and a little intuitive thought.

However if we turn to the ancient world we will find that on many occasions the wings are placed at the bottom of the staff rather than at the top. This however need not bother us too much, for in depictions of the god Hermes he will be found to have winged shoes as well as a winged helmet. This implies that the whole of the human psychic makeup is capable of flying upon spiritual wings, not just the higher centres. We will find this point brought out in the symbolism of the winged bull, in Dion Fortune's novel of that name. It is not only birds and angels that fly.

ix) By Secret Well and Sacred Tree...

As the review in *"The Inner Light"* Magazine remarks, Jane Harrison's *"Prolegomena to the Study of Greek Religion"* is of particular interest to the student of the Mysteries in that it charts the rise in the belief that man can pass from the human to the divine.

Fragments of a ritual for the dead, (which also means an entrance to the underworld for initiates,) have been found inscribed on thin gold amulets. These are quoted in full in an Appendix to Harrison's book and also in the review. They are worth reproducing here, alongside parts of a Rite of Isis which appear in *"The Sea Priestess"* and *"Moon Magic"* for the light they throw on the source of some of Dion Fortune's work.

The Petelia Tablet

Thou shalt find on the left of the House of Hades a Well-Spring
And by the side thereof standing a white cypress.
To this Well-spring approach not near.
But thou shalt find another by the Lake of Memory,
Cold water flowing forth and there are no guardians before it.
Say: "I am a child of Earth and of Starry Heaven
But my race is of Heaven (alone). This ye know yourselves.
And lo, I am parched with thirst and I perish. Give me quickly
The cold water flowing forth from the Lake of Memory."
And of themselves they will give thee to drink from the holy
Well-spring,
And thereafter among the other heroes thou shalt have
lordship...

The Rite of Isis

Sink down, sink down, sink deeper and more deep
Into eternal and primordial sleep,
Sink down, be still, forget and draw apart,
Sink into the inner earth's most secret heart.
Drink of the waters of Persephone,
The secret well beside the sacred tree.
Waters of life and strength and inner light -
Eternal joy drawn from the deeps of night.
Then rise, made strong, with life and hope renewed,
Reborn from darkness and from solitude.
Blessed with the blessing of Persephone,
And secret strength of Rhea, Binah, Ge.

SPIRITUAL AND ELEMENTAL ENERGIES

The Circuit of Force Part 2 [May 1939]
Dion Fortune

We must conceive of the personality as receiving energy from two sources - the spiritual energy drawn into it through the realisations of the mind, and the elemental energy flowing into it through the etheric double. It will be observed that I do not refer to the body as a source whence energy may be taken up by the personality, and upon this omission hangs the whole theory of yoga as the culture of the etheric double. The physical body is of the earth, earthy. Its processes are a matter of chemistry and physics; its activities a matter of mechanics, hydraulics and magnetics. The contact between a man and his body is made by means of his etheric double just as the contact between him and his car is made by pressure of foot and hand on pedal, lever and wheel. The analogy is an exact one, for the body derives its energy from electrically determined internal combustion even as does a car, and the consequences of depriving a car of petrol are precisely the same as the consequences of depriving a man of food and water. It is with the etheric double that we are concerned in the study of yoga and the physical body only comes into it in so far as its postures determine the nature of the circuit in which its magnetism operates.

The primary unit of matter is agreed to be the electron, which, as its name implies, is a unit of electrical energy believed to be of the nature of a vortex. No man has seen an electron with the naked eye, however; nor yet the atom, which is held to be composed of a constellation of electrons; nor yet the molecule, which is believed to be formed of a group of atoms; any one of these is, taken by itself, too small for our perception. We have to conduct our investigation of matter en masse as it were, and deduce from our study of its bulk the nature of its units. We know enough to know with certainty and precision that matter is not self-existent in the form in which we perceive it but is the end result of the organisation of pre-existent energy. It used to be believed that energy was the result of the breaking down of physical molecules, but we know nowadays that electrical and radioactive forms of energy exist apart from the combustion or chemical combination of material substances; but as we do not know of any form of existence of physical substance, even the most inert, that does not possess its own inherent energy, we may reasonably conclude that the existence of energy preceded the existence of matter, and that there may be a transitional phase which can aptly be termed pre-matter or materialising force according to which way we look at it.

Physical science is beginning to tell us something about the nature of the magnetic field of the physical body which esotericists call the aura, but for any detailed information on the subject, based on extended observation and experiment, we must go to the East and learn from the yogis, with, however, the handicap and complication that there is little love lost between East and West, and even less understanding, and that the yogis, having no scientific tradition of the pooling of knowledge, are masters of the sister arts of *suppressio veri* and *suggestio falsi*. The Indian initiate will not give out the truth, the whole truth, and nothing but the truth, and the white initiate may not.

I, however, who am an initiate of the Western but not the Eastern Tradition, stand in a position of peculiar advantage, for I can take the eastern teachings and methods, and comparing them with what I know of the western methods, say: "This is what you really mean, quite apart from what you choose to say." The sources of my information are the works of Sir John Woodroffe, which are the only scholarly investigations in the field of yoga, and those of Madame Blavatsky, who knew a great deal, and knew a great deal more than she told. These, throwing light on each other and interpreted with the help of a working knowledge of the principles of physics and a pretty intimate knowledge of not only the principles, but the practical applications of psychology; combined with a quarter of a century's experimenting and observing in this remote and rocky field, have supplied me with such explanations as I have to offer concerning the science and art of yoga, and I do not fancy I am very far out so far as I go, though I do not for one moment flatter myself by believing that I know all there is to know - it is only a mortal as ignorant as he is rash who will set a limit to knowledge in any direction.

I have no doubt that what I have to say will be criticised and discredited as not according to the oriental equivalent of Cocker by those qualified, or who consider themselves qualified, or who are believed when they say they are qualified, to speak from within the Veil. Nevertheless, I believe that I have in some measure at any rate succeeded in drawing back that Veil because what I have to say can be tried out experimentally and proved to work.

It must be borne in mind, however, that the occidental viewpoint diverges fundamentally from the oriental, just as the European's physical habits differ from the Asiatic's. I do not, therefore, admit the plenary authority of oriental experts on the subject of yoga for Europeans, but regard them as sources of information, rather than a kind of multiple Papacy.

I have observed unfortunate, and even disastrous consequences follow upon disregard of this precaution, ranging from nervous exhaustion and incoordination, through various degrees of mental unbalance to a death in acute mania. Yoga is not fool-proof, and it is possible, by the indiscreet use of its methods, to disorganise one's etheric double very thoroughly - and one then sees the part the etheric double plays in one's economy. It affords the key to more than is realised.

I define the etheric double as the magnetic field of the physical body, the existence of which requires no demonstration by me, being a well-established fact. We will therefore proceed to the next question: "Whence does the etheric double derive the energy that animates it?" Physical science regards it as the emanation of the physical body and its energy is derived therefrom; esoteric philosophy disagrees with this, believing the physical body to derive its existence from the etheric double, and that the magnetic field surrounding living creatures, of which the scientist is well aware, is the unabsorbed portion of this basic energy.

The esoteric philosopher, therefore, does not regard the physical body as the source of magnetic energy, and therefore he does not, if he is well-informed, regard the diet and regimen of the body as directly affecting consciousness, but rather as affecting the body itself and thus rendering it either an efficient or an inadequate instrument of consciousness, just as the mechanical condition of a car does not make any difference to the health of the chauffeur, though it makes a very great difference to the efficacy of his work.

The principal sources of our knowledge of yoga are Hindu, and the Hindu not only has religious objections to the eating of meat, but is condemned by custom and circumstances to exist on a diet which all authorities agree to be definitely unsatisfactory. He is born and bred in malnutrition; this applies to the well-to-do as well as the less prosperous sections of the community, because Indian ideas on dietetics and hygiene in general, are, to put it mildly, not well-informed. What is luxury for an Indian is privation for a European and their respective physiological processes have adapted themselves accordingly.

It is a well-known fact that fasting leads to what are called hallucinatory or revelatory visions according to the viewpoint, but let us bear in mind that hallucinatory visions can be revelatory, as Freud pointed out in respect of dreams. Even though they bear no relation to the facts of objective existence, they may, and often do, bear a very definite relationship to the facts of subjective existence. All religious disciplines, Catholic, Mohammedan and Buddhist as well as yoga, have availed themselves of this principle in order to afford their devotees direct mystical experience.

For this and such methods are undoubtedly efficacious, but so is the use of hashish, mescal, and other hallucination producing drugs, and these have been used from time immemorial for precisely this purpose, mescal being the sacred plant of the Indians of the New World and hemp, from which bhang, a form of hashish, is made, occupying a similar position in Asia.

Whether the method of extending consciousness by the chronic method of restrictive dieting, or the acute method of drugging or fasting, the results, though psychologically efficacious are physically disastrous. These results are, in my opinion, obtained by altering the balance of energy between the physical and etheric bodies till their normal polarity is reversed and the latter predominates. The physical body, so far as its physiological processes go, is under normal conditions a self-regulating mechanism; but there are certain states in which the automatic level of the mind suffers invasion by the subconscious level. Hysteria is an outstanding example of this condition; but there are also subtler and less readily recognised conditions among the neurotic states and even more elusive forms of dual control when prolonged emotional tension reacts on all levels of the being. It is this latter condition which affords the fruitful field tilled by the various forms of mind-healing, and to say this is not to disparage them, for they meet a great need which orthodox medicine cannot deal with. A man is no less ill if the working of his stomach or his kidneys is upset by prolonged anxiety than if they are disordered by invading bacteria.

But in addition to such unconscious and undirected interference with the automatic control of the bodily functions, it is possible to achieve conscious and directed control of them, of your subconscious mind, and through it you can acquire control of your automatic mind, and so of the physiological processes usually regarded as beyond the influence of the will.

Yoga practices, by concentrating the attention on the breathing, the heartbeat and the principal nervous plexuses, cause us to become conscious of them, and as we become conscious of them, we acquire control of them. The yoga method of picturing in the imagination the inflowing and out-going of the pranic force as rays or clouds of light is an effectual method of manipulating the sub-conscious mind which responds to the imagination but not to the will.

The yogi employs this method for the culture of the etheric double, which is as responsive to exercise and regimen as its physical counterpart, and can yield very remarkable results both as to physical energy and the extension of consciousness when thus trained and developed; but the line is narrow between the achievement of control of the etheric double and the breaking in upon the automatic control of the physiological processes, and it is here that danger lies, and to avoid it the guru must be careful and experienced, and the chela obedient, properly prepared and working under suitable conditions. These conditions consist in good general health, a harmonious emotional life, and circumstances wherein freedom from disturbance for prolonged periods may be secured, so that the practitioner of these methods shall not only be able to build up his condition step by step without being in any way obliged to force the pace but shall have ample leisure to "convalesce" from the higher states of consciousness, which cannot be borne by the mind for unduly long periods without disintegrating it.

The building-up process is well understood but the coming-back process is not so well understood, because the Asiatic regards the higher trances as the supreme good and has not the slightest objection to it disintegrating his mind, the resulting lunacy being regarded as sainthood. The European, however, has different values, and though he may esteem the illuminations of extended conscious quite as highly as his eastern instructor, he also values what the Asiatic devotee does not value in the very least - the integration of the personality - knowing that if he fails to maintain this and becomes incapable of self-maintenance, he will not be supported by voluntary contributions as a saint, but become chargeable on the rates as a pauper lunatic.

Everything depends on the viewpoint in these matters, and it is not well to accept as a leader one who is heading for the next world as fast as he knows how unless one has finished with this world. One may regard the body as an encumbrance from which the spirit must be freed, or one may regard it as an instrument through which the spirit must be expressed. These are divergent viewpoints and lead to divergent ends, and one needs to be quite clear which one subscribes to when one selects a guru, or one may find oneself in the position of the passenger who was taken on to Manchester when he wanted to go to Crewe. It is for these reasons that I do not recommend the practice of yoga to Europeans, but I fully acknowledge the value of its study by western occultists and frankly admit my debt to it. There can be little doubt that it was something of the nature of yoga that Mrs Atwood found to be the key to alchemy, though she described it in terms of "animal magnetism" of her day, and it was a realisation of its dangers as well as its powers that caused her to destroy the whole edition of her *"Suggestive Enquiry"*.

CURRENTS OF FORCE
IN THE ETHERIC DOUBLE

The Circuit of Force Part 3 [June 1939]
Dion Fortune

The energy substance out of which the etheric double is organised is called by various names and divided into various grades according to whether yoga or the Qabalah be the tradition that is followed. To call it etheric energy, as is often done in the west, is to confuse it with the better-known ether of the physicists, which is undoubtedly an aspect of it, but by no manner of means the whole. It was referred to by the older mesmerists as *Od*, or odic force, and unquestionably formed the basis of their experiments. Another of its manifestations has been described as ectoplasm. In the east the well-known terms of *prana* and *kundalini* are used to describe different aspects of it. We, however, cannot do better than adopt the term elemental force to distinguish it from the purely physical forms of energy on the one hand and astral force on the other.

This elemental force appears to vibrate like an alternating current between Earth and Heaven, and also to run as a circuit of force round the earth. Living creatures, and in a lesser degree, inanimate objects, appear to pick up their share of elemental force from these sources of energy, and build and maintain their etheric bodies with it just as the physical body has its intake of nourishment from physical sources.

Every creature and object seems to have its normal charge of elemental force, but under certain conditions can be super-charged; the technique of this super-charging is called talismanic magic or consecration when applied to inanimate objects, and yoga when applied to human beings.

Yoga, then, is a form of psycho-physical culture wherein the mind directs the currents of elemental energy in the etheric body and thereby develops that body just as its physical counterpart is developed by gymnastics; the centres of force, and the channels connecting them being as susceptible to cultivation as the muscles and senses.

A great deal is recorded in tradition, both oral and written, concerning the etheric body and its channels of force, but in a matter where suggestion and auto-suggestion play so large a part, it is not easy to distinguish between objective force and psychic convention. A good deal can be learnt by comparing the eastern and western systems, yoga and the Qabalah; for those things in which they agree may be taken as being established in objective experience and not as auto-suggested conventions, bearing in mind, however, that auto-suggested conventions have their very definite uses in the *modus operandi* of the psychic, provided they are never mistaken for anything but what they are, for that way lies superstition and hallucination.

Both eastern and western systems agree in recognising a main current of magnetic force corresponding to the central line of the body. Qabalists call it the Middle Pillar; I hesitate to be dogmatic as to what the yogis call it, for there are so many schools of yoga, and such a multiplicity of subtle subdivisions of terminology that I can hardly hope to escape the charge of inaccuracy from one source or another if I enter on that thorny field. Let it suffice to say that east and west are in agreement concerning the central vertical line of force.

The east also recognises two side channels of force, which it calls *Ida* and *Pingala*, and the west recognises the Pillars of Mercy and Severity; but whereas the yogi locates these channels centrally, as subdivisions of the central channel, the Qabalist places the Pillars of Equilibrium, as they are called, outside the body, in the aura, and equates them with the limbs. Both east and west, however, are agreed in recognising these side channels of positive and negative force after the analogy of a magnetic circuit; whether they are located alongside the spine or projected into the aura being, in my opinion, entirely a matter of where they are placed and cultivated according to the system that is used, and I have worked with both systems, and obtained results with both.

There is a certain amount of difference concerning the location of the centres or chakras between the two systems. The Hindu locates the basal one in the sacral plexus, and the Qabalist places it under the feet. This difference of position is readily understood when it is remembered that the Hindu habitually meditates squatting, so that it is his sacrum which forms his earth terminal, and the European meditates either sitting, standing or lying down, with his lower limbs extended and his aura consequently extended with them.

The most important point in this connection, however, is to be found in the fact that the yogi invariably meditates in one of the asanas, or special postures, with one or both feet tucked into his groin, and works on his etheric body while it is in its normal relationship to his physical body; it is for this reason that he contorts himself into what the European considers fantastic postures in order to bring the magnetic currents into the position in which he wants them to function. The Qabalah-trained European, on the other hand, relaxes his physical body and works with the etheric double projected, and this is a very important distinction of method.

I have tried both methods, and in my opinion the Eastern method is incomparably the more efficacious. In actual practice, so far as my experience goes, the western adept merely throws his etheric double out of gear and projects his astral body when he tries to do this operation; and the result, whatever else it may be, is not Hatha Yoga, and it is quite certain that, although psychism is developed by this method, the etheric body is practically unaffected. It is also my experience that a far more powerful concentration of force is obtained when the lower legs are bent on themselves in the squatting posture, and the aura consequently retracted.

Most Europeans, however, cannot achieve this position, being much more heavily boned and muscled than the Hindus, owing partly to racial characteristics and partly to the fact that an inadequate diet produces a laxness of ligaments that permits of contorted attitudes. I myself can speak of these postures with some degree of experience, for, being born at a time when the science of nutrition was not as well understood as it is now, I am blessed, or more accurately speaking, cursed with elastic ligaments, and from my earliest childhood to the present day, habitually sit cross-legged. *Siddhasana* is a normal posture with me, and *Padmasana* presented no particular difficulties after a little practice.

Speaking from my own experience, I find the cross-legged posture invaluable for meditation, but do not think *padmasana* worth the trouble of achieving. The point to be borne in mind in this matter is that the aim of the posture is to make the sacral plexus the earth contact of the Central Pillar, and that this is achieved if the aura is retracted to the size of the torso and the legs folded upon themselves in such a manner that the soles of the feet are turned upwards and raised above the level of the base of the spine. This can be done by sitting cross-legged and putting a small cushion under the ankles; and although the agonies of achieving padmasana are no doubt an excellent discipline for the soul, and save the expense and dirt of a hair shirt, it has not been my experience that they have any beneficent effect on the etheric body that cannot be achieved by the use of a small cushion, though I admit that the cushion does not make so impressive a display as a pair of legs tied in a bow-knot. Another spectacular feat, the power to retract the right or left rectus abdominus muscle at will, is a mere trick achieved by digging the thumbs into the groins at the appropriate spot. It can, of course, only be done when a high degree of control of the muscles of the abdomen has been achieved. What bearing it has on the spiritual development of the performer I do not know, though it undoubtedly has a great deal on that of the onlookers.

All these psycho-physical exercises have, so far as I can see, their value as means to an end - the end being the concentration of the attention upon the currents of force that constitute the etheric body, which is much more effectually achieved by means of the Hatha Yoga methods of the east than by the purely psychological methods of the west; therefore I advocate the study of yoga principles, though I do not consider it necessary to break any bones in their practice, for it is in the mental aspect of these psycho-spiritual exercises that the real value lies.

THE SUBTLE BODIES

The Circuit of Force Part 4 [July 1939]
Dion Fortune

The anatomy of the etheric double has been the subject of many treatises and much speculation. Different psychics report different things, and although psychics trained in the same school may agree, the schools disagree among themselves. Broadly speaking, however, all schools agree in describing an ovoid of light surrounding the physical body in the same way as the white surrounds the yolk of an egg. Less advanced psychics described this light as grey, silvery, and pale or bright gold according to their power of perception and the type of aura. Highly developed psychics describe a rainbow appearance surrounding the human form.

Which is correct? In my opinion both are correct; the colourless, greyish light is the basic etheric substance, increasing in brightness to silver or sparkling white according to what may quite accurately be described as the voltage. When the golden radiance appears, a higher type of force seems to be manifesting through it; the basic silver-grey cloud, however, persists, but is suffused by the brighter radiance of the golden light. These two types of radiance I think all schools would agree in referring to those factors in manifestation which are represented by the Lunar and Solar spheres. The rainbow colours perceived by still more highly developed psychics can, though with less unanimity of agreement, be referred to the various planetary spheres of the manifestation of force. Thus we obtain a working scheme of agreement concerning the anatomy of the subtle body so variously and variegatedly described.

We may, for all practical purposes, consider the human make-up as consisting of a physical body of dense matter which is subject to the known laws of chemistry, physics and mechanics; a subtle body, obeying laws which appear analogous to what is known concerning electro-magnetism and radio-activity; a mental body concerning which psychology has something to say, and could have a great deal more to say if it were not as deaf as the scriptural adder to all that does not fit in with a materialistic viewpoint; and at the core of all, a spiritual nucleus concerning which no one knows a great deal, save that it is to the man what the grain of sand is to the pearl.

This spiritual nucleus is apparently the channel for a limitless flow of force from the Unmanifest, which, far from being the inert emptiness pictured by the untutored imagination, is the power-house of the whole manifested universe. The other bodies, or vehicles, if the term be preferred, derive their pabulum from the basic substance of their respective planes in exactly the same manner as the physical body has its necessary intake of raw material in the form of food and drink.

It appears to me important, from the practical point of view, to distinguish between the intake of form-building and maintaining substance on each plane, and the dynamic energy emanating from the Great Unmanifest and coming in through the channel afforded by the spiritual nucleus. The exact nature of this spiritual nucleus, and the nature of its relationship to the Great Unmanifest, can only be a subject of speculation; but so far as I can see, what may best be called the Divine Spark, or unit of manifestation, itself belongs to the Plane of the Unmanifest, and the spiritual body is its first-formed vehicle of manifestation.

It is, I believe, very important to distinguish between the spiritual force which supplies the energy of the whole being on all planes of existence, and the material for form building that has to be derived from each plane for the formation and upkeep of the vehicle of that plane; it is the failure to make this distinction which causes the prevailing uncertainty and inefficiency in manipulating the subtle aspects of our make-up. It is as if we took no account on the physical plane of the presence or absence of life in the body and tried to feed a dead man, only to find ourselves much perplexed when, in spite of our best efforts, he began to decompose instead of putting on weight; or if, contrariwise, we thought it unnecessary to supply a living person with food on the ground that, being alive, he drew all the energy he required from his own vitality.

These are things we see done daily by the various schools of thought, from the most materialistic to the most mystic, who forget to take into account the exact working of the phrase: "man cannot live by bread alone," forgetting that he cannot live without bread either. Fanatics of whatever type, whether materialistic or mystic, always appear to be people singularly lacking in common sense; it is also an odd fact that the term fanatic is reserved exclusively for application to the mystic and idealist, entirely ignoring the fact that the materialist and the rationalist can exhibit exactly the same traits of emotionally determined bias and absence of good sense and balanced judgement.

Bearing these points in mind, we see that it is not only possible theoretically, but vitally necessary for practical work, to distinguish between the development by intensive training of the spiritual, the mental, the astral and the physical vehicles of man. Equally we must bear in mind that they are all inter-acting, and we can no more develop one and ignore the others than we can cultivate the muscles while neglecting the corresponding development of the heart and lungs, an error that is made by many athletes, resulting in the premature death which so often befalls them.

Even more clearly do we see the same principle exemplified in the case of such men as Darwin, Herbert Spencer and Carlyle, whose physical infirmities, which we now know to have been purely nervous in origin, greatly handicapped them in their work. Or again, we see physically gifted people with such undeveloped mental vehicles that they were unable to avail themselves of their physical endowments. Each was entirely dependent on their respective managers, and, left to their own devices, was helpless. We must now consider a point which is the key to the whole question of yoga and psychic development: "Why is it that, by the culture of the etheric double, we can produce psychism and magical powers?" A great deal of advice has been given as to how this task should be carried out, but very little thought has been devoted, or at any rate, very little has been published, concerning the rationale of the proceeding, which consequently has been left on a rule of thumb basis.

It is well known to those who study such matters that the etheric double – that subtle, electrical counterpart of the physical body

– is the link between mind and matter. Orthodox science knows something about its manifestations in relation to the central nervous system, but psychology is entirely innocent of any realisation on the part it plays in sensory consciousness. It is the culture of this etheric double, the link between mind and body, that is effected by Hatha Yoga with such remarkable results on both mind and body. Let it be carefully noted, moreover, that the results of such cultivation are neither merely physical nor merely psychic, but concern the powers of the higher psychism as well, and lead on to genuine mystical experience. Taking into consideration all that can be learnt not only from tradition, but also from personal experimentation in its degree, it appears highly probable that the different levels of consciousness are correlated with the centres in the aura recognised independently by the practical systems of both yoga and the Qabalah.

THE PSYCHIC CENTRES AND THEIR USE

The Circuit of Force Part 4(continued) [August 1939]
Dion Fortune

We now come to the detailed consideration of the chakras or psychic centres, and their practical use. The Indian yoga tradition undoubtedly enshrines the widest and profoundest knowledge available, for the Qabalistic teaching on the subject, as I learnt it at any rate, is negligible. The best course of this knowledge is to be found in the works of Arthur Avalon (Sir John Woodroffe) upon Tantra. These books, however, are written in a very guarded manner, so that the casual reader can glean little from them, and what he does obtain is profoundly misleading.

Sir John Woodroffe only defines his terms when using them in relation to purely metaphysical implications; when using them in relation to practical psychic or magical matters, he leaves them untranslated; consequently what the student needs is a translation of Arthur Avalon's translations. This I had laboriously to equip myself with before I could make any headway, for a Sanskrit dictionary is no use in this connection, the *tantric gurus* employing a kind of *double entendre* known only to the initiated. But as "Hudibras" has it:

"Patience and perseverance made a bishop of his reverence."

And the same made a yogi of me. I learnt what I know by the dangerous method of self-experiment, and more by good luck than good management, survived to tell the tale, despite all sinister prognostications. The fruits of my experience, such as they are, I am prepared to give out in order that they may form the basis of future research. No doubt my knowledge is limited and imperfect as compared with that of Indian experts, born and bred in the yoga

64

tradition, but I am inclined to believe that it will prove to be of more practical use to western students than any scholarly adherence to the traditional texts, for it is the fruit of actual experience of working in a western body under western conditions. My records are admittedly incomplete and imperfect, but so far as they go, they are personal and practical, and they will, I believe, form more efficient guideposts for the experiments of others than the more elaborately documented, but more abstract and doctrinaire genre. It will certainly be said, and not without justice, by the orthodox exponents of the art: "But this is not yoga." To which I reply: "I never said it was." It is my own recipe, compounded from the works of Sir John Woodroffe on the *Tantra*, Mme. David-Neel on Tibetan mysticism, Baudouin on auto-suggestion, and the Qabalistic method of the Middle Pillar as I learnt it in the Order of the Golden Dawn; those who want to study this latter will find it exposed in the works of that able renegade, Israel Regardie.

The Qabalist, accustomed to using the Middle Pillar, will find it necessary to make careful distinction between his Malkuth and Yesod and the yogi's *Muladhara* and *Svaddisthana Chakras*. The yogi locates both these in the auric equivalent of the pelvic region of the spine; the Qabalist locates Yesod, the Moon Centre, there, but places Malkuth under the feet in the same way as Kether is over the head, thus indicating that it likewise is a link with objectivity. In the Qabalistic method, Malkuth is used as the earth contact, and the operator visualises himself standing on it as if it were the globe of the Earth swinging through space, and a remarkable magnetic flow is thus received.

This current, derived according to tradition from the Earth's aura, rises straight to Yesod in the sacral plexus and there becomes personal to the individual. Yesod, in fact, is a transformer of the universal, elemental energy into personal magnetism, and this is a very important practical point. Therefore, although it is customary to equate Malkuth with the *Muladhara Lotus*, and I have done this myself in previous writings, I have come, after practical experience of both methods, to doubt whether this is correct. It must be remembered, in equating the Lotuses with the Sephiroth, that the yoga method is concerned with a single line of Centres, arranged one above the other, and the Qabalistic method is concerned with three lines of centres related to each other in triangles, and we must consider the functions rather than the locations of the centres in equating them.

Malkuth occupies a position in the aura analogous to that of Kether, that is to say, it is outside the body and has no physical analogue; and just as Kether picks up the cosmic forces, so Malkuth picks up the earth magnetism. Kether, therefore, equates accurately with the *Sahasrara Lotus*, but the function and "feel" of Malkuth is quite different to that of the *Muladhara*.

Moreover the colouring is different. Malkuth has attributed to it the four colours of Elemental Earth – whereas the Muladhara is wine-coloured. Yesod, on the other hand, has among its colours in the four colour scales, indigo, very dark purple, and violet-purple, and the Paths surrounding it have various shades of crimson, dark blue and wine-colour among their symbolism. In my own experience, moreover, I have found what is said of the *Muladhara Lotus* to equate with my experience of Yesod, which, for practical working purposes is unquestionably the reservoir of magnetic force so far as the individual is concerned. Traditionalists will not agree with this, but I was aware of the workings of Yesod before I had ever heard of yoga, and the results I obtained from that centre exactly equate with what is reported of the *Muladhara* with its Sleeping Serpent. An ounce of experience is worth several pounds of tradition and the citing of authorities who copy one from another, and in taking my own experience in conjunction with the traditional colouring of Yesod and its converging Paths, I think we have here a useful indication of the practical working.

There are certain places on the Tree where the Paths connecting the Pairs of Opposites, the Equilibrating Sephiroth on the Side Pillars, cut the Middle Pillar. These nodes are obviously important points. I believe we shall be on the right track if we equate certain of the chakras with these nodes and recognise in them the equilibrated forces of the Pairs of Opposites of the different levels of manifestation. The *Svaddisthana Lotus*, according to this system of notation, would correlate with the equilibrium of Hod and Netzach.

Now Hod, Netzach and Yesod are called the Magical Triangle; Hod equating with Thoth-Hermes, is characterised by an intellectual, austere method of operation of the Hermetic type; Netzach, equating with Aphrodite and the Lady of Nature, is characterised by the Greek type of magic, such as is seen in the Dionysian rites; and Yesod, equating with the Moon, which according to the most ancient tradition is the magnetic aspect of the Earth, is characteristically represented by the magical methods of Egypt.

According to Mme. Blavatsky's *"Secret Doctrine"*, the Moon is the reservoir of magnetic force for the Earth because evolution was at the etheric phase of development when Moon and Earth parted company. If this be true, and I attribute high authority to *"The Secret Doctrine"*, then it is to be presumed that what Qabalists call the Moon Centre in the microcosm will fulfil the same function; that is to say, Yesod will be the reservoir of magnetic force at the base of the spine where the *Serpent Kundalini*, which possibly equates with the Qabalistic Dragon, sleeps in Her coils. It will be remembered by Qabalists that it is in Yesod that is the Place of Severest Judgements, to which Leviathan raises its seven crowned heads, and allowing for the ascetic influence of Christian thought upon the doctrine of western initiates, it is quite probable that the *Goddess Kundalini* of the east is referred to as "that old serpent" – and here again we have a useful piece of information.

I do not believe that the magnetic circuits in the aura are normally closed circuits at all, but that the real secret of certain types of yoga lies in knowing how to pick up the different types of force at the different levels from sources outside ourselves. At any rate, whatever the pupils of eastern gurus may be taught to do, the Qabalist is accustomed to pick up the earth currents through his Malkuth.

The elemental energy which feeds the etheric double is picked up from the Earth aura through the Malkuth Centre just as definitely as the food that feeds the physical body is taken in by the mouth. There is a widespread belief that it is picked up from the physical earth by the soles of the feet, and people refuse to wear rubber soles on their boots because they believe that to do so insulates them from the earth magnetism.

Such beliefs are superstitions, due to the error of confusing the planes. Aura picks up from aura, and because for practical purposes the aura follows the conformation of the physical body, it is convenient to assume physical postures and make physical gestures because the body carries the aura with it; but it is not the physical form that is doing the work, which can be done quite independently of physical acts when the imagination is sufficiently trained to be able to visualise the aura without adventitious aids. The inhibiting effect of rubber soles is simply due to the fact that what we picture in the imagination we build in the astral kingdom, and if we imagine a barrier to exist, that barrier comes into being. This is another important key to the practical workings. It may of course be said that such activities are pure auto-suggestion, but the initiate believes them to be something much more than that; he believes that the subtle levels of the human make-up can enter into relationship with the corresponding levels of objective existence and so extend the range of our experience and function beyond the physical body.

Initiates, though under no delusions concerning the part played by physical agencies in such matters, nevertheless make use of the physical forms of the elemental energies when seeking to contact the earth magnetism. Such an act is ritualistic rather than of the nature of a physical exercise. It is the mental effect of the physical action that counts, not the action as such. It is one thing to fall to our knees over a fold in the carpet, and another to fall on our knees in ecstasy before a high altar. Nevertheless, because places tune mood, it is well worth while when seeking the elemental contacts to seek them where the elements are present in their strength. By so doing we not only aid ourselves in the establishment of contacts, but may enjoy experiences of great interest and value. But although the beginner needs all the help that physical conditions can give him, the experienced worker ought to be independent of them. It is the very amateur and "precious" author who has to have something special in the way of a desk or inkpot to enable him to function – all the experienced writer requires is pen and paper and a quiet corner.

It is my experience that we ought to be very careful to balance the subjective and objective in our occult work, and not allow ourselves to become exclusively habituated to either in our methods of working. If we do, we produce a one-sided development and may make of ourselves dissociated introverts, cut off from the world of form just as effectually and limitingly as the worldly man is cut off from spiritual things. In this matter we shall be unwise to allow the advice and example of the saints of the west and the yogis of the east to influence us unduly, for many things pass for spiritual that are really pathological, and I shall always maintain that there is little profit in saving the soul at the expense of the mental balance.

It is this difference in viewpoint and divergence in aim between east and west which forces us to approach the practice of yoga by the traditional methods with great caution. For this reason I prefer to apply the theory of yoga to the practice of the Qabalistic methods rather than pursue whole-heartedly an imperfectly understood and alien method.

THE EARTH
AND MOON CENTRES

The Circuit of Force Part 5 [September 1939]
Dion Fortune

For practical purposes the Qabalah-trained Western initiate is accustomed to pick up the earth-forces through his Malkuth, located under the soles of the feet, and to regard the sacral or pelvic centres as constituting Yesod, the Moon-sphere of personal magnetism, and this appears to be a useful practical concept. Working with the microcosmic Malkuth we contact the elemental forces, and working with the microcosmic Yesod we contact our own reserves of magnetism and set them in motion.

Malkuth, as we have already seen, is charged from the Earth-aura, but whence does Yesod receive its magnetism? This raises an important point, and one that needs to be carefully examined and thoroughly understood, for it is here we have the possibilities of both power and chaos.

We have got to face the all-important matter of the real nature and function of the Moon Centre; the fact that it is correlated with the sacral plexus in both eastern and western systems should have put investigators on the track of its real nature, for the sacral nerve plexus controls the generative organs. In the Moon Centre the impersonal magnetic vitality derived from the Earth is transformed into very personal sex force, and if anybody questions that statement, I suggest they put it to the test of practical experiment and see for themselves.

It is well known to all students of the subject who have penetrated below the surface that sex plays a very important part in *Hatha Yoga*, and as *Hatha Yoga* is the basis of all the other forms of yoga and has to be mastered before they are attempted, it is obvious that we have here one, and possibly the chief, of the secret keys

70

which are perpetually being hinted at but never explained. The fact that the eastern and western views on the subject of sex are widely sundered is probably the good and sufficient reason why this mystery is not explained to the European enquirer, the *guru* fearing that if he were too explicit he would lose his pupil. Nevertheless, allowing for the difference of viewpoint and social conditions, it can be explained rationally, and, I hope, without offence. It is because this is not done that so much trouble results from the practice of yoga by Europeans.

It is very necessary to know these things if the study of yoga is to be pursued with safety, let alone efficacy. The key to the whole of the practical workings really lies in the fact that the force of the Moon Centre is carried up to the higher centres and there utilised for the purposes appropriate to those centres; in other words, we have an example of the principle which western psychology is familiar with under the name of Sublimation.

In the practical workings we pick up elemental force from the Earth through the Earth Centre; we transmute it into magnetic force in the Moon Centre, and we raise it again to the Sun Centre where the actual work begins. If we fail to maintain thought control when the force is at the Moon level, sexual images will arise in the imagination and the force will short-circuit through sensual channels; if, however, we maintain a rigid control, which we can only do if we are experts in the practice of concentration, then the force rises out of the sexual sphere and gives no more trouble in that direction but becomes available for the purposes of higher magic. Without this basis of personal magnetic force I do not believe it is possible to work magic effectually. It is because in the west we are both ignorant and afraid of this that our magic is inefficacious and our occultists of ill repute; for either they fail to function at all or fall into pits that they have all unknowingly digged. In my opinion we ought to understand these powers and keep them clean, neither refusing to face them, nor basely exploiting them.

Bearing in mind the distinction I have made between the Qabalistic Malkuth and the *Muladhara Lotus* of *Hatha Yoga*, with which it is usually equated, we are now in a position to study the nature of Yesod by equating it with the Muladhara, and to avoid confusion I will refer to this *Yesod-Muladhara* equation as the Sacral Centre.

The *Muladhara Lotus* is usually described as a reservoir within the aura wherein magnetic force is stored in the form that is called the Sleeping Serpent, or *Kundalini*. With all due respect to the learned traditionalists, I believe this explanation to be lacking in certain vital particulars, for it is my experience that the Qabalistic teaching is better upon this point when it says that in normal circumstances vital force is picked up from the Earth and not stored in the aura.

So far as I can see, the aura is the channel of an alternating current that flashes from heaven to earth and back again; the methods of *Hatha Yoga* aim at transforming this alternating current into a circuit in which the individual, by insulating himself from the Earth, prevents the earthing of the magnetic force and turns himself into a storage battery, thus raising the magnetic voltage of his own aura. These analogies are crude, and should be regarded as metaphoric, not descriptive; but as a far better understanding can be arrived at by those untrained in the discipline of philosophy if we employ analogies rather than attempt to expound the subtleties of metaphysics, it is well worth our while to borrow the terminology of electricity, whatever the purists may be able to allege against such methods.

It will be seen from what has gone before in these pages that the Tree of Life represents the magnetic configuration of the natural man, whereas the Lotus diagram of *Hatha Yoga* represents the magnetic configuration of the magician. When, therefore, the Qabalah-trained western student tries to adapt the methods of *Hatha Yoga* to his own system, he must remember to cut out Malkuth and by thus insulating his Earth-contact, render himself a storage battery. This being done, he applies to Yesod what is said of the *Muladhara Lotus*, and the system immediately becomes workable which previously was misleading and abortive. In confirmation of this, let me remind the Qabalists among my readers that Yesod is referred to in the *"Sepher Yetzirah"* as the "Receptacle" wherein all forces are gathered together, and this description accurately fits the Muladhara Lotus with its Coiled Serpent, the sleeping *Kundalini*.

Now let us consider what happens when we cut out Malkuth and the Earth contacts and turn ourselves into a storage battery. One of two things must happen - either we depend entirely on the spiritual forces received through Kether, or we establish a new circuit via Yesod. A little consideration of the respective natures of Kether and Yesod will reveal to us the practical implications of these two procedures.

If we cut ourselves off from the Earth-contacts we soon find ourselves beginning to be reabsorbed into the plane of spirit. This is the well-known aim of *Raja Yoga*, and its discipline, both mental and physical, is designed with this end in view, as, in fact, are all ascetic disciplines that repudiate the world and the flesh. The alternative method, which works the Yesod circuit, is known as the *Tantrik*, and to the *Tantrik* texts we must go in order to learn what this means.

Tantrik magic is a method of exceedingly ill repute, and can unquestionably lead to the grossest moral abuses. On the other hand, to the ascetic ideal can be traced that vast mass of nervous and mental trouble which is due to sex repression. We have, therefore, to steer between Scylla and Charybdis in this matter, remembering that because Charybdis is admittedly dangerous, Scylla is not necessarily a haven of refuge.

In judging *Tantrik* methods we must bear certain things in mind if we are to form an adequate opinion. Firstly, we must not take the missionaries' viewpoint, reinforced by the lurid revelations of sensational travel books, as being an impartial presentation of the subject as a whole. Modern scholarship has shown that the views of the Early Fathers on the pagan civilisation of their day were very far from a fair presentation of the facts; and since though manners change, human nature does not, it may quite well be that the missionaries may have failed to appreciate the significance of a system so widely different in viewpoint form their own. As for the sensation mongers among the travellers, we must remember that pornography dished up as ethnology is always sure of a public, and that India caters in exactly the same manner as Montmartre for tourists who wish to be shocked.

Serious enthologists are beginning to give us data apart from moralising, and if to this data we apply the teachings of psycho-analysis, we realise that we are dealing with folk who see no evil in sex and act accordingly, though taking a serious view of marriage. From them we may learn much that is of very great value, and that serves as a much-needed corrective for neurotic Europe.

The Tantra, the Qabalah, and Freudian psycho-analysis form a trinity in unity which is the key that not only admits to the Mystery temple but releases from the lunatic asylum. This may seem a hard saying, and is hardly likely to be a popular one; it is likewise very quotable, and, if lifted from its context, very damaging; but I believe it to be the truth, and truth is a thing of which I have a very high opinion, though no doubt Mark Twain is right from the worldly point of view when he says that as truth is so rare and precious, we ought to use it very economically. Truth, alas, partakes more of the nature of a high explosive than a negotiable commodity.

Commentary B

WESTERN APPROACHES TO THE EASTERN TRADITION

Gareth Knight

There seems to have been a spate of elementary books on yoga just before Dion Fortune began writing *"The Circuit of Force"*, most of which she felt would have been better left unread if not unpublished. However, in more recent times classes in elementary yoga have become a popular part of the curriculum of many an adult education college, so as a form of physical exercise, relaxation and elementary meditation technique, this approach to yoga would appear to do no harm and may well do a considerable amount of good.

Futhermore, changing patterns of population in the postwar years together with the exodus of Tibetan lamas as a consequence of Chinese intervention in their country has caused a considerable body of Hindu and Buddhist teaching to become available in the west. So those who feel they may have a call to follow the eastern traditions now have authentic means more readily to hand to test their vocation.

Arthur Avalon and the Serpent Power

For most of her information on yoga, Dion Fortune turned to the books of Sir John Woodroffe, who wrote under the pen name of Arthur Avalon. He was perhaps the first Westerner to approach the doctrines of yoga sympathetically and upon their own terms, and spent half a life time searching for key documents and an Indian guru willing to help him translate the texts in a form accessible to Westerners.

"The Serpent Power" appeared in 1918, which after several chapters of introduction to the chakras, mantra, and the theory and practice of yoga, provides a translation of two important texts

on kundalini yoga *"Description of the Six Centres, or Chakras"* and *"The Fivefold Footstool"* (which covers the seventh and highest chakra, the Sahasrara at the top of the head.)

Kundalini yoga forms a part of laya yoga and in a collection of essays and lectures, *"Shakti and Shakta"*, published at the same time, Woodroffe differentiates the four main types of yoga, (mantra yoga, hatha yoga, laya yoga and raja yoga), the general characteristics of which are described in *"The Serpent Power"*.

The general principles and meaning of kundalini yoga had never before been published, although they had long been subject to a great deal of western curiosity and ill-informed speculation. This had been encouraged by a specious veil of mystery drawn by self-proclaimed experts for their own financial or prestigious benefit.

The system is not exclusive to India and Sir John acknowledges similar notions in Islamic Sufi mysticism, and in Amerindian Maya scripture, the *"Popul Vuh"*. This form of yoga is called tantrik because it appears in various manuals of Hindu worship and occultism, which are called tantra. The particular form of tantrik yoga that is known as kundalini yoga is concerned with raising a power in the body that Sir John Woodroffe calls the Serpent Power. This power is said to be a divine cosmic energy that is a form of prana, (vitality or life principle). It is figuratively called the goddess Kundalini, and may be visualised in the form of a sleeping serpent coiled at the base of the spine.

When aroused, the kundalini passes up three channels that run parallel to the spine on an inner level. The central one is called the Sushumna, and the two others that spiral round it are called Ida (pale in colour and regarded as feminine and carrying a negative lunar current) and Pingala (red in colour and regarded as positive and carrying a positive solar current). Each of the latter is associated with one of the nostrils, which is why one technique of yoga is learning to breath through each nostril independently.

The central channel, the Sushumna, runs from the Muladhara Chakra at the base of the spine, through an opening called the Door of Brahman. The three channels pass through six centres of consciousness or chakras as they proceed upward in line with the spinal column. These centres of subtle force should not be too closely associated with organs of the physical body. They are visualised as lotus flowers, of differing numbers of petals. These normally hang downwards but become erect as kundalini passes through them. At the Ajna Chakra at the brow the three channels become one and proceed to a twelve petalled lotus that is in the pericarp of the Sahasrara Chakra, or thousand petalled lotus, at the top of the head.

Each chakra has a number of visualised symbols associated with it, and in this respect resembles the symbolic attributions of the spheres and paths of the Qabalistic Tree of Life, although of course the detail of the symbolism is oriental rather than occidental. It consists of various animals, gods and goddesses, with geometrical sigils of the elements (or tattvas), and letters of the sanskrit alphabet, which is a holy alphabet of the orient as the Hebrew alphabet is a holy alphabet of the west.

The red Muladhara lotus has four petals and is associated with the region midway between the genitals and the anus in the male human body. Within this lotus, the tattva or element is Earth, whose strength, firmness and solidity is signified by a yellow square and an elephant. Here also is the goddess Kundalini, (she who maintains all living creatures), lying coiled asleep, shining as bright as lightning, covering with her head the Door of Brahman.

The vermilion six petalled Svadhisthana lotus comes next and is associated with the root of the genitals. The Water tattva reigns here in the form of a white crescent moon and the animal symbol is a white makara, similar to an alligator.

Next comes the ten petalled Manipura lotus, lustrous as a gem, associated with the region of the navel, wherein is to be found the Fire tattva, a red triangle, and a ram, which in eastern mythology is carrier of the Lord of Fire.

The Anahata lotus, in the heart region, is also red and has twelve petals, its element/tattva a smoky coloured six pointed star of Air, and its animal a swift black antelope.

At the region of the base of the throat is the Visuddhu lotus, a smoky purple colour with sixteen petals, its elemental tattva a white circle of Ether, and its animal a white elephant.

Then between the eyebrows, we come to the Ajna lotus, of two white petals, whose tattva is Mind. Finally there is the Sahasrara or thousand petalled lotus at the top of the head.

This is a very basic outline of the chakra system, which in its fullness is of considerable complication, and details vary from school to school. As in western occultism there is no "one and only true" secret system of symbolism, although many may darkly hint at having possession of one, and may even believe this to be true, naively assuming that because their own system works for them it must be of unique and universal validity. The general principles may agree, but the detail varies quite legitimately from school to school and between individuals. The simplified tattva system employed by the Hermetic Order of the Golden Dawn, for example, differs in several respects from the system described in *"The Serpent Power"*.

Sir John Woodroffe was at pains to point out that raising kundalini is not the be all and end all of yoga, despite the belief amongst many westerners that this is the case. The traditional Indian approach is, according to Woodroffe, more concerned with states of consciousness than with raising powers, and in particular the raising of lower consciousness into states of higher consciousness.

The aim of the yogi is to raise consciousness from the limitations of physical world experience to the unlimited wholeness which is Perfect Bliss. It follows that the highest aims of yoga can only be allied to a religious disposition, whether that disposition be in terms of monism, (where all is identified with god), or theism, (where creator and creation are defined as separate). Practitioners of yoga, by nationality and culture, may be followers of a variety of Hindu or Buddhist religious beliefs, and there seems no reason why there cannot be practitioners with a western cultural background. However, it is doubtful if anyone could get very far who assumes the system to be no more than a kind of interior "body building" through the practice of breathing techniques and physical postures with the object of acquiring strange or miraculous powers.

Attention is paid to the physical body as a vehicle for the spirit, purity of mind is identified with purity of body, and the meditation postures, or asanas, are intended as an aid to clear and correct thought, apart from hygienically and callisthenically securing a healthy physical condition in an unhealthy climate.

The Chakras of Besant and Leadbeater

With this in mind we may turn to a line of teaching based upon the yoga chakras that was energetically popularised by the

Theosophist writers C.W. Leadbeater and Annie Besant. Their inspiration derived from the monumental works of H.P.Blavatsky *"Isis Unveiled"* (1877) and *"The Secret Doctrine"* (1888) which were in turn largely based upon eastern esoteric and religious thought. Blavatsky indeed deserves credit for pre-dating most efforts to open up eastern wisdom teaching to the west..

Leadbeater and Besant set out to render much of Blavatsky's teaching into more accessible form, and one of Leadbeater's most popular books was *"The Chakras"* complete with coloured illustrations. This did not appear until 1927 but he had published the gist of it as early as 1910 in a publication called *"The Inner Life"*. Thus his views were well known to Sir John Woodroffe, who spent some space in his introduction to *"The Serpent Power"* pointing out how Leadbeater's teaching diverges from the traditional Indian yoga systems.

This accusation of divergence from native tradition would not have been a source of surprise to Bishop Leadbeater nor very much cause for concern, for he honestly considered that his method was an advance on the native traditions. He had similar views with regard to Christianity and set about adapting and developing the creeds and liturgy of the Liberal Catholic Church with great gusto in works such as *"The Science of the Sacraments"*.

One major difference between the chakra system that is promulgated by Leadbeater on the one hand and by Woodroffe on the other is that Leadbeater declines to recognise the Svadisthana Chakra. He is unhappy about its sexual connotations, and substitutes for it a Spleen Chakra instead.

In giving his reasons for doing so he cites the dangers of "phallic sorcery" and schools of Black Magic that use kundalini for the purpose of stimulating the sexual centre. Sir John Woodroffe claims never to have heard of such kind of abuse and points out that concentration upon the lower centres in the yogic fashion should quiet the passions rather than arouse them, although he concedes that it is quite possible that approaching the centres with another attitude, practice or purpose might well produce other results.

A more fundamental difference lies however in the different sense or shade of meaning that the Theosophical writers put on some of the traditional yoga terms, and this can be confusing when one tries to establish points of correspondence between the two systems. Sir John Woodroffe would, for example like to have seen the word "principles" used instead of "planes", for although the concept of "planes" may be useful in devising elementary diagrams, it simplifies the realities involved to the point of distortion.

In particular Woodroffe challenges the conception and definition of the terms astral and etheric, which, it has to be said, Madame Blavatsky treated somewhat inconsistently in her major works.

Leadbeater describes the chakras as vortices of etheric matter into which astral forces rush, as from a higher plane, at right angles to the whirling disc. The impact of these forces upon the discs causes secondary forces to be set up at right angles to the inflow of astral force, which gives the appearance of "petals" to the lotuses. The incoming astral forces each bring a particular Logoidal influence, or aspect of divine life, into the physical body via the etheric double. Each of the chakras so formed is thus a potential link to higher consciousness. By raising the "serpent fire" they can be consciously activated, and this brings about different forms and levels of astral consciousness.

Woodroffe's objection to all of this is that it is at variance with traditional yoga aims and beliefs, and that the term "astral" is indeed one of western origin. Also that the aim of the Indian yogi is not astral consciousness or clairvoyance but spiritual aspirations far beyond that. He also takes issue with Leadbeater's assertion that kundalini is of a different order of nature from prana.

Nonetheless, whether they be distortions, misunderstandings, adaptations or improvements, the teachings of Leadbeater and Besant have permeated modern western occultism to a considerable degree, often quite unconsciously. One may find, for example, even died in the wool followers of "western native traditions" happily incorporating into their esoteric vocabulary ideas and terms which come from the east via the popular publications of the Theosophical Publishing House.

There are indeed many who consider that the lines of teaching derived from the works of Madame Blavatsky constitute the genuine western tradition, although this is to ignore established streams in western culture such as the Rosicrucian, Qabalistic and Hermetic Traditions, which indeed were well known to Blavatsky and acknowledged in her original works.

The proof of the pudding is of course in the eating. Leadbeater claimed that his system had been developed from personal experience and there seems no reason to doubt him on this point. It is no more than Dion Fortune similarly claims, in the right to find her own way in these matters, choosing those ideas that seem to be congenial and testing them against her own experience.

Tibetan Yoga

Sir John Woodroffe's works, upon which Dion Fortune largely depended for her information on yoga, are based upon Indian Hindu traditions. Another important source of information comes from the Buddhist traditions of yoga found in Tibet.

Apart from the travellers' tales of Madame Alexandra David-Neal the great pioneer in giving us access to Tibetan yoga was the American anthropologist W.Y.Evans-Wentz. As a young man he created quite a stir with *"The Fairy Faith in Celtic Countries"* (1906), a long report of anecdotal field work on faery traditions and sightings, aided and abetted by informed mystics and occultists of the order of W.B.Yeats and George Russell (A.E.).

Subsequently he went east, and began to publish informed translations of yoga texts in the Tibetan tradition. These included *"The Tibetan Book of the Dead"* (1927), *"Tibet's Great Yogi, Milarepa"* (1928), *"Tibetan Yoga and Secret Doctrines"* (1935), and concluded with *"The Tibetan Book of the Great Liberation"* (1954). He finished his life in California, working upon Amerindian traditions, marked by the post-humously published *"Cuchama and Sacred Mountains"* (1981).

In the field of Tibetan yoga he blazed a trail in much the same way that Sir John Woodroffe had done with the Indian traditions. In this he made a considerable advance on the kind of patronising and culturally blinkered commentary that had previously been attempted. L.P.Waddell's *"Buddhism of Tibet, or Lamaism"*, (1895), previously regarded as the authoritative text on the subject, contained remarks to the effect that lamaism was nothing but idolatry and demonology, it's mantras "meaningless gibberish", and it's mysticism "a silly mummery of unmeaning jargon and magic circles"!

With guides like this, who needs esoteric secrets? There are no doubt experts around who would find similar things to say about the opinions and activities of magical practitioners in the west today. This particularly so perhaps as, of all the eastern esoteric disciplines, Tibetan Mahayana Buddhism has elements remarkably close to western magical belief and practice.

Lama Anagarika Govinda's *"Foundations of Tibetan Mysticism"* (1960), the work of a German national who spent more than twenty years at the feet of masters in Tibetan hermitages and monasteries, is a lucid description of the techniques of Tibetan yoga and his book summarises much of the detailed material of Evans-Wentz's commentaries and translations of original texts.

We find that Govinda's delineation of the chakras has more in common with the general scheme of Sir John Woodroffe than that of Bishop Leadbeater. Similarly terms such as astral or etheric planes are conspicuous by their absence from his work. This does not mean to say that the states that we understand by astral or etheric do not exist, but rather that viewing the subject matter from a different perspective entails different definitions and identifications of the inner side of things.

We also find parallels between Tibetan yoga and western Qabalistic magical practice that do not appear so readily in the Hindu system. An example of this is Dion Fortune's suggestion that the lowest psychic centre can usefully be located beneath the feet. When used in this way it could be regarded either as representing the path that the initiate treads, or as the magic circle in which the magician stands. In this respect the diagram known as the Five Dhyani Buddhas is very close to the classical form of magic circle known to the west. A dhyani buddha is an ideal or archetypal god form of a certain type and aspect, and five of them are visualised, one at each of the four cardinal directions, and another balancing on in the centre.

In Figure B.1 we see a typical western magical circle compared with the similar structure of Tibetan yoga. There is a similar archetypal function attached to each of the four quarters, and to the equilibrating centre. The only difference lies in the detail of the symbolism chosen, designed to appeal respectively to those of either an occidental or oriental cultural background.

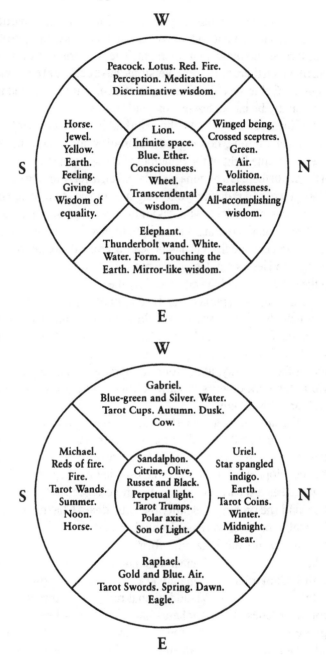

Fig. B.1. Typical Tibetan and Western magic circle symbolism.

The Tibetan system has a god or buddha-form of a particular colour, associated with a goddess or dakini, together with a particular type of throne and magical implement. The western type of magical circle, of which there are several versions, has occidental equivalents. Thus in the Celtic system the animals of east, south, west and north would usually be eagle, horse, cow and bear.

In the Tibetan circle we find in the east a buddha and dakini embracing on an elephant throne, holding a thunderbolt wand, and from whom radiates the white light of the principle of consciousness.

In the south there is a buddha with dakini on a horse throne bearing a precious jewel and radiating yellow light of the wisdom of equality.

In the west is a buddha with dakini on a peacock throne holding a lotus blossom and radiating the red light of discriminating wisdom.

In the north is a buddha and dakini bearing crossed sceptres on throne of winged goddesses amid the green radiance of wisdom in action.

In the centre is a buddha embraced by the divine mother of infinite space, and from them radiates the blue light of heavenly wisdom.

In much the same fashion would a western magician invoke archangelic forms of Raphael in gold and blue, Michael in the reds of fire, Gabriel in blue-green and silver, Uriel in star spangled indigo of the night sky, at the four quarters, with Sandalphon at the centre in the dark colours of earth, citrine, olive, russet and black, the colours of Malkuth.

Dion Fortune raises the question of correlating the chakras of the eastern system with the Middle Pillar of the Tree of Life, and initially, (in Part 1.4,) she suggests a straight linear correspondence, but in her further development, (in Part 4,) suggests that the Sephirah Malkuth be regarded as a separate entity as it is more objective than the other centres, and she prefers to identify the Muladhara Chakra, the seat of the kundalini powers, with the Sephirah Yesod.

We can lay this out in tabular form:

Kether	Sahasrara chakra	- top of head
Binah + Chokmah	Ajna chakra	- brow
Daath	Visuddhu chakra	- throat
Geburah + Chesed	Anahata chakra	- heart
Tiphareth	Manipura chakra	- solar plexus
Hod + Netzach	Svadisthana chakra	- genitals
Yesod	Muladhara chakra	- base of spine
Malkuth	Source of earth energy	- beneath feet

There is a lot to be said for this configuration, although Dion Fortune also has some reservations about allocating Daath to the throat centre, for reasons that she gives in Part 7. However, her concern, which with cogent reasons places Daath at the point where skull and spinal column meet, does not necessarily vitiate Daath's continuing association with the throat and the powers of speech, which physiologically take in the organs and cavities of nose and mouth as well as the larynx. Identifying the Muladhara Chakra with Malkuth, however, has the disadvantage of disrupting a certain natural connection between Daath and Yesod, although the situation is resolved when the yogi tucks his feet up into his pelvis in one of his asanas. On this point Dion Fortune was able to speak with some practical experience, for those who worked closely with her have remarked with no small wonder on her ability to take up the yoga asanas of which she speaks in Part 3 despite lacking the lissom build of a yoga ascetic.

There is plainly room for debate on divergences of eastern and western theory and practice on these matters, but this can be instructive by virtue of the insights that the elements of one system can throw upon the other. There is no point however in trying to make one system into a Procrustean bed for the other.

An interesting sidelight from one system to the other is Lama Govinda's observation of a certain connection between the Muladhara and the Svadisthana chakras so that in some respects they may be considered to be conjoined. This adds a certain amount of support to Dion Fortune's readiness to associate the Muladhara Chakra with Yesod.

On the other hand C.W.Leadbeater will have none of the Svadisthana Chakra, appropriating this title for the spleen. Nonetheless there is an interesting and unexpected correlation of function between the Malkuth centre placed beneath the feet by Dion Fortune and the Spleen centre favoured by C.W. Leadbeater. In his system the function of the Spleen centre is to gather energy from the objective world, and this is much the same function that Dion Fortune ascribes to Malkuth, a centre to draw in earth energies.

In "The Hidden Side of Things" (1913) Leadbeater developed this into the doctrine of "vitality globules" in the atmosphere, emanating from the Sun, which are absorbed by the etheric vehicles of all living things. In the case of man they enter by the Spleen centre, and from here the energy is distributed to the various other centres within the etheric body.

Alice Bailey, a more recent follower of the Blavatsky tradition but with her own unique contribution, also recognises the Spleen centre, although not at the expense of omitting or displacing the Svadisthana Chakra. In her system the Spleen has a similar function of channelling vitality, including higher correspondences up the planes which relate to the various seed atoms about which the different subtle bodies of man are formed.

Despite differences in terminology there is a general correspondence between systems in the esoteric anatomy of the human psyche. Thus Lama Govinda's description of the five sheaths of human consciousness is quite useful as a reference point between systems, particularly as it can be accompanied by a useful diagram that has similarities with the Theosophical "planes" system although is not identical to it. In his system the levels of consciousness are shown as surrounding the central spiritual being, with the physical body upon the outside, (see Figure B.2.)

The physical body is built up and sustained by food, and within it is a subtle fine material sheath consisting of prana that is sustained by the breath. Then comes the thought body, or personality, which is formed by active thought, and with that is what Govinda calls our potential consciousness, containing the totality of our spiritual capacities. Central to all is universal consciousness, whose natural condition and abode is great joy, which is only experienced in a state of enlightenment in high yogic meditation.

It is important to realise that the sheaths are not separate layers but are mutually interpenetrating forms of energy. The body is penetrated by the breath, the breath is imbued with thought or intelligence, and all three are motivated by an indwelling deeper consciousness that is based on past experience. The spiritual body penetrates all the five sheaths, although in the normal course of events is only experienced in advanced states of meditation, as a flame of inspiration and spiritual joy.

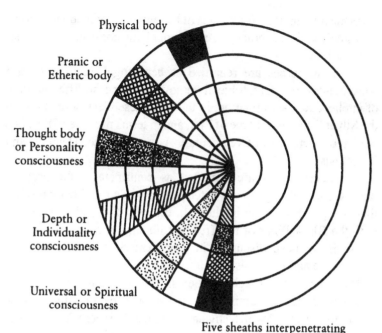

Physical body

Pranic or
Etheric body

Thought body
or Personality
consciousness

Depth or
Individuality
consciousness

Universal or Spiritual
consciousness

Five sheaths interpenetrating

Fig. B.2. The Five Sheaths of Consciousness in Tibetan Mysticism.

We can tabulate rough correspondences between this system and that generally regarded in the west, along with the appropriate spheres of the Tree of Life:

Govinda diagram	Western system	Tree of Life
Inspirational body	Spirit/Essential Self	1 - 2 - 3
Depth consciousness body	Higher Self	4 - 5 - 6
Thought body	Personality	7 - 8 - 9
Pranic body	Etheric body	10
Physical body	Physical body	10

For the Tibetan yogi the path of meditation is the spiritualisation of the body by means of the most immediately available form of spirit, that is to say prana, the vitality or life force, which is carried by the breath, informed with thought and motivated by deep conscious and spiritual intention.

As the human body is a replica of the universe, or a universe itself on a small scale, the polar currents through the body are called solar or lunar forces.

The solar forces are regarded as centrifugal, tending toward conscious awareness and objective knowledge, and the differentiation of intellectual discrimination. In the west these ideas correlate with the Silver Pillar of the Tree of Life, and in terms of some of the gods we have discussed in Commentary A, with Apollo, Demeter and Bright Isis.

The lunar forces are regarded as centripetal, subconscious, undifferentiated, regenerative, tending towards reunification of all that is separated by the intellect. In the west these ideas correlate with the Black Pillar of the Tree of Life, and in terms of some of the gods we have discussed in Commentary A, with Dionysos, Persephone and Dark Isis.

The forces flow through the body as psychic energies in two main channels - Pingala, pertaining to the sun, and Ida, pertaining to the moon, from each of which emanate innumerable secondary nadis or channels. Spiralling round the hollow channel of Susumna they are all three conjoined at the base of the spine.

The Susumna, like Mount Meru, the mystic world axis, establishes a direct connection between the seven centres and thus is also the vehicle of another polarity, that which exists between the highest centre and the lowest, as well as containing the synthesis of solar and lunar currents. The integrated solar and lunar energies are sublimated and raised from centre to centre until they reach the thousand-petalled lotus, the state of highest multi-dimensional consciousness. This polar integration is experienced in successive stages, in successive chakras, each of which represents a different dimension of consciousness.

In practice the Tibetan descriptions do not emphasise the spiral movement of Ida and Pingala round Susumna in the circulation of force but tend to see the three fold column like a figure eight upon its side with Ida on the left and Pingala on the right. The seed syllables of all the vowels of the Sanskrit alphabet are visualised going down the left channel, and those of the consonants down the right, in brilliant hair-fine red letters, moving in and out in harmony with the breath. The hollow canal of Susumna runs through centre, and is closed at the lower end as long as kundalini is not awakened. In this state, like a coiled serpent, it blocks the entrance of Susumna and its energies are absorbed in subconscious bodily functions. The aim of kundalini yoga is to awaken these dormant forces and by directing them to the higher centres, release, transform and sublimate their energies until their perfect unfoldment is achieved.

The awakening and raising of kundalini is by no means the sole aim of yoga however. The Tibetan poet and saint Milarepa, for example, took the Yoga of the Inner Fire as the main subject of his teachings and of his spiritual practice. This technique uses only the four upper centres, and takes place on an entirely different plane from kundalini yoga.

The creation and contemplation of the inner fire is focussed upon the navel centre, from whence, in conjunction with the visualisation of the appropriate seed syllables, a flame is seen like a fiery pearl, rising up to the crown centre, from whence the elixir of life flows down like white nectar.

The intensity of the flame grows and decreases in ten stages. At first the rising flame is seen as fine as a hair, then as thick as little finger, then the thickness of an arm, then as wide as the whole body, after which the whole world becomes an ocean of fire. The ocean of fire is then re-absorbed by the body, becomes the thickness of an arm, then of a little finger, then is as fine as a hair, until it disappears altogether in the great void.

This meditation upon fire arouses man from the slumber of worldly contentment. It fills him with the warmth of spiritual emotion, which can become the flame of inspiration, leading to that which may appear to be renunciation and asceticism, although a buddha who lives in the fullness of perfect enlightenment does not feel that he has renounced anything.

The aim of the yoga of inner fire is not the production of bodily heat even though this may be one of the qualities that may be witnessed as the snow and ice melts round an advanced practitioner as he meditates. The purpose is purely spiritual, and it is a common misunderstanding to think that the discipline was intended to enable the yogi to survive in the icy mountain heights of Tibet. Yoga in any case originated on the hot plains of India. The spiritual evocation of fire brings with it all its possible manifestations, ranging from bodily warmth to purification, radiation, enlightenment, transfiguration. A similar idea is evoked in Charles Williams' novel *"The Greater Trumps"*, where by meditating upon the element of Earth in conjunction with the appropriate suit of the Tarot, earth begins to appear between the shuffling fingers of the adept and his apprentice. Later a storm is raised by magical concentration upon other elements.

In simple terms, the Buddhist system confines itself to the five main centres, which can be divided into three zones:

1. the head and throat centres;
2. the heart centre;
3. the solar plexus and lower centres; between which there is a
   three-fold polarity.

The head and throat centres, which could be equated with Kether and Daath on the Tree of Life, pertain to the level of eternal cosmic or universal laws, of timeless knowledge, (which from the human perspective is felt as an ideal future state or goal yet to be achieved,) and spiritual awareness of the Infinite, (which may be symbolised in boundless space and the realm of stars, in form or formless terms.)

The heart centre represents the human plane of individual realisation, and can be aligned with Tiphareth on the Tree of Life, wherein the qualities of earthly and cosmic life, the forces of the earth and of the universe, and their relationship become conscious in the soul as a constant deeply felt reality.

The solar plexus and lower centres, equating with Yesod and Malkuth on the Tree of Life, represent the earth-bound consciousness of the elementary forces of nature, of material corporeality (which also may be held in consciousness as memory of the past).

However, even the brain centre in its unsublimated or unregenerated form represents the mundane activity of the intellect, separating us from the true source of life and the inner unity of all beings. In this condition, when it is outwardly directed, it entangles us intellectually in the world of material form, the illusion of separateness and therefore of death. While if it is turned inwards, the intellect loses itself in a maze of conceptual thinking, a vacuum of abstractions, the death of mental petrification.

If however brain consciousness catches a brief glimpse of the true nature of things, its conceptual world may collapse, threatening chaos and destruction. To the spiritually immature the unveiled truth, like the face of God, whether Jehovah, Zeus or Isis Unveiled, can appear in terrible form - and it is for this reason that in Tibetan iconography there are the terrifying images of the blood drinking deities. Their mandala is associated with the brain centre, and the blood that they drink is the elixir of knowledge, (fruit from the Tree of Knowledge,) which, if it is not combined with the qualities of love and compassion, acts like a deadly poison.

The solar centrifugal force of Pingala contains the principle of individual self-consciousness, which carries within it the limitation of mortality. The lunar centripetal force of Ida represents the principle of immortality but at the same time contains the blind urge to existence, which causes the endless round of rebirths. In like manner the brain centre of the unawakened man contains the seeds of death and principle of mortality, whilst the root centre contains the seeds of life and thus the infinite cycle of rebirths. The root centre of the unawakened man is the source of unifying but blindly creating vital forces, whose functions exhaust themselves in the instinct of self-preservation.

In the awakened man a discriminating cognition gives meaning and direction to these blind forces, raising and regenerating them from the realm of sexual expression into that of psychic and spiritual activity. The first transformation of the centres is to make them conscious; the second is to make them into vehicles of enlightened consciousness; and this double transformation enables them to receive new impulses and forces by the interaction of the fiery and liquid currents of consciousness, which respectively ascend and descend, influencing and interpenetrating each other, with the five centres relating to each other like the five elements.

Thus the head centres are transformed into an organ of universal consciousness, corresponding to the element of space or Ether.

The throat centre becomes the organ of mantric sound, where physical breath is transformed into conscious prana and the spiritualised vibration of mentally and audibly formulated knowledge. Its element is the Air.

The heart centre becomes the organ of intuition or spiritualised feeling, manifesting as an all-embracing compassion, where the cosmic principles are transformed into human experience and realisation. It is thus associated with Fire, the fire of inspiration, psychic fire, the fire of religious devotion, for which reason the heart is often symbolised as a brahmanic fire altar.

The solar plexus and lower centres provide the vessel for the transformation, equilibration, and the assimilation of subconconscious forces, and are associated with the element Water.

The body itself may be regarded as corresponding to the Earth element and we may see it as being in the centre of a magic circle, much as we have visualised the ground pattern of the Sephirah Malkuth. In Tibetan yoga this principle is extended to other levels, for each centre within the body may be regarded as the centre of a magic circle, or mandala, upon its own level. In this tradition indeed the term chakra is often used as a synonym for mandala. This is not so far distant from Qabalistic practice, where a magic circle may be constructed using the symbolism of any Sephirah.

The yogi imagines himself in the centre of the mandala as an embodiment of the divine figure of perfect buddhahood, which is a high equivalent of what in the west we would describe as a magical body. He then sees the things of the outer world combine and transform themselves into a sacred circle in the centre of which his body becomes like a temple, with the psychic centres of the body that we have described becoming the five storeys of this sacred temple, each of them containing a throne and the associated mandala of a dhyani buddha.

The lowest storey is the root centre, represented by a yellow square or cube, corresponding to Earth. The second storey is the navel or solar plexus centre, depicted by a white disc or sphere in the form of a drop, representing Water. The third storey is the heart centre which has a red triangle, cone or pyramid, and contains the sacrificial altar of Fire. The fourth storey is the throat centre which is dedicated to Air, symbolised by a semicircular bow or green hemisphere, open side upwards. The fifth and highest storey is the head and crown centres, represented by a blue flaming drop, symbol of space or ether, and the wisdom of universal law.

The whole system can be resolved into a simple diagram that is reproduced in Figure B.3. and in its fundamental simplicity it can be likened to the basic Sephiroth of the Tree of Life, with the five Sephiroth of the Middle Pillar giving rough approximations of the Tibetan system.

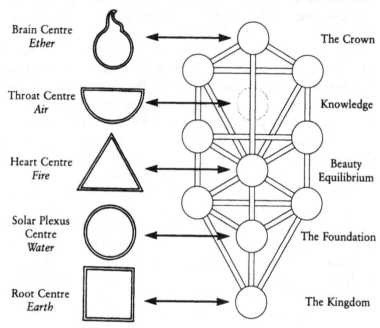

Fig. B.3.   Tibetan Symbol System and Qabalistic Tree of Life.

Both eastern tantrik and western Qabalist systems, simple in their general principles, can be developed into very complicated ancillary symbolism. However neither the yogi or the Qabalist allow themselves to be shackled to the minutiae of symbolism. The symbols of meditation are principally imaginative tools that we create for ourselves, which may vary to suit temperament and circumstance. In yogic or magical meditation we are constructing channels in consciousness through which psychic energies may flow and be consciously controlled. Within the broad principles of the general tradition, each school of meditation and sect has its own system, developed and maintained by experience and passed on from master to pupil.

The importance of Tibet as a source of traditional wisdom is that it is the last living link that connects us with the civilisations of a distant past. Other mystery cults have perished with the destruction of their civilisations. In this respect Tibet, due to its natural isolation over past centuries, until Chinese communist invasion, has preserved and kept alive traditions of the distant past, comprising knowledge of the hidden forces of the human soul.

It is therefore perhaps not without significance that Tibetan traditions were an early influence upon the great occult polymath H. P. Blavatsky who prior to the efforts of Woodroffe, Evans-Wentz, Govinda and the rest, opened up eastern traditional wisdom to the west, albeit after her own fashion and with her work elaborated in diverse ways by later disciples. She spoke no less than seven languages and was widely travelled in Asia, Europe and America, and had in her time been an experienced medium.

She was exposed very early in life to Tibetan culture through the influence of her grandfather who was the government administrator for the Kalmuck tribe which practised Tibetan Buddhism near Astrakhan and about which her mother wrote a novel. The idea of Masters of the Wisdom with which she later became publicly associated did not originate with her, for as a teenager she had the run of the extensive occult library of her great-grandfather, Prince Pavel Dolgorukii, who was a member of a German Rosicrucian Masonic Rite founded in 1754 which claimed authority from a world wide body of superiors. When she claimed contact with similar sources of wisdom in the 1880's it was principally through two such hidden masters, named Koot Hoomi and Morya, apparently resident in Shigatse, Tibet.

After Madame Blavatsky's death, in 1891, followers of her teaching, such as C.W.Leadbeater and Annie Besant, whose work we have noted, continued to maintain and expand her teaching as they understood it. There was eventually a reaction against this form of popularisation and in course of time a "back to Blavatsky" movement turned emphasis to the study of Blavatsky's original works, which amount to no less than fourteen volumes in addition to the seminal titles *"The Secret Doctrine"* and *"Isis Unveiled"*, a vast compendium of esoteric lore that Madame Blavatsky had picked up during her extensive travels and association with various occult personalities and movements.

Alice Bailey and Djwal Khul

A more innovative development was that which commenced in 1922 with the beginning of the esoteric literary career of Alice A. Bailey who found herself to be the amenuenis of one of the original but lesser known Blavatsky masters, named Djwal Khul, who is usually simply referred to as "the Tibetan".

In the course of time this body of teaching developed its own momentum and forms another important example of western approaches to eastern mystical traditions. The major works start with *"A Treatise on Cosmic Fire"* (1925) proceed to a five volume *"A Treatise on the Seven Rays"*, which includes esoteric astrology, esoteric healing, and a stellar oriented guide to advanced initiation. Of more immediate concern to our present considerations however are two very practical works *"A Treatise on White Magic, or Guide to the Disciple"* (1934). and a slim volume entitled *"Telepathy and the Etheric Vehicle"* (1950).

This last volume was written with a specific purpose and in answer to a genuine need, that esoteric students were paying far too little attention to the etheric vehicle. Because attention was too much attracted toward the supposed glamours of the astral plane a gap in conscious awareness had opened up, neglecting the very important links between the personality and the physical body that are provided by the etheric vehicle, which are largely neglected by science and medicine. The Tibetan thus insisted that one of the main obligations of occult students was to testify to the fact of the etheric body, for while many might be ready to acknowledge its existence in theory, very few did anything practical about it.

This was in 1950 and in the intervening years much of this gap has probably been made good by the increasing use and recognition of alternative therapies that, whether they realise it or not, often work directly upon the etheric vehicle. There has also been a great resurgence of interest in ley lines and other etheric power lines and centres within the body of the Earth. Dion Fortune's concern with the etheric level, which is largely the concern of *"The Circuit of Force"* and features largely in her novels, may thus be seen as anticipating this concern of the Tibetan.

In Djwal Khul's teaching, the etheric body is the dominant subtle energy to which mankind in all times reacts, and there is nothing in the universe that is not imbued with it. It is an interlocking system of circulating lines of force, subject to ceaseless change, that emanates from all planes of the universe and controls and makes us what we are from moment to moment.

As has already been described, its force-streams focus in seven principal centres within the etheric body, and as well as interpenetrating the physical vehicle extends beyond it to form the aura.

Beyond this personal application there is also the planetary etheric body from which it follows that any sense of personal isolation is an illusion, for every form of life upon the planet is interconnected by this etheric net. It is a vast circulatory medium which is the vehicle for a universal telepathic system between spiritual beings of whatever type or grade.

This telepathic network will however work at various levels of quality, according to the centres of the chakra system that are being used. Thus there is an instinctive telepathy which interconnects mother and offspring, whether animal or human. This form of telepathy works principally at the emotional level and so is activated through the centres which lie below the diaphragm, principally the solar plexus. Indeed as the Tibetan rather tartly remarks, what is often described as a heart to heart talk is technically speaking usually a solar plexus conversation. The heart centre, above the diaphragm, is more concerned with ideals and aspirations.

All this implies that people are more telepathic than they realise, at whatever level. The spontaneous emotion in a crowd or a theatrical audience is one of the more obvious forms but it may also act at a more general level when ideas or enthusiasms sweep through the nation or humanity at large, forming part of the zeitgeist, or spirit of the times.

By esoteric extension of this we move into all kinds of areas and possibilities, including communication between masters and disciples, whether inner plane or outer plane or both, whether individually or as part of a group. This aspect forms the subject matter of *"A Treatise on White Magic"* (1934), which is not a guide book to ceremonial magic as the title might inadvertently suggest, but rather a detailed analysis of the process whereby a disciple tunes personality consciousness into rapport with his or her own Soul or higher nature, and thence to telepathic rapport with the master or his personal group or *ashram.*

The mode of training suggested is largely based upon a system of occult meditation upon a series of affirmations that aim at stimulating the higher psychic centres. There is an emphasis on service to the wider group, to humanity and the world at large, in which the United Nations Organisation is regarded as playing an important role, whilst for the individual the principal goal is building a rainbow bridge, or antaskarana, between higher and lower consciousness.

In terms of the chakra system the emphasis is very much upon the higher centres, of heart, throat and head (all the centres of the head being regarded for practical purposes as one). The centres are regarded as being located in the etheric body but are differentiated as to sub-plane, there being seven sub-planes to the physical/etheric plane. Thus:

the head centres are said to reside in the 1st etheric level,
the heart centre in the 2nd ether,
the throat centre in the 3rd ether,
the centres at the base of the spine, generative organs, solar plexus and spleen in the 4th ether,
below which are the gaseous, liquid and solid elements of the dense physical body.

It will be seen that this totals seven sub-planes in all, that together comprise the physical/etheric plane. As we have mentioned, traditional yoga commentators such as Sir John Woodroffe have their reservations about the concept of "planes", preferring to think in terms of qualities. However, the concept of planes has the convenience of setting out in diagrammatic form relationships between qualities that might otherwise be difficult to conceptualise, even if there is a risk that simplifying distorts the reality. Accordingly, we give an example of a planar diagram of the general system in Figure B.4. which, as will be seen, mounts to a scheme of some complexity, with seven planes to the universe, (each divisible into seven sub-planes), and each of these seven universal planes being but the seven sub-planes of the densest of seven cosmic planes.

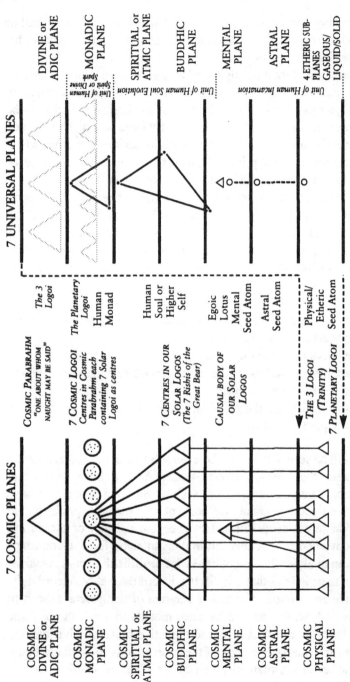

Fig. B.4. Scheme of Cosmic and Universal Planes, showing psychic structure of human being and of a Solar Logos and related divine beings.

It will be seen that within this system the etheric chakras of the human vehicle have their corresponding equivalent upon the astral plane, (which is again similarly split into seven astral sub-planes), and yet again into further corresponding equivalents upon the manasic or mental plane. Here the lower centres are reckoned to be a part of the personality vehicle, whilst the higher centres are part of what is known as the Egoic Lotus.

It is important to understand the terminological parallels between one esoteric system and another. In Alice Bailey's work the Soul or the Ego means the Higher Self, and not the general religious or psychoanalytic application of these terms. In the terminology of the Hermetic Order of the Golden Dawn it might be called the Holy Guardian Angel; in Dion Fortune's usage it was the Higher Self or Individuality.

The disciple, or white magician, is one who is in touch with his or her own Soul, Higher Self, or Holy Guardian Angel, is receptive to it and aware of its plan and purpose, and capable of registering impressions from it in brain consciousness. Everyone has a higher consciousness of course, but in the untrained person the downflow of Soul energy is unconscious, rhythmic and cyclic. In the esoterically trained initiate it is conscious and steady, and this is the hallmark of the white magician.

Thus the meditating and aspiring disciple is one who seeks to learn a new internal rhythm, and through this to enter a new field of experience; that of spiritual perception. This new awareness grows slowly and surely as brain consciousness becomes capable of being illuminated by the soul - by the inner light. As the intuition (or "inner-tuition") develops, so the radius of awareness grows, new realms of knowledge unfold and the form side of life becomes a field for service.

The Rainbow Bridge

The whole corpus of "the Tibetan's" work extends over a period of twenty years and more and represents a sizeable body of work and a considerable intellectual challenge. As occurred with the works of Madame Blavatsky therefore, efforts have been made in some quarters to render some of this teaching more accessible. A typical example of this is *"The Rainbow Bridge"* under the aegis of a group called the Triune Foundation in 1981, whose authors remain anonymous, simply describing themselves as "Two Disciples".

Getting down to fundamentals their method aims straight at Soul consciousness, invoking its involvement in the affairs of the everyday personality by simple techniques of the visual imagination. The powers of the Soul are evoked by imagining a point of light about six inches above the head, which is called the Soul Star. This is no great distance in concept from the Sahasrara Chakra or Thousand Petalled Lotus in traditional yoga doctrine, or the Limitless Light around Kether, the highest Sephirah upon the subjective Tree of Life.

This visualisation is accompanied by a simple vocal invocation, to wit: *"I am the Soul, I am the Light Divine, I am Love, I am Will, I am Fixed Design."*

Such a formula is deceptive in its simplicity and to the critical brain consciousness may appear to be no more than a sequence of self regarding platitudes - mindless generalisations passing as some kind of higher wisdom. Its components are, however, far from meaningless, for in their fullness they are the equivalent of the famous and universally used mantra of yoga tradition OM MANI PADME HUM which might roughly be translated as *"The Jewel in the Lotus"*. This in itself is also a simple enough formula but one so packed with meaning that Lama Govinda can use each word of it as an overall title for parts of his book on the foundations of Tibetan mysticism. Its western equivalent might be regarded as the Qabalistic formula and codex to the Lord's Prayer, *"In thy hands is the kingdom, the power and the glory, for ever. Amen."*, in this instance being addressed specifically to the Higher Self or Soul, which ultimately contains within it the God Within, the Spark of Divine Fire, or Jewel in the Lotus.

This invocation is the essential preliminary to any exercise that follows, and in so doing affirms that all actions within the world of the personality must be validated by the Higher Self, which projected the personality in the first place. This initial visualisation is sufficiently important in itself not to need further exercises. It is sufficient to go about one's ordinary business in the world, recollected as to the source of one's actions as being located in that Soul Star above the head.

However, to follow up from this preliminary focussing of awareness upon the Soul Star centre above the head, the lower centres of consciousness can also systematically be activated and purified. This is done by drawing a line of light down through the centre of the body and into the Earth, with pauses at specific steps along the way to focus attention upon the Brow, the Throat, the Heart, the Solar Plexus, the Sacral Plexus, the Base of the Spine, the Knees, the Soles of the Feet, and then to a point that is called the Earth Star beneath the feet, which is analogous to the Soul Star above the head.

As Lama Govinda has explained in regard to Tibetan yoga, these visualisations are imaginative constructs that work indirectly, and thus safely but by no means ineffectively, upon whatever real power centres may exist within the subtle and physical bodies. The method of working recommended is one of building successive triangles of flows of force, as shown in Figure B.5.

Thus, after stating the spiritual intention the Soul mantram, the Soul Star is visualised about six inches above the head, like a small bright sun. Then by a process of imagination it is seen to descend diagonally to take up a position about a foot before the brow. From this position it is drawn back into the centre of the head, from whence it slowly rises back to its original position by an act of will.

This triangular process is repeated two or three times before moving on to a similar pattern with regard to each lower centre in turn. The full cycle of work is built up to gradually, at a rate of one or two more centres each week.

Such a basic visualisation technique will be seen to be one broadly in line with traditional yoga techniques and in common with similar light visualisation exercises represents a type of aspirational training that can be effective in a western urban environment without some of the problems that might be experienced from a full yogic regime in like circumstances.

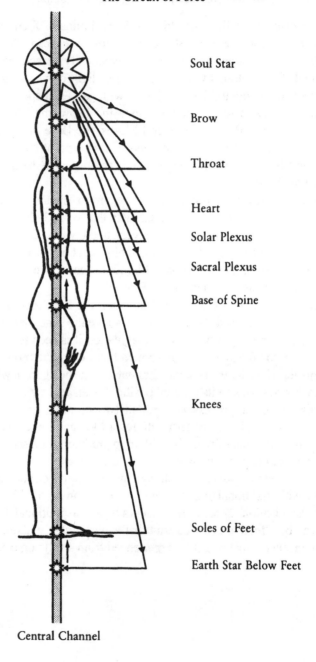

Soul Star

Brow

Throat

Heart

Solar Plexus

Sacral Plexus

Base of Spine

Knees

Soles of Feet

Earth Star Below Feet

Central Channel

Fig. B.5. Method of Triangle Working with Soul Star system.

MAGNETIC INTERCHANGE

The Circuit of Force Part 6 [October 1939]
Dion Fortune

I do not know what the teaching of the accredited exponents of the science of yoga may be, never having seen the point referred to in their writings, but I have observed that the Centres always work in pairs, and it seems impossible to bring one into function unless it is supported by another. Malkuth, for instance, supplies the force for the functioning of Yesod just as Kether illuminates the Supernal Triad; equally, Yesod supplies the motive power for Tiphareth.

In these matters I speak with no other light than my own personal experience, for they are practically a lost secret in western occultism, and the Eastern Tradition does not commit its secrets to writing in a form comprehensible to the uninitiated. One can pick up hints here and there, and check experience against traditional practice, but that is as far as one is able to go. But I am weary of the practice pursued by so many writers on these subjects of making a living by taking in each other's literary washing, so let us at least go as far as we can, confident that the methods of the Mysteries must have originally been worked out in the light of practical experience, therefore practical experience will always have the power to recover lost secrets.

Yesod, as we have already noted, is the Moon-centre, intimately connected with the functioning of the sex forces. Although the knowledge of sex psychology has made notable strides since the First World War, it is still in its infancy, and there are obvious and dangerous gaps in both its theory and practice. I do not propose in these pages to deal with the subject of sex in its physiological or social aspects, but solely in its magnetic one, touching upon the physical and moral in so far as it may be necessary to explain or qualify the practical application of what I have to say.

It is well known to all who have observed life with their eyes open, that a great deal more is necessary to a marriage than is specified in the church service. The physical and social aspects of that relation, as the Prayer Book frankly and sensibly states, are essentials, but, as life affords only too many opportunities for observing, they are by no means all-sufficing for a harmonious marriage. There is another factor, quite unrealised though keenly experienced, and that is the magnetic factor.

The subtle magnetism of a living creature is a very curious thing, and in human beings it is quite as much mental as physical. Esoteric science teaches that it forms a magnetic field or aura around each individual of varying degrees of potency. When the voltage is high, it can emanate a ray like beam-wireless; when it is low, it can exercise a kind of absorbing or draining influence upon its environment.

When aura impinges upon aura, if the vibrations are in tune with each other, interchange of magnetism takes place. They do not need to be of identical pitch for this interchange, but, on the analogy of musical tone, provided the wave-lengths of their vibrations are multiples of one another, they will harmonise, but if they possess no common factors, they will form dissonances. And so it is with human magnetism. The analogy is closer than is realised. Consequently we observe that there are some persons with whom interchange of sympathy is easy, and some with whom it is impossible. We also observe that when people of dissonant magnetism are forced to live in close relationship to each other, that the more potent will tend to tune the less vital to his or her own keynote. This may be well enough when the pair form a harmonious chord, but it is a fatal proceeding when they are in different keys. The only thing to do in such circumstances is to live and let live in mutual freedom and toleration.

We also observe that magnetism flows from the highly charged to the less highly charged, and that both benefit by the exchange, the former being relieved of pressure and congestion, and the latter being vitalised and inspired. Presently, however, when two persons are associated together permanently and exclusively, a state of equilibrium is reached, and they cease to benefit by the association to the degree that they once did; though the fact that, if parted, they soon become conscious that something is lacking and miss each other, shows that a low pressure circulation of magnetism is going on between them unobserved.

Fresh magnetism, from a new source, serves as a stimulus, and revivifies those who have settled down into a quiescent condition of mutual satiation. This magnetism does not need to be that of a liaison or love affair; ordinary social intercourse with congenial people will suffice. Much magnetism gets exchanged in perfectly decorous dancing, and a visit to the theatre or cinema is a very definite outlet and a stimulus.

The fact that the shadows on the film are as magnetically effective as the flesh and blood performer on the stage is a matter that gives us a good deal to think about, and throws light on certain aspects of ritual. Obviously the shadow on the screen cannot emanate any personal magnetism; therefore it follows that each stimulus as is received is due to the release of reserves of the spectator's own latent magnetism, set free by the emotionally stirred imagination. Some would say that all magnetism is thus subjectively stored and emotionally released, and that the art of raising Kundalini consists in releasing it for subjective use in the absence of an emotional object to drain it off. Others would say that all magnetism is derived from either the Earth-soul or the Unmanifest.

Yet others say that we derive additional magnetism to supplement our own supplies by sitting in a circle or the laying on of hands.

I believe, in the light of such experience as I have had, that all these statements are true, and that they are in no way mutually exclusive. We draw magnetism, as I have already shown, from both the Earth and the Unmanifest; we unquestionably have reserves of latent magnetism in our organism under the control of our subconscious minds which are released whenever that level of consciousness comes into action - spontaneously, when the deeper emotions are stirred, and deliberately when the yoga or the occult techniques are made use of. The yoga technique taps these reserves - or in the language of its exponents, rouses the Sleeping Serpent, by direct methods of conscious approach; the occult method uses ceremonial to energise the imagination so as to arouse the emotions, thus causing the subconscious energies and controls to come into action.

The two methods are usually employed separately, the exponents of one decrying the use of the other; but far the most potent results are obtained when they are combined. The person who has developed his etheric body by means of yoga is an incomparably more effectual ritualist than one who has left the magnetic side of his nature to gain such development as it may incidentally receive in the practice of ceremonial. One may compare such methods to that of a would-be dancer who set to work to learn the movements of a ballet without first undergoing the preliminary exercises that build up the muscles.

The exponents of yoga, on the other hand, seldom, in my experience, appreciate the value of ceremonial. This might, of course, be due to the fact that they have had no experience of ritual effectually performed, and judge of it by the dreary routine of church service and Masonic lodge; but such European exponents of yoga as I have conversed with appeared to give no place to ritual in their philosophy. In India, however, *Mantra Yoga*, or achievement through ceremonial, is one of the recognised paths to enlightenment, and in the *Tantrik* system the *Charkra*, or rite performed while sitting in a circle after the manner of the spiritualists, is a vital part of the method of working, to which, in fact, all else leads up. It is a noteworthy fact that both in the *Charkra* and the séance it is customary, as far as possible, to seat men and women alternately; in fact in the *Charkra* such an arrangement is regarded as indispensable, and numbers are regulated accordingly. Those who have experience of ritual know that better results are obtained if persons of opposite sex work opposite each other, and if the proportion of the sexes in the lodge is kept balanced. I have never had experience of a lodge in which men predominated, but I know only too well the disastrous effect in a lodge of the predominance of women.

From the testimony of these varied sources of experience and practice, we are, I feel, justified in drawing the conclusion that, in addition to the subjective and impersonal sources of magnetic force, there is a very definite exchange of magnetism between individuals, and that this is greatly enhanced when they work in series, after the manner of a battery of electric cells.

It should not be beyond the wit of man to devise exact experiments to demonstrate, if not the nature of this force, at least its mode of working. One can see the effect of the magnetic relationship in the lives of individuals and in the working of rituals. One can see, only too plainly and frequently in our psychologically unhygienic civilisation, the effect of the deprivation of magnetic polarisation in the stultifying and drying up of both mind and body of those whose circumstances or viewpoint cut them off from all emotional experience and sympathetic rapport with others.

But I have also seen an even more interesting thing - that ritual rightly performed can set the static magnetism circulating, vitalising those to whom it is lacking and relieving those in whom it is congested, and this is no small contribution to the solution of one of the most tragic and baffling problems of our civilisation.

In order to understand how this comes about and, by understanding, learn to control and direct it at will, we can turn for illumination in two directions - to the séance and the cinema. We know how, in the séance, the individual sitters pool their magnetic resources to be used by the spirits for manifestation, or, as some think, by the medium for additional psychic power. We also know how the incidents pictured on the screen, by stirring the imagination, rouse the emotions and so discharge latent magnetism. It cannot be the actor who emanates the magnetism, for he is not present; it is the emotion-stirring image in our imagination. Equally we shall find that if we are able to formulate images in our imagination with sufficient clarity to be emotion-stirring, that they will cause the discharge of magnetism in our etheric bodies to take place. If, in addition to this, there is the pooled magnetism of a circle to be drawn upon, very important results are obtained.

All this, of course, is plain psychology and the ordinary psychic practice of the spiritualist movement; but if, in addition to these subjective factors, we admit the occult hypothesis of the astral light and its denizens, we open up a vast new field of possibilities.

AUTO SUGGESTION
AND THE ASTRAL LIGHT

The Circuit of Force Part 7 [November 1939]
Dion Fortune

The whole of magical theory and practice turns on two points –
autosuggestion and the astral light. These two points must therefore
receive the careful consideration to which their key position entitles
them, and not be employed as stick-on labels – terms of abuse that
explain nothing but discredit everything.

Auto-suggestion is a method of manipulating one's own
subconscious mind and persuading activities that go on beyond the
control of the will to obey its behests – performing their subliminal
work and delivering the results to consciousness in the form of a
finished production whose fabrication one has had no conscious
part. Remarkable results can be obtained in this way, character and
habits being changed and unsuspected energy released to a degree
that has to be experienced to be believed.

The technique of this operation is simple – so simple that
it eludes our rational minds as an object held too near the eye
becomes indistinct – the subconscious mind has to be approached
by means of the imagination, completely disregarding reason, will
and concentration. One has, in fact, to rely on cannoning off the
cushion, for a direct approach defeats itself. There is a knack in this
procedure which has to be laboriously acquired, and its satisfactory
use depends on the right understanding of one's condition and needs.
It will be observed that I say "satisfactory", and not "effectual",
for it is possible to use autosuggestion most effectually with very
unsatisfactory results if one's philosophy of life is remote from the
facts – a by no means uncommon state of affairs.

The effectiveness of an appeal to one's subconscious mind by
means of the imagination is greatly enhanced if one reinforces

one's subjective operations by an objective appeal in the shape of symbolism and ritual. We all know how much more vivid is the film than the story; how much more vivid sound film to the old silent movies. Obviously all the trappings and paraphernalia of ceremonial magic afford most potent appeals to the imagination, and through it to the subconscious mind with all its but dimly realised resources. Is this appeal to subliminal energies the beginning and end of occultism?

There was a time when I was inclined to believe that it was, but wider experience has convinced me that it is not, though I am not prepared to subscribe to the school which believes that magic is purely magical. A very large psychological element unquestionably comes into it; for if the appeal to the imagination is ineffectual all that follows is nullified, being counter-suggested. A sense of humour is the great enemy of magic. Anything that distracts the attention or appeals to one's sense of the ridiculous effectually destroys the power of a ceremony. Makeshift cardboard symbols, painted plywood instruments, crumpled and skimpy sateen vestments, the drawing-room furniture pushed into the corners and a smell of cooking coming up the back stairs will destroy all magical power as effectually as an exorcism with bell, book and candle; while, on the other hand, a ceremony performed with the simplest dignity will not fail to achieve its purpose. The occultist can do what the Elizabethan play-goer did – provide his own Forest of Arden on an empty stage, but he cannot overcome the banal effects of home-made props borrowed as like as not from the housemaid's cupboard.

It is amazing to me that occultists fail to realise that a magical rite is a religious ceremony, and treat it as if it were amateur theatricals before an uncritical audience. A Temple of the Mysteries may be as bare as a Little Bethel, but at least it should be a consecrated place that does not outrage one's sense of good taste. Even if the cardboard impedimenta and the cotton vestments are held to deceive the Powers invoked, they do not deceive either operators or spectators, and effectually nullify the psychological appeal of the ceremony. That ritual can be effectual under such circumstances proves conclusively that another factor besides autosuggestion comes into it.

This other factor we will call, for want of a better name, by the traditional terms of the Astral Light. This, of course, is the great stand-by of occultism that is used to explain everything. Occultists of the credulous, traditionalist type cling to the Astral Light as if it were a solid object; the word auto-suggestion being a shibboleth which proves the user to be not of the elect. I cannot accede to this, for autosuggestion so obviously plays an important part in magic, as is clearly discernible by all who know what to look for. Equally, however, I shall write myself off as unscientific and superstitious by making use of the term Astral Light, but I beg leave to define my terms.

To argue with the crass materialist is as useless as arguing with the bigoted believer, these twin attitudes being the two sides of the same psychological coin; so I will content myself with an appeal to the experience of those who are sufficiently sensitive to have had intimations of supersensible realities. They will, I think, be able to confirm the statement that these are of more than one kind, and represent distinguishable strata of tangibility. The densest type is perceived semi-physically as a tingling sensation, like a weak electric current, a wave of heat, or a draught of cold air; even, sometimes, as a sense of touch or generalised weight. A subtler type is perceived as a kind of emotional tenseness in the atmosphere, as when waiting for some important event to take place before one's eyes, surrounded by a crowd who are all expecting the same thing.

This emotional tenseness can, and is in fact deliberately employed to produce all manner of subjective effects, ranging from mental stimulus right up to hallucination. It is easy to show the psychological factor in so-called occult phenomena, but it is not so easy to account for the stimulus that regularly and under willed control calls those phenomena into being and determines their type. Anyone who is, as I am, intimately acquainted with both psychotherapy and ceremonial magic, cannot fail to be aware of the difference not only in the degree but in the kind of influence exerted by them. I am fully prepared to concede the psychological factor in ceremonial, but I would also ask for the astral factor to be taken into consideration, for it unquestionably exists; on this point I think I may be excused the criticism of persons who have not had any experience of the working of occult rituals.

Let us now consider in detail, and elucidate by contrasting, these two types of subtle energy that experience and occult tradition both declare to exist. The denser we will call etheric energy, and the subtler, astral energy.

Etheric energy we have already studied at considerable length in these pages, though our approach has been empiric rather than philosophical, so it must suffice to say that it is the magnetic field of a living creature, and refer the reader to the orthodox presentations of electro-magnetics for further information concerning the nature of a magnetic field. This will be found to apply, allowing for the fractional voltage, equally well to the aura and its extensions as to the more obvious forms of electrical activity. All that is needed for its detection is an instrument that can magnify an electrical current in the same way as an amplifier magnifies a sound, for etheric force is purely physical and entirely objective. Sensitivity to it varies within as wide limits as sensitivity to musical pitch, and depends likewise on a basic natural capacity and its cultivation.

The perception of the astral influences is a subtler affair, and is entirely subjective; that is to say, they are of the kingdom of mind, not matter, and we perceive them with the mind, and not with the physical sense organs; but in a manner that is well known to those who have experience in such things, but of which I have never heard a satisfactory explanation, these subtle impressions are best perceived by focusing the attention on certain spots in the etheric double. These are the *chakras* of the yogi, or the Sephiroth of the Central Pillar of the Qabalist, and the principal of these, for clairvoyant purposes, is the centre in the forehead between the eyes, which is called in the east the *ajna chakra*.

In the west, the Qabalist regards the mysterious Sephirah Daath, which has no place on the Tree of Life or symbolism in the *"Sepher Yetzirah"*, as the centre concerned with extended consciousness. He, however, locates it at the back of the neck. The superficial correlation, therefore, is with the Visuddhi, or Throat Centre of the yoga system, but this, I am satisfied, is incorrect. The true location of Daath is where the spinal cord joins the brain; that is to say, at the base of the cerebellum; the direct developmental association of this with the forebrain, where the Ajna Centre is located, will be obvious to anyone acquainted with anatomy. At any rate, whatever arguments back and forth there may be, it is in the spot at the root of the nose that the sensation is felt when the psychic senses wake up and perception is willed; but there is, in my experience, and that of others with whom I have compared notes, a sensitive spot at the back of the neck where one is aware of an uneasy sensation when consciousness is being called up by an incoming message from subconsciousness. Perhaps this is due to the fact that the cerebellum, or little brain, is the old, original brain of the vertebrates, developed at the same time that what we now call subconsciousness was developing, and is therefore its appropriate and habitual organ; the main brain being the organ of consciousness, developed when the higher mind was developing in the course of evolution.

There are, so far as I can see, likewise two kinds of psychism - that which depends upon the development of the centres in the etheric body to act as sense organs and transmitting centres, and that which depends upon a change in the mode of consciousness. This change of consciousness involves oblivion on the physical plane while it is in function, and has been called the higher trance, or samadhi. Its link with consciousness, if such exists, and it often does not, is through the dream channels of the subconscious mind, expression being formulated by means of vision-symbols after the manner well understood in dream-psychology. It is one of the aims of the occult technique to forge the link between superconsciousness and subconsciousness and aid the formulation of those subconscious cartoons representative of superconscious experience. It is one of the aims of the *Hatha Yoga* technique to develop the etheric double into an effective instrument of the astral forces.

STAGES
IN THE GREAT WORK

The Circuit of Force Part 8 [December 1939]
Dion Fortune

The training of the mind that enables it to transcend sensory consciousness and achieve the direct superphysical awareness described in the preceding chapter is the function of Raja Yoga in the east and contemplative mysticism in the west. We are, however, concerned in these pages with the method that forges the etheric body into a magical instrument, so will confine ourselves to that viewpoint only, for the moment, though in no way underestimating the validity and efficacy of the other.

The two methods form, not so much two different lines of development, as two different stages in the evolution of the soul. This can only be understood when considered in the light of the esoteric doctrine concerning evolution as a whole. This teaches that force issues from the Unmanifest as formless energy, and only becomes differentiated in type and organised into forms in the course of long aeons of evolution.

It passes through phases in the course of its development which still remain in existence and functional, and it is these that constitute the subtler planes of existence, the subtlest being the earliest to evolve and therefore the most remote from our mode of consciousness; the densest, the material, being the last to evolve, is represented by the nadir, or lowest point of the outgoing arc of evolution when the phases are depicted schematically as planes of manifestation.

The vanguard of evolving life has rounded the nadir and is now on its return journey back to the Unmanifest. Having attained the organised stability of material form, it is now freeing itself from the limitations of matter while retaining the power thus acquired to maintain co-ordination. This process we can observe going on in the case of the higher type of psychism, where a mystical sensitivity exists in addition to a high development of intellect and personality.

There is a marked contrast between this and the primitive type of psychism which appears as a forerunner of rational intellectualism. One might say of these two forms of mind-working that they exist on the same plane of manifestation, one remove from the material, but that the primitive type manifests in people who have not yet completed the outgoing arc of evolution and the evolved type in those who have rounded the nadir of dense matter and are on the returning arc of evolution.

Bearing this in mind, it is easy to see how people who are at that stage of evolution which takes place on this physical earth, instead of making the effort to master matter which is demanded of them in order that they may round the nadir and set out on the return journey to the kingdom of the spirit, may shirk the effort involved and double back on their tracks, reverting to an earlier non-intellectual type of mentation in order to avoid the effort required to control matter by means of the mind, which is the goal of the out-going arc, the achievement of which alone entitles them to enter upon the return journey that leads to the Sabbath rest of spiritual attainment.

If we consider the popular aspects of the psychic and occult movements, and many of the modern variants of traditional Christianity as well, we shall see, only too often, that this tendency to shirk life's experience is cultivated as a remedy for suffering, and its exponents are regarded as saints and initiates.

This is an utterly false concept. Escapists and shirkers do not provide the stuff out of which great souls are made. The exploitation of a shrinking sensitiveness is no basis for the heroic qualities. Such as these are the weaklings, not the great ones. The older religions are wiser in their experience and do not encourage escapism, but require works as well as faith for salvation. The spurious mysticism receives a veneration to which a very cursory examination of the lives and works of its exponents show it to be unentitled. They are unprofitable servants of god, however loud may be their cries of: "Lord, Lord!" Their withdrawal into quietism means that they bear no burdens save their own.

It may be argued that the greatest of the Illuminati are withdrawn into solitude and practise the mystical contemplation that is beyond magic and psychism. This is true; but these can easily be distinguished from those others by the fact that they have passed through a phase of active work done in the world of men, and have fulfilled the law of the Mysteries in that they have handed over to successors they have themselves trained the burden that they have received from their predecessors. It is only such as these, with a record of work fulfilled and ripe experience achieved, who are entitled to withdraw into the Lodge in the Wilderness and lead the hermit life of mystical contemplation, and they go, not by their own choice, but when summoned.

For those others, whose task is to achieve the mastery of mind over matter, another type of training is necessary, and this is known in the east as Hatha Yoga and is represented by the viewpoint of the Shakta philosophy (the Divine Power often expressed in the form of a Goddess or Mother of the Universe) which, as a matter of fact, is at the back of far more eastern mysticism that is realised by European students. This cult represents the worship of God made manifest in Nature, and has its analogue in the method of the Qabalah, which is developed on its practical side into a technique for dealing with the various types of manifesting force which go to build up the world of form. The doctrine of Adhikara, or Competency, is one to which great importance is placed in Hindu thought, and it is a very wise doctrine, and we would do well to learn its lessons and apply them to western religion. This doctrine teaches that all men are not ready for the supreme renunciation of the mystic, but still need to attain their full stature of human development by undergoing the full range of experience which the body is designed to give, for however far advanced a soul may be in its evolution, in each life it needs to recapitulate life's experience before entering upon the Mystic Path. Consequently it is a condition of initiation in the east that a man shall have fulfilled his duties to the race as a householder and begotten a son.

There is great wisdom in this teaching, and we have only to consider the number of religious and psychic persons who can best be described by the vulgar epithet "half-baked" to see how wise it is, and how little good is to be obtained from a philosophy of escapism which renounces that which it has failed to acheive.

It is in order to aid this achievement of the control of matter by mind that the methods of the Tantra and the Qabalah have been developed. Mind, however, cannot master matter by direct action, as is so often attempted. Dense matter has its own laws, which are enunciated by the sciences of physics, chemistry, mechanics, mathematics and their various subdivisions and applications. Living things, however, which are studied by the science of biology and its subdivisions of physiology, anatomy, organic chemistry, and their specialised applications in botany, zoology and bacteriology, need to take into account a factor that failure to reckon with which upsets all calculations and falsifies all results, and that is the factor of the etheric double. This is the real vehicle of the life forces to a body which in actual fact is inanimate matter.

The etheric double is the link, and the only link, between mind and matter. It is the failure to realise this which makes psychology, and especially its applications in psychopathology and psychotherapy, even more uncertain and inconclusive in its workings than the biological sciences. Mystical and psychic methods, because they have at least a notion of such a subtle vehicle and its forces, achieve in a hit or miss manner things that science entirely fails to explain and therefore tries to explain away.

It is the occult initiate, and he alone, who has any real concept of the nature of this subtle aspect of the body and understands its relationship to the mind. Occult methods of development have as a fundamental basis, if they are to be effective, the development of the etheric body and the acquirement of skill in its control by the mind. Until this is achieved no one can hope to be effectual in the practical work of occultism.

No-one can fail to observe how many mystics and psychics are delicate and sickly, or show unmistakable signs of mental stress and strain. An occult initiate, on the other hand, is invariably a person of power and vitality; they live to a great age, and retain their youthful appearance in a very remarkable manner. The mystic, in his withdrawal from life, tends to disorganise his etheric double by cutting off the flow of life force to the physical plane. This is especially marked when his withdrawal is premature from the point of view of evolutionary development, resulting in his doubling-back to a higher plane on a primitive aspect, as already described. And even when the soul is ripe for such development, it will disorganise the etheric double, and consequently the physical health, if it takes place before recapitulation has been completed in this incarnation. In my opinion it is absolutely essential to obtain the control of mind over body by means of the cultivation of the etheric double if disorganisation of both mental and physical health is not to supervene upon spiritual development. Once the etheric double is developed and the mind has become conscious of it and acquired control of it, the distribution of the vital and magnetic forces can be regulated as required, and need not be allowed to become disorganised or unequally distributed among the levels; but if concentrated power is brought through in unregulated rushes, or vital force is withdrawn unduly and inconsiderately to higher levels, both mind and body go all to pieces and orthodox medicine and psychiatry have no remedy to offer.

Commentary C

ANIMAL MAGNETISM
AND ETHERIC PHENOMENA

Gareth Knight

We tread on shifting sand on any scientifically based evaluation of the Unseen. Despite all attempts at an "objective" approach, the assumptions and the evidence, the questions asked and the answers given vary from generation to generation.

Great excitement arose toward the end of the eighteenth century when Benjamin Franklin channelled electricity from the upper atmosphere, by the highly dangerous method of flying kites in a thunderstorm, and when Walsh found that electric shocks were given off by certain forms of deep-water fish.

Then Galvani made the sensational discovery that dead frogs' legs could be made to twitch by the discharge of electricity. In a spectacular experiment he connected a limb from one of his specimens to a conductor on the top of his house at the height of a storm, to show the dead limb violently twitching each time there was a flash of lightning. It seemed that electricity might be the source of life, and it was but a short step of the imagination to Mary Shelley's novel *"Frankenstein"* where a monster was brought to life from various disparate human parts.

This was an added twist to existing folklore, of the golem and other man-made monsters, and in the field of science it led to much experimentation, applying electric shocks to ailing patients and even attempting to bring the dead back to life. Ironically this technique is still in use in a somewhat crude fashion in resuscitation after heart attacks, associated with which there has been a number of accounts of experiences of those who have thus been "brought back from the dead".

More controlled electrical experimentation became possible when Volta invented the electrical battery, and this led in turn to the discovery that magnetism was part of the same phenomenon. When an electric current passes through a wire it produces a magnetic field at right angles to its direction of flow. If the wire is then wound into a coil the effect is greatly amplified, and will magnetise a soft iron core placed inside it. Thus was the electromagnet discovered and by whirling coils in a magnetic field Faraday invented the generator and electric motor.

What we now take for granted as simple experiments in school physics were, two hundred years ago, fascinating researches upon the very borders of life, and they attracted a considerable following, amateur and professional. These interests also embraced other subjects perceived to be on the frontiers of spirit and matter, such as mesmerism, animal magnetism, "odic force", and communication with discarnate spirits and associated phenomena.

Dr. Antoine Mesmer

At much the same time as the early observations of electricity an Austrian doctor, Antoine Mesmer (1734-1815), attracted great attention by effecting remarkable cures by what he called "animal magnetism". On graduating from the University of Vienna in 1766 he wrote a thesis on *"The Influence of the Planets on the Human Body"* in which he proposed the existence of a "subtle or universal fluid" that penetrated all the bodies within the universe. As he saw it, this corresponded to what Newton had discovered in the principle of gravitation, another force which appeared to affect bodies at a distance. By recourse to his theory Mesmer explained the periodic menstruation of women and almost all the cyclic crises found in various illnesses.

He established a successful practice in Vienna but faced with hostility from the church and his fellow medical practitioners he removed to Paris where he was patronised by high society, and began to publish works upon the history and practice of "animal magnetism". His theories were quite complicated and based on occult theories that some consider stemmed from the influence of the legendary Comte de St. Germain, whose mysterious presence and strange powers were reported in the courts of Europe over a long period that extended between from as early as 1710 to as late as 1822! However there were also earlier published sources such as the works of van Helmont, Robert Fludd and Paracelsus.

Mesmer did not concern himself much with details of medical physiology but kept to general principles. He compared the human body to a magnet, which was also, in its way, capable of acting upon other bodies at a distance. To maintain the body in a state of health it was necessary for its internal magnetism to be in a state of equilibrium. Disease was a condition found when these forces were unbalanced.

The principle of any cure therefore was simply to apply more magnetism according to the rules Mesmer formulated in order to restore harmony to the flow of magnetic forces ebbing and flowing within the body, although he was also willing to prescribe various standard health measures where appropriate.

He considered the left and right sides of the body to be of opposite polarity, like the arms of a horseshoe magnet, and the hands of the magnetic healer were looked upon as conductors of magnetism of the appropriate polarity. Human or animal bodies were the most powerful source of magnetism, followed by growing vegetation; and iron or glass were the most effective conductors.

His methods were very simple, mainly concerned with magnetically touching the patient, either with the hand or with a wand of glass or metal. Sometimes he treated patients individually himself, sometimes assisted by a "chain" of healthy people linked in a circle about them. Above all he treated patients in groups, assisted by various reservoirs of magnetism, of which the "baquet" is the best known, a large container of magnetised water, with which he could treat fifty or sixty people at a time.

The effect of applying animal magnetism was often to bring about a sudden curative crisis, sometimes with violent hysterical reactions, that would end in some form of trance or deep sleep. Mesmer believed no disease would be cured without the production of some more or less violent crisis, a crisis being the means by which nature endeavours to get rid of the disease. There were two kinds of crisis, a symptomatic one produced naturally in the course of an illness at more or less extended intervals resembling the symptoms of the disease, or a critical crisis developed under the influence of magnetism. The aim was to do all one could to get rid of the first kind of crisis and seek out the latter, which would restore harmony to the system.

To establish a flow of magnetism in individual treatment, the operator would stand facing the patient; his right side being opposite the patient's left, and vice versa, to set up the conditions for magnetic polar interchange. To establish an initial rapport the magnetiser would place his hands on the patient's shoulders, sweep them down the length of his arms to the fingertips, grasp the thumbs for a moment, and repeat this action several times. Then passes would be made from the patient's head to his feet. If all went well, a combination of touching the patient and talking with him or her, should lead to an awareness of the seat of the problem. In most cases, it was found, the real seat of the disease lay on the opposite side of the body, especially in cases of rheumatism and paralysis. The seat of almost all illnesses was also found to be below the diaphragm, and the best conductors of magnetism within the body were the nerves, hence the importance of the solar plexus, which was often called the seat of the soul.

The patient might be magnetically touched either with the thumb or the palm of the hand, or simply a finger, and to touch at a little distance from the actual body of the patient was often found to be magnetically stronger than actual physical contact. Alternatively a wand of glass, iron, steel, gold or silver could be used.

By means of such a rod a basin of water could be magnetised by making passes within it, often in the form of an equal armed cross. The "baquet" was in effect a very large basin containing a number of bottles of magnetised water which were submerged under more water, or else buried in some conductor such as glass, iron filings or sand. Thin iron rods protruded from the baquet, which were used to touch the affected parts of patients. A long cord attached to one of the rods could enable those about the baquet to wrap it around the affected part of their anatomy. They could also form a "chain" about the baquet by linking thumbs with each of their neighbours, (the thumbs being considered important magnetic conductors), although the power could be increased if they sat in a close chain with thighs, knees and feet touching so as to form a continuous circle for the flow of magnetic fluid.

Mesmer's public treatments had an imposing and mysterious ambience to them. They took place in magnificent surroundings, in large salons whose thick curtains allowed in only a half light, soothing music was played and delicate perfumes scented the air, whilst he himself, in a lilac robe, directed proceedings.

In these public treatments nearly all the patients fell into crisis. With some this might simply be yawning, shivering, weeping or laughing immoderately. Others, particularly the women, would suffer nervous spasms, contractions and often violent nervous attacks, rolling around the floor in contortions, drumming the floor with their heels, their fists, or even their heads at some physical risk to themselves. When possible, those in crisis were individually looked after by an assistant to prevent them from harming themselves, but when the number of patients increased an assistant could be overwhelmed by having to look after six or eight patients at once. Mesmer then introduced padded rooms into which those in crisis could be carried and where they could do themselves less harm.

The Marquis de Puységur

An early disciple of Mesmer who simplified his theories and improved some of his practices was the Marquis de Puységur (1751-1825). A distinguished soldier in his youth, a colonel at the age of 27, rising to brigadier general, he resigned his commission during the French Revolution and returned home, where he gave refuge to many who were fleeing from persecution.

He was well read in the physical science of his day, understood the physical manifestations of electricity, and regarded animal magnetism not so much a circulation of invisible fluid but more a state of vibration. His experiments convinced him that the head and solar plexus were the parts of the human body most susceptible to magnetic emanation, and particularly the eyes. An important contribution of his was the discovery, in 1784, of "magnetic somnambulism" with its accompanying unusual powers.

He did not describe many detailed techniques of magnetic passes because he considered thought and will to be of main importance. He also realised that magnetic practitioners varied in their ability, although this might also be dependent upon the practical training and theoretical instruction they had received. Like Mesmer he used auxiliary equipment including the baquet, but preferred the use of trees, which he said already contained their own power, and could also be augmented by human magnetism. His favourite was a great elm tree in the grounds of his mansion with cords fixed to the branches hanging down to the ground, which the sick could wind about themselves

Whilst the most dramatic effects that Mesmer attained were through crises, which he believed got rid of morbid elements within the organism, de Puységur did not think such crises indispensable. In fact he described the rooms that Mesmer set aside for his more violent patients as "convulsion hells". He considered the true curative crisis to be, on the contrary, a calm and tranquil state. This form of crisis he called "the magnetic state" or "lucid somnambulism".

He observed this for the first time on May 4th 1784 when he magnetised a young peasant who had been confined to bed for four days with pneumonia. He had his patient sat up in a chair to receive his treatment, and to his astonishment, found that after a few minutes of magnetisation he fell asleep in a completely different way from ordinary sleep. He was able to speak, and discussed his outstanding affairs. When de Puységur saw that these included problems that were affecting his patient disagreeably he sought to inspire happier thoughts within him, and found he could do this by means of silent mental commands. This came to the extent of inducing the patient to make dancing movements whilst seated in his chair, simply by silently running a song through his head. From this he discovered that response to suggestion, even mental suggestion, was a condition of the somnambulistic state. It was not long before anaesthesia was discovered and also the remarkable faculty possessed by sick somnambulists to describe the means of cure for their illness.

Whilst de Puységur recognised the advantages that somnambulism can give he also anticipated some of its dangers. Assuming somnambulism to be a state of crisis, and not a particular disposition of the nervous system, he thought that it must disappear with the illness, and this is what he almost always observed. In his hands the greater number of patients fell into somnambulism but as their cure approached the state was obtained less easily, until it disappeared completely when the cure was achieved.

When he was a member of Mesmer's school de Puységur had accepted that the human body is polarised and that opposite polarisation calmed and similar polarisation excited the patient, but later, discovering the importance of the will, he came to the conclusion that this polarity did not exist. In touching the sick at Mesmer's establishment by what were called friendly or alien poles, one calmed or excited them it is true, but this was because the training caused both sick and operator to think in those terms. In fact it was all a matter of suggestion.

De Puységur also found that all somnambulists, upon waking, forgot all that they had said, some even refusing to believe that they had been asleep. In one celebrated case, to convince a particularly obstinate and argumentative patient, manacles were forged upon him, which the local blacksmith then struck off without the patient being aware of it, whilst he was in somnambulistic trance.

In the course of his practice de Puységur increasingly saw the will as playing an important role, and in his memoirs he summed up his credo for successful magnetism as:

> Active WILL toward the good;
> Firm BELIEF in its power;
> Complete CONFIDENCE in employing it.

According the will such an important role, his procedures were often rudimentary, for he attached no great importance to them. The magnetised tree and the baquet were eventually abandoned, although he retained a high opinion of the curative effect of magnetised water and gave it to patients to drink.

Deleuze

Another important figure in the field of animal magnetism was Deleuze (1753-1835) Librarian at the Museum of Natural History, whose works included a history and a practice of animal magnetism. He lived not far from de Puységur's country establishment and when he first heard of the remarkable cures associated with the place refused to believe them, as they appeared to be pure folly beyond all common sense. However, after one of his friends had gone to see Mesmer and reported favourably on the subject, he decided to investigate for himself.

At de Puységur's establishment he found several people, one of whom was sick, forming a chain. He joined the chain, and soon saw the patient fall asleep, and did so himself. On returning home he tried magnetising himself, obtained satisfactory results, and having been convinced, from then on devoted himself passionately to the study and practice of the subject.

He is the most cautious of early writers on magnetism as he concentrates upon facts and observation rather than speculative theories, and writes up either what he has seen himself or has received from those he considers worthy of trust. He shows the similarity of results in experiments undertaken in different times and different countries and by those of differing opinions, and assumes illusion in all cases where this is likely.

He thought Mesmer's theories obscure, too complicated and not in agreement with several physical principles. Although he admitted that a universal fluid might be the cause of major phenomena he could not accept that anyone had the power to direct it over great distances. Also, although the human body might be polarised, if the polarity could be changed, destroyed or reinforced then, he thought, it might just as well not be taken into account. In this he was a disciple of the Marquis de Puységur, who admitted neither human poles nor the influence of the stars. He differed from de Puységur however by insisting on the paramount importance of the will which, he considered, would obtain effects without need for belief.

Despite his emphasis on the importance of will, Deleuze also placed great emphasis on techniques which, he said should vary according to the nature of the illness being treated. He admitted however that the techniques he used were not indispensable for he knew good magnetisers who obtained results by different methods. In a simple style he described techniques precisely, showing the advantages of each one, with diverse considerations and precautions in the light of common sense. Like the Marquis de Puységur he attached great importance to the state of somnambulism and gave much useful teaching on how to obtain it and how to follow it up. His instructions are valued by schools of magnetism in France to this day.

He particularly advised that magnetism be practised only between members of the same sex on account of other sympathies that might be aroused by the process. Should it be necessary that a man magnetise a woman he prescribed detailed rules of conduct.

He considered magnetised water to be one of the most powerful curative agents that one can employ, capable of producing remarkable results. His method for magnetising water was to take a vase containing it and make passes alternatively with each hand from top to bottom. Magnetic fluid could also be introduced to the water through the opening of the vase by making passes towards it with the finger ends. One might also breathe on the water or stir it with the thumb. To magnetise a glass of water it was sufficient to take the glass by the bottom in one hand and project magnetic fluid from the other hand down through the glass.

A procedure he preferred in magnetising a bottle of water, if he was sure the practice was not disagreeable to the patient, was to put his mouth over the opening and breathe into the bottle balanced on his knee, whilst making passes with his two hands over its whole surface. He believed this procedure highly effective although it was not absolutely necessary, as magnetism could be achieved simply by use of the hands. A carafe of water could be magnetised in two or three minutes, a glass of water in one. These methods were of course quite useless if not employed with close attention and determined will.

He also recognised that different objects could be magnetised, acting as storage conductors and producing magnetic effects upon those with whom they were in rapport. These included linen or cotton handkerchiefs, leaves from trees, and plates of glass, gold or steel, which placed at the seat of discomfort would serve to ameliorate it. He had often seen magnetised booties produce a warmth to the feet not obtainable in any other way, conserving their property over four or five days before needing remagnetisation.

He observed how employing a chain of people could be very efficacious, but required certain conditions not always easy to fulfil. It was absolutely necessary that:

1. all those composing it should be in good health;
2. they all take a sympathetic interest in the sick person;
3. none of them try to introduce their own ideas to the unanimous action, be it for curiosity or any other reason.

In other words it was important for all to be of one mind in one place.

He recommended that the chain be ranged in a circle, including the sick person, joining hands by means of holding the thumbs. The magnetiser formed part of the chain but to enable him to make passes with his hands the two persons on each side of him could place their hands on his shoulders or knees. If the magnetiser wished to work from the centre his immediate neighbours should approach the centre too so that the chain is not broken.

Magnetism has always been explained by recourse to current physical theories and Deleuze possessed the notions of his day, when several invisible fluids were admitted. Heat was the result of a calorific fluid emanating from a warm body. Light was luminous fluid. Electrical and magnetic phenomena were explained by two fluids acting one upon the other, by attraction when of opposite pole and repulsion when of similar pole. Supported by these hypotheses the human body was seen as the focus for an animal magnetic fluid that could be directed by the will.

Normally this magnetic fluid escapes continually from us and forms an atmosphere round the body, but having no point of polar discharge, is not felt by those around us. But when our will propels and directs it, it can act with all the force with which we impel it. While convinced of the importance of religion Deleuze was no mystic, and if he sometimes advised recollection and prayer it was in order to concentrate the mind on the forces and direct them better. Above all, the magnetiser must be in good health and of irreproachable morals, yet magnetism was no mystery and it could be explained by the laws of physics. Man simply possessed a fluid that could be directed by his will and which could powerfully augment the healing forces of nature. Even so, magnetism was no universal panacea and should be used in conjunction with normal medicine.

However, the lucidity of the somnambulistic state could be of great service, particularly when the somnambule talks about his illness during treatment. No experiment should be practised simply for the sake of curiosity, for the whole attention of the magnetiser must be on the treatment, of which the sole end is the cure or at least the relief of disease. He considered that magnetic treatment was not needed for those in good health, for fluid in natural circulation has no need of extra force. He wanted above all to see magnetism practiced in the family, as a system of home remedy, and outside of man and wife practised only between those of the same sex.

Baron du Potet de Sennevoy

Following upon these three pioneers, Mesmer, de Puységur and Deleuze, one of their most successful nineteenth century successors was Jules-Denis, Baron du Potet de Sennevoy, (1796-1881) more succinctly known as du Potet.

His career as a magnetiser began in quite spectacular fashion, in 1820 in front of Dr. Husson the head of the Hotel-Dieu hospital. The doctors at this establishment not only denied that magnetism could effect any cures but doubted its very existence. However, Dr. Husson declared that if any magnetiser presented himself they would put his power to the test.

The next day a young medical student put himself forward and was given the case of a young woman reduced to a state of exhaustion by constant vomiting which nothing would allay. She was brought in on a stretcher and was magnetised for about twenty minutes after which the vomiting stopped.

The doctors were not convinced but agreed to further experiment along these lines. After several more treatments she went into a somnambulistic trance after which an appreciable improvement was declared. Four weeks later the patient was able to leave hospital in a much more satisfactory condition and a report was drawn up describing the case. The student in question was du Potet.

Like Deleuze and de Puységur, du Potet recognised that the effects of magnetism came from two different causes, one material and the other in the mind, but magnetisers have never been able to agree on which is the first or most important cause. The majority favour a material action transmitted from one individual to another by an unseen fluid from the human body under the direction of the will. Others do not admit the existence of this fluid, and claim that all effects are achieved through the action of the mind.

Du Potet tried to reconcile these two positions, considering the more usual phenomena to be due only to the transmission of magnetic fluid, but that phenomena of a higher order were more directly due to the lucid somnambulism brought about the action of the mind. At the beginning of his career as a practician he leaned towards the material explanation but later in life placed more importance upon the action of the mind.

Du Potet describes few techniques and hardly mentions passes, for if the will is the principal factor in directing magnetism to the patient, then precise details of actual gestures are of little importance. He even considered forms of massage to be only a degenerate form of magnetism. He magnetised his patients individually but on occasions when he treated a group, he did not form them into a circular chain like Mesmer or Deleuze but put them in indian file seated one behind the other.

He employed magnetised water but attached no very great importance to it. In magnetising it he considered it necessary simply to hold the vase of water between the hands and apply thought to it; the thickness of the vase being no impediment to the magnetism, although if the vase had a large enough opening one could make passes with the fingers a little way above the surface of the water. Three of four minutes should be sufficient to magnetise a litre of water.

Whatever his theories as to its action, du Potet seems to have been admirably gifted as a magnetiser, possessing a very high degree of medical intuition, that is to say an instinct for diagnosis and prognosis that seemed superior to reason. He practised and taught with an apostolic fervour. Sometimes mystical, always enthusiastic and persuasive, and with a highly poetic style, he violently attacked priest and doctor, not always without good reason. For him, magnetism was a truth of nature, long misunderstood, which should now be generally recognised, to the great benefit of all who suffered. It was the medicine of the future, and one of the most powerful means of healing that nature had given us. He wrote a major work on magnetic therapy and 20 volumes of a Journal of Magnetism besides various other treatises and monographs.

He was a great advocate of the importance of the somnambulistic state and the remarkable faculties sometimes developed under it, and although he admitted that magnetism was not a universal panacea, he insisted that if it could not cure all illnesses it could

certainly cure a great number of them, particularly when all
ordinary medical means seemed to have failed.

Charles Lafontaine

Another great nineteenth century figure in the annals of magnetism
was Charles Lafontaine (1803-1892), who after studying the work
of Deleuze and de Puységur devoted himself seriously to its practice,
travelling all over France giving public demonstrations and curing
the sick. In 1841 he came to England where he met Braid, the
discoverer of hypnotism, who attended to observe at least one of his
theatre performances. He returned to France in 1848 and then left
for Italy where he was granted an audience with the Pope Pius XI,
who helped and encouraged him. He returned to France in 1851 and
eventually spent the rest of his days in Geneva.

He contributed little to theory, and his works are mainly
summaries of observations rather than didactic works. He was
convinced of the emission of a magnetic fluid that he considered
to be a physical agent, closely akin to physical magnetism. He
eschewed supernatural theories and sought above all to demonstrate
and propagate magnetism by way of experience. He believed that
will played an important part in magnetisation, in serving to make
the magnetiser more efficient, but not in the sense of imposing his
will upon the patient.

He also attached great importance to the somnambulistic state,
with its curious and diverse phenomena. He describes it often
as a singular mode of consciousness that is neither waking nor
sleeping nor dreaming. The somnambule enjoys the fullness of his
faculties. His intelligence is often greater, his perceptions more
delicate, and sometimes he demonstrates faculties that he does not
ordinarily possess. These may include seeing at a distance without
the help of the eyes, prevision of events, knowledge of hidden
things, and an instinct for remedies. Through this last faculty the
somnambulist can be of great help to the magnetiser, directing the
treatment in certain complicated cases. It is, however, necessary
to allow the somnambulist the freedom of his own perceptions. It
may be permissible to guide him gently, but to make demands that
are beyond his aptitude risks causing considerable distress and the
loss of these particular faculties.

Through his wide travels in France, England, Italy and Switzerland giving public demonstrations, Lafontaine was a great populariser of magnetism. His theories were admirably simple, disengaged from all metaphysics and resting only on physical laws. His demonstration that the will of the magnetiser was not imposed on the patient gave the lie to fears of the abuse of power such as were featured in the dark figure of Svengali in George du Maurier's novel *"Trilby"* where a beautiful girl becomes the somnambulistically gifted automaton of the mesmerist. This conception goes right back to Coleridge's *"Rime of the Ancient Mariner"* (1798) in a scenario where the luckless wedding guest is held by the "glittering eye" of the mariner, unable to proceed to the wedding feast for "the mariner hath his will".

Other elements of Lafontaine's observations have, however, been challenged by latter day magnetisers and in particular his belief that the attitude of mind of the magnetiser is of no account to his patient. The point was disputed by Hector Durville, founder, in 1893, of a modern school of magnetism in Paris, who insists that the thoughts and emotions of the magnetiser are very easily communicated to the patient, whether he intends or realises this or not.

Through the efforts of teachers and practitioners such as Hector Durville and his son Henri, to whom he handed on his school in 1914, the practice of animal magnetism has continued to thrive in France. It is to the 1956 fifth edition of his book *"Théories et Procédés du Magnétisme"* that we owe much of the foregoing information on a subject which seems to have been much neglected in the English speaking world, although the American Colonel Olcott, the early associate of Madame Blavatsky, was a skilled magnetic healer, who on railway journeys throughout India would attend to hundreds of patients.

Dr. James Braid and Hypnosis

However, the general thrust of animal magnetism was hi-jacked, so to speak, as early as 1841 by the Scots doctor James Braid. when he claimed that all the phenomena of mesmerism could be achieved by mechanical means, and in particular by tiring the optic nerve with a persistently flashing bright light. His medical colleagues fell with delight upon this apparent disproving of the theory of animal magnetism and all its occult associations. So, modern "hypnotism" was born, a term coined by Dr. Braid from the Greek word for "sleep".

When Dr. Mesmer was enjoying widespread popularity in Paris, he attracted such hostility from the medical profession that he asked for an independent enquiry to be set up to investigate the claims for animal magnetism. A government commission was duly appointed that included the distinguished American statesman and scientist Benjamin Franklin. They concluded, however, that wonderful though some of Mesmer's cures might seem, there was no evidence that conclusively proved his magnetic fluid theory. They put down his results to the "imagination" of his patients and concluded that the subject was therefore not worth further scientific investigation.

In light of the subsequent growth of the psychological sciences in the twentieth century this dismissal of "imagination" as unworthy of scientific investigation seems a staggering blind spot. However, such was no doubt the spirit of the times of the rationalist Enlightenment. Only a century before, Charles II, as founder of the Royal Society, could not bring himself to conceive the existence of air and dismissed efforts to investigate it scientifically. It would take at least another century to come to the realisation of the importance of the human imagination as something to be taken very seriously.

Mesmer was subsequently driven into exile and died in 1815 but the exploits and researches of his followers, such as de Puységur and Deleuze, raised so much interest that the Royal Academy of Medicine in France ordered a new investigation. This continued from 1825 to 1831 and confirmed much that was claimed by the mesmerists, but this apparent triumph of the magnetisers infuriated the conservative establishment. The Academy refused to print the report and another committee was appointed, headed by a hostile chairman, with the inevitable required result.

So things remained for a decade until Braid claimed to produce much the same phenomena simply by using a bright intermittent light. The academicians were mollified, Mesmer's theory of animal magnetism had apparently been demolished and a new method introduced that was simple and easy to apply, the new science and technique of hypnotism.

However, there seems good reason to believe that there is a significant degree of "higher phenomena" associated with the somnambulistic state that cannot be produced by mechanical methods and suggestion alone.

Braid's experiments were confirmed and extended in various quarters including the Paris Salpetrière Hospital where the highly influential Professor Charcot insisted that the hypnotic state was simply a result of a diseased condition of the nerves, that much of the phenomena could be produced without the use of suggestion, and the whole subject was explicable in terms of the physiology of the brain and nervous system.

Emile Coué and Auto-Suggestion

Nonetheless the subject of suggestion came to loom very large indeed in other schools of hypnosis, including the work of Liebault in what became known as the Nancy School, as opposed to Professor Charcot's Paris School. Liebault approached the subject in terms of mental action alone. He insisted that phenomena were best produced by those who were sound in body and mind and that all results were the result of some form of suggestion. This line of thought and practice eventually attracted enormous publicity in what became known as the New Nancy School under the influence of the practical results obtained by a practitioner known as Emile Coué.

Coué was essentially a practitioner rather than a theorist and his methods were largely popularised in 1920 by the book *"Suggestion and Auto Suggestion"* by his disciple Baudouin.

The theory and practice of induced auto-suggestion took the subject to the point where a practitioner was hardly needed at all, except as a means of inducing the process within the patient. An important element in the technique was avoiding getting the patient's conscious mind too intellectually involved, for this could invoke the Law of Inversed Effort, whereby the harder one tried, the more difficult it was to get results. One gets a similar kind of effect when "racking one's brains" to remember some forgotten name. The more one tries, the less successful one is, until having forgotten about trying, the name may then pop up automatically into consciousness. The same principle applies in trying to induce an auto-suggestive cure.

After his initial good results in Troyes and at Nancy, Coué's practice was helped very considerably by his reputation which induced a kind of snowball effect of increasing belief and faith in him and his methods. Anyone going for treatment would find a waiting room crammed full of people all confident of being cured of their problems, some of them very remarkably so. Thus a high expectation of success was generated.

Coué would begin his individual instruction by demonstrating to the patient the effectiveness of the patient's own powers of auto-suggestion and he would do this by methods which, in other circumstances and with other intentions, might well have been regarded as occult experiments.

He would, for example, give the patient a pendulum and after telling him to try, by muscular effort, to keep it quite still, then ask him to visualise it moving in a particular way, either in straight swings or in a circle. When the pendulum began to behave in this way, Coué would tell the patient that this was proof positive of the power his own mind to affect his bodily or nervous condition. He might then go on to put out a circle of letters of the alphabet, again telling the patient consciously to try to keep the pendulum steady, but then to think of a letter or a word. This would usually then be spelt out by the swing of the pendulum, as another demonstration of the powers of self-suggestion.

We know that techniques of this nature are, in certain circles, popular means of seeking spirit communication and Coué had other little experiments like this that came very close to table turning. Dowsers also use pendulums as a means of detecting lost or hidden objects or subtle energy fields.

Coué, however, was not interested in any theories of this nature. As far as he was concerned the aim was to activate the subconscious mind as a tool of the subject's own conscious mind, and not as a vehicle of communication with any disembodied spirit or as a means of extra-sensory perception. He had sometimes to reassure superstitious or religiously conservative patients that they were not somehow in contact with demonic agencies.

Having convinced his patients of the power of auto-suggestion, he then put them onto a regime of repeating a verbal formula many times a day, affirming that they were getting better, in what might be regarded as the equivalent of an oriental mantram or Catholic rosary prayer.

This would need to be rehearsed several times a day, and repeated over and over. Even gabbling it quickly was no barrier to success, and could even be more efficacious as a means of by-passing the critical objective faculties. He also found that it was effective to add a general clause to the effect that the patient was getting better "in every way" as well as referring to the particular symptoms or ailment.

In time this became promulgated as a general formula which anyone and everyone could use, and a highly popular New Thought movement sprang up whose famous litany was "Every day and in every way I am getting better and better". Promoted as the power of positive thinking, it had many ramifications including schools of salesmanship and general psychological self-improvement.

Coué would use any means to obtain the faith of the patient in the efficacy of what he was doing, even to the extent of telling the patient that he would be co-operating in "absent healing". That is to say that, at the same time as the patient was performing his affirmations, Coué would be concentrating upon him and aiding in the healing process. The fact that Coué had probably gone fishing or was indulging in some other spare time occupation, whilst the patient still got better, was proof to Coué that the technique worked and was based entirely upon auto-suggestion. Faith in the power of auto-suggestion might have been induced by him in the first instance, and continuing consultations might help to bolster the patient's faith in this, but, at root, it was the patient's own faith, will and efforts that effected the cure.

We are now of course a long way from conceptions of animal magnetism and the somnambulistic trance. Yet, we would do well to bear in mind that because these techniques and theories were passed by, after Braid's introduction of hypnotism in 1841, that they cease to retain any validity. A fact of nature still exists whether or not an influential body of opinion chooses to ignore it, and if Braid demonstrated that he could keep up his trousers with the belt of hypnosis instead of the braces of animal magnetism, it does not mean to say that braces do not still exist and remain an efficient means of retaining decency.

Faith healing or magnetic healing?

I had a vivid and somewhat painful demonstration of the reality of animal magnetism in my youth by getting rather too close to a faith healer who still used these methods, even though he was generally regarded as a Faith Healer, operating by means of the Holy Spirit, which he probably also believed himself.

Invited to accompany someone to a meeting of his, which took place in a packed church, I happened to be personally introduced to him just before the event. In what may well have been his usual practice in such circumstances, he grasped my hand strongly, fixed me in the eye with a powerful gaze, with the verbal affirmation positively expressed, "God Bless You" or words to that effect. Such was the intensity of his gaze that I felt an instant tingling in my brow at the point that is usually regarded as the ajna psychic centre. This passed away however and I took my seat near the back of the church.

Before the healer began the laying on of hands to the sick he began to walk up and down the aisles of the church making sweeping movements of his arms and hands as if drawing in some form of power from the congregation; then he proceeded with his healing of individuals before the altar. As he did so, I began to feel myself getting weaker and feeling increasingly unwell, as well as intensely emotionally irritated, particularly at the repetition and tone of his repeated "Thank you, Father" which he got all the patients to say after he had laid hands on them. Eventually I was sufficiently distressed to leave early and having fortified myself with a hot drink at a nearby cafè, went on home.

The next morning however I woke to find I had a most uncomfortable point of irritation right between the eyebrows. What is more, the discomfort increased as the day wore on until it was very painful indeed at about midday, after which it decreased in intensity until the sun went down. The next day the same thing happened again, the pain coming and going with the light. On the third day I sought medical advice and the doctor diagnosed it as sinusitis, dispensed an inhalant but implied that the only thing to do, short of an operation, was to grin and bear it. However, the problem wore off over a matter of days and I have fortunately never been bothered with it since.

It was a salutary demonstration to me, however, of the reality of some forms of the unseen and also a warning that some alternative healers may have little idea of how and what they may be doing in the course of their empirical healing practice. I imagine no harm came to most people to whom this particular healer projected his magnetic handshake but to a young initiate sensitised by meditation and magical ritual methods it plainly broke a temporary hole in the etheric vehicle, so that I was being literally vampirised in the church, with physiological repercussions following on.

Anecdotal evidence may not cut much ice in scientific circles but it is none the less convincing to those who bear the brunt of the actual experience. It certainly convinced me that although doctors may write off much of alternative healing as an application of the placebo effect, it was more than a placebo that hit me between the eyes on that particular night.

Dr. Thomson Jay Hudson and the Objective and Subjective Minds

In our review of the development of the techniques of animal magnetism and of hypnosis through to induced autosuggestion, it has been apparent that considerable differences of opinion could exist about the causes of various phenomena. It is possible that if suggestion is as important as Coué and his followers suggest then a great deal of the cures and theories could be due to the expectations of healers and patients. Much the same has been said of modern schools of psycho-analysis, where Freudian analysts come up with case studies that bear out Freudian theory and Jungian analysts with case studies that bear out Jungian theory, and so on through the whole gamut of psychotherapies.

In 1892, at a crucial point just before the waters were about to be further muddied by the advent of psycho-analysis and the various psychiatric disciplines that depend upon the theory of the subconscious, an American savant, Thomson Jay Hudson Ph.D., Ll.D., produced a book *"The Law of Psychic Phenomena"* that attempted a fair and balanced assessment of all that had gone before. His work can provide a useful vantagepoint in time for us, falling midway between Mesmer's first appearance and the post psycho analytic age where we are now.

Dr. Hudson made a list of the principal methods of what we would now call "alternative healing", namely:

1.   *Prayer and religious faith,* as at Lourdes and other shrines, or cures effected by prayer alone, often called Faith Healing;

2.   *Mind Cure,* which rests on the supposition that all diseased states of the body are due to a problem within the mind, and can thus be cured by a direct mind to mind process between healer and patient;

3.   *Christian Science,* a religious movement based on a disbelief in the reality of matter, from which it follows that if our bodies are unreal then there is no such thing as disease, must also be illusory if properly understood;

4.   *Spiritualism,* which has also taken on the trappings of religious belief, the healing side of which is based upon the assumption that the spirits of the dead, often deceased doctors and surgeons, are operating a subtle form of therapeutics through a medium or faith healer;

5.   *Magnetism,* which includes all systems of healing based on the supposition that there exists a fluid that can be projected onto another person at the will of the operator and which will effect a healing;

6.   *Hypnosis,* which is based on the law that persons in a hypnotic condition or light trance can be controlled by means of suggestion so that pain can be suppressed, bad habits or addictions eradicated, nerves calmed.

Each of these can be further subdivided into various schools, movements and individual practitioners, and there may well be an overlapping of function, whether consciously realised or admitted or not.

Having reviewed all the evidence available to him Dr. Hudson considered that most of the phenomena could be explained by supposing that man has two minds. One of these he called the objective mind, and the other the subjective mind.

The objective mind is the one with which we are all familiar. It is the means whereby we make contact with the physical world, and its means of perception are the five physical senses. It seems to be very largely a function of the physical brain, for its powers can be affected by ageing or damage to the brain. It might be regarded as the outgrowth of man's physical necessities, and in this respect would seem to be very similar to the generally accepted occult doctrine of the Personality or Lower Self, as a projection of the Higher Self into material conditions for the purpose of gaining experience.

The subjective mind is rather more than what we would nowadays call the subconscious mind, although in some respects it perhaps has an affinity with Jung's concept of a collective unconscious which can be accessed in certain circumstances by the individual. The subjective mind seems aware of the physical environment but by means that are independent of the physical senses. It operates by means of a kind of direct intuition, and is the seat of the emotional drives as well as being a storehouse of memory. Whilst the objective mind has access, by conscious recollection, to a relatively small amount of memory for utilitarian use, the memory of the subjective mind is a comprehensive recording. Within it, all past sensory and mental images are stored, in what we would nowadays call a vast database of past experience.

The subjective mind thus has very remarkable powers, far beyond those of the objective mind, and of a different order. However, its powers are not available consciously unless the objective mind is put into abeyance - one form of which is the state of somnambulism discovered by the mesmerists. In this state the subjective mind has been shown to be capable of vision without use of the physical eyes, of travel to distant places, of thought transference, and of reading the contents of sealed envelopes or closed books. In other words it demonstrates a panoply of what are usually called clairvoyant powers.

Some investigators have likened the subjective mind to the immortal soul, on the grounds that the closer the body approaches the condition of death, with the functions of the objective mind suspended, the stronger become the demonstrations of the subjective mind. However, the subjective mind does have its limitations.

The objective mind is a fairly rigid structure, built up on a foundation of reason and positive knowledge through the evidence of the senses. It is capable of rational argument and is resistant to suggestion, and whatever its limitations in terms of extra sensory perception or universal memory, it forms a centre of identification and control.

The subjective mind, on the other hand, is highly amenable to suggestion, and will accept without hesitation any statement that is made to it. It also seems incapable of inductive reasoning. It is very effective at producing examples from general principles, but avoids building up a general conclusion from observation of particular evidence and examples, or arguing a point through by logical analysis.

An ideal situation would be the objective mind working on conscious harmonious terms with the subjective mind, and this might be regarded as a condition resulting in the manifestation of genius, the secret of producing a William Shakespeare. In less spectacular cases it is a working arrangement with the subjective mind that produces flashes of creativity in the various fields of human endeavour. However, a subjective mind that breaks out of its normal confines and runs wild beyond the control of the objective mind leads only to eccentricity, neurosis and lunacy.

One intriguing speculation of Dr. Hudson's was that magnetic operators tend to get higher phenomena from their somnambulistic patients because, by virtue of their technique, they too are in a form of trance as opposed to the rationally detached hypnotist with his mechanical devices. This would suggest once more the importance of the matter of polarity in consciousness, and the advantages of a group, be it only of two, being of one mind in one place.

Séance-room phenomena

Phenomena associated with disembodied spirits runs parallel to research into animal magnetism and the somnambulistic state. The eighteenth century Swedish statesman, scientist and mystic Emanuel Swedenborg differed from previous visionaries in that he believed himself able to walk in heaven and hell and converse with the illustrious dead of previous generations. His newly founded church exercised an influence on William Blake and later upon early spiritualist communicators who proliferated in the wake of the events in the small town of Hydesville, New York, in 1848, where the Fox sisters reported strange rappings upon the wooden frame of their bed and interpreted them as attempts of a discarnate spirit to make itself known.

This rapidly became a huge movement in the 1850's that spread to Europe and reached its height in the 1870's, when the distinguished scientist Sir William Crookes began actively to investigate it, allied to his experiments on the behaviour of electricity within a vacuum. Having pumped as much air as was mechanically possible from a tube he saw beautiful evanescent light forming within it. Since the premature death of his brother he had resolved to try to find the borderland between physical life and death and had attended many séances. He had observed ethereal lights at some of them which, he thought, very much resembled lights within his vacuum tubes.

He hoped that his scientific researches had brought mankind to the edge of a supersensible world and gave public demonstrations in 1879 of what he called "radiant matter" to be seen in the tubes. In his accompanying lecture he declared:

"We have actually touched here the borderland where Matter and Force seem to merge into one another, the shadowy realm between Known and Unknown, which for me has always had peculiar temptations...I venture to think that the greatest scientific problems of the future will find their solution in this Borderland, and even beyond; here, it seems to me, lie Ultimate Realities, subtle, far-reaching, wonderful."

The world that he had discovered however was the beginnings of the technology of the neon and sodium lights of the twentieth century advertising industry and the cathode ray tube that graces all our television sets and computer terminals, as well as the world of quantum mechanics and its resulting technology, which, by a further twist of fate, has led to a serious questioning of the fundamental state of matter and the mystical dynamics that may be contained within it, in such works as Frithjof Capra's *"The Tao of Physics"* (1975) or Gary Zukav's *"The Dancing of the Wu Li Masters"* (1979) and more recently Dana Zohar's *"The Quantum Self"* (1990).

The scientific world of the 1880's was however completely unsympathetic to William Crookes' psychical assumptions. His paper *"On Phenomena called Spiritual"* was totally rejected by his contemporaries and he had to contend with their opposition as long as he embraced this line of research. He therefore abandoned his investigations, deeply disillusioned at the lack of sympathetic response from his colleagues, although he later served as President of the Society for Psychical Research and continued to express his personal views on the subject.

Nonetheless, spirit phenomena continued to be demonstrated despite the attitude of the scientific community. Whilst the bulk of séances consisted of private households indulging in table turning and the ouija board there was a certain number of mediums who produced phenomena of a remarkable nature. Whether or not their phenomena was false or genuine, or a mixture of the two, their reported exploits helped to keep the movement alive and encouraged the more modest attempts of home circles.

Dr. Hudson, our guide to how things appeared to the plain man of 1892, is quite sure on the matter. He states quite categorically that

"the man who denies the phenomena of spiritism today is not entitled to be called a sceptic, he is simply ignorant,"

and continues,

"Modern scientists have an easy way of treating such phenomena, which consists in denying their existence and refusing to investigate. Such men would plug their ears against thunder and deny it if they could not account for it by reference to familiar laws."

Such comment would have been welcome to Sir William Crookes but the existence of phenomena did not convince Dr. Hudson that it came through the agency of the spirits of the departed. His orthodox Christian belief tended to militate against such an interpretation. There were, on the other hand, sincere and intelligent commentators such as his near contemporary Frank Podmore, author of *"The Newer Spiritualism"* (1910) who could accept the idea of communication with spirits but because of his respect for the "familiar laws" of physical science could not bring himself to accept the validity of séance room phenomena.

It would take us far beyond our present purpose to review the complex question of spirit communication, and whether or not any messages received in trance or other forms of psychic receptivity come from a disembodied mind, or by telepathic rapport from another person, or from the subjective mind of the individual involved. Suffice to say that any material obtained by these means should be judged upon its content rather than on any claims as to its ultimate source.

One of the most remarkable of mediums as regards phenomena was Daniel Douglas Home. He was born in Edinburgh in 1833 but moved in childhood to America where he lived with an aunt until 1850, when he started to practise as a spirit medium, first in America and then in England and Europe. He charged no money for his services although he lived quite well as a result of them, through the friendship and patronage of influential and wealthy admirers. In addition to his mediumistic gifts he was a reasonable musical performer, an excellent reciter of poetry and a talented sculptor.

He was, by all accounts, a man of considerable charm, and made two financially advantageous marriages before giving up his public activities in 1872 shortly after his second marriage. His most remarkable séances were conducted in the twelve years up to this date.

During his time as a medium in America, from 1850 to 1855, he had been but one of a host of physical mediums. The Fox sisters, and others such as Gordon, Cooley, Abby Warner, E.S.Fowler, all produced phenomena of the order of moving tables, the autonomous playing of musical instruments and the appearance of spirit hands and faces.

A typical professional séance would have first the production of raps and knocks, then vibration of the table, its levitation, touches on the hands of the sitters or of their dress beneath the table, and a simple mechanical instrument such as an accordion playing itself. If circumstances were favourable there might follow the appearance of hands and arms, even heads in luminous clouds, movement of various articles including furniture from distant parts of the room,and a general distribution of flowers.

Home was capable of even more spectacular phenomena, such

as a polished table inclining at a steep angle while articles upon it remained in place. Occasionally he would appear to become elongated, or be carried bodily through the air above the heads of the sitters, touching them as he passed, or he would plunge his hands in the fire and walk about the room carrying a flaming coal.

Such sessions were never under any very vigorous control conditions. Few details are recorded as to the placing of the sitters, let alone attempts at monitoring the movements of the medium. The light might be fairly good at the beginning when minor phenomena were taking place, with gas light or candles, but these were generally extinguished before any higher phenomena took place, with the fire screened or damped down.

The general attitude of sitters in the 1860-70's was one of exalted excitement, partly religious and partly personal sentiment, stimulated by expectation of the messages of love and consolation that they hoped would be relayed to them from deceased loved ones. We should remember that in those days of comparatively primitive medical science there was considerably greater infant mortality than today, and husbands, wives and sweethearts dying in comparative youth. Whilst cunningly phrased spirit messages might well have been part of an unscrupulous medium's stock in trade there was hardly need for any very sophisticated trickery when seekers were fervently willing to believe their own fond imaginings of the presence of their dear ones.

Home encouraged a religious atmosphere by interspersing the phenomena with sermons and moral homilies, frequently invoking the name of Christ and the heavenly angels. He was also remarkable for the insights he showed into the lives of his sitters, although it has to be said that he was often on terms of close friendship with those for whom he gave sittings.

He won the affection and respect of many eminent people, including Sir William Crookes, although the poet Robert Browning remained convinced that he was an impostor and lampooned him as Mr Sludge the Medium. Yet there was never any direct evidence of Home ever cheating in his production of phenomena.

The substance of any case against him could only be on thecircumstantial grounds that he might be a skilled conjuror who could dictate the conditions under which he worked before an audience of his own choosing, and with the further advantage that he need only produce his phenomena when he felt like it and circumstances were propitious. Sir William Crookes, in his *"Researches in Spiritualism"* (1874) for instance, lays Home open to such a sceptical interpretation when he remarks:

> "the experiments I have tried have been very numerous, but owing to our imperfect knowledge of the conditions which favour or oppose the manifestations of this force, to the apparently capricious manner in which it is exerted, and to the fact that Mr. Home himself is subject to unaccountable ebbs and flows of the force, it has but seldom happened that a result obtained on one occasion could be subsequently confirmed and tested with apparatus specially contrived for the purpose."

In the same publication Crookes also laid down some principles which ought to guide scientific research into seeking proof for the existence of supernormal physical forces:

> "The spiritualist tells of flowers with the fresh dew on them, of fruit, and living objects being carried through closed windows and even solid brick walls. The scientific investigator naturally asks that an additional weight (if it be only the thousandth part of a grain) be deposited on one pan of his balance when the case is locked. And the chemist asks for the thousandth of a grain of arsenic to be carried through the sides of a glass tube in which pure water is hermetically sealed."

Neither Sir William nor anybody else has managed to find this desired scientific proof, yet sometimes we are baffled by the circumstances that seem to militate against deliberate fraud. A case in point is the Reverend Stainton Moses, a pillar of the English establishment, an Oxford M.A., clergyman of the Church of England, English Master in a public school, who in mid-life blossomed forth as a spirit medium. He received a large number of philosophical spirit communications that he wrote up into various books but these were accompanied by quite remarkable physical phenomena.

In his sittings brass candlesticks, plaster statuettes, flowers and seed pearls were apported into the séance room, pencils wrote by themselves, spirit lights floated about, perfumes came from his head, strains of ethereal music could be heard, and sometimes he himself would levitate. All this was under quite casual and unscientific conditions: complete darkness, a circle of close friends, no physical restraints, tests or precautions of any kind, and most of the phenomena reported by himself. The argument against trickery in this instance is the character of the man. Even if one considers that he might have been tempted to try to spread belief in his new faith by a fraudulent demonstration of conjuring tricks we are faced with the prospect of an extraordinary psychological abnormality on his part.

After Home retired there was no immediate successor to match his abilities and between 1870 and 1890 the movement entered a new phase. Sitters became more sceptical in attitude and insisted on holding the medium's hands or imposing more severe measures of restraint. On the other hand it became the trend for circles to be held in almost complete darkness, with the medium seated in a cabinet with the intention of producing ectoplasmic materialisations.

This was the high period for spirit photography and slate writing, (messages written on two slates bound together with a piece of chalk inside). It was also a period marked by frequent exposures of fraud - of double exposed photographs, trick slates, spirit lights of phosphorised oil, muslin passing for ectoplasm, false beards, stuffed spirit hands and the deft manipulation of hidden apparatus with threads or hairs by hand or foot.

The subject began to fall into increasing disrepute and after experimenting with several mediums a distinguished committee of psychical researchers came to the conclusion that psychic phenomena deteriorated in proportion to the precautions that were taken to prevent trickery, until a point was reached when manifestations disappeared altogether. The Society for Psychical Research on its foundation in 1882, to avoid fraud, declined to undertake experiments with professional mediums. It invited the co-operation of private persons with similar powers but received little response.

Then Eusapia Palladino appeared, a semi-literate Italian peasant woman who had apparently possessed remarkable mediumistic powers since adolescence. From 1892 onwards she appeared before a series of investigating committees in England, France and Italy, that included distinguished scientists such as Madame Curie on the one hand and practical conjurors and fraud hunters on the other.

She proved capable of conscious and deliberate fraud on occasion and also rejected or evaded a number of tests, and displayed a rooted antipathy to scientific apparatus of any kind. Nonetheless much of her phenomena was not only impressive but seemed unimpeachable.

It therefore seems inconclusive to try to sift the evidence of remarkable cases, and the trend in the spiritualist movement in any case began to move away from the production of startling phenomena by a few remarkable individuals. It may thus prove more productive if we turn our attention to the evidence of one or two practising mediums closer to our own time, who seem to demonstrate intelligence, common sense and personal integrity, and who are familiar with all aspects of séance room phenomena. It immediately becomes apparent that some of the conditions required for success run counter to the attitude of mind and conditions of working that scientific committees, quite understandably, will want to impose.

For instance, Ursula Roberts, in her booklet *"Hints on Mediumistic Development"* insists that the medium should be free of all worry and responsibility while the sitting is in progress, should be allowed to fall into a trance, go to sleep, or simply rest. If he or she feels uncomfortable in one chair, should be allowed to sit in another. This because any tension within the medium, whether in body, mind or emotion, will inhibit the release of ectoplasmic force upon which the success of the sitting depends.

If the sitters and medium cannot trust one another then there is no point in having a sitting in the first place. An atmosphere of patience, kindness, cheerfulness and complete freedom from suspicion is the keynote for success. These conditions of course approximate to the séances of the hey day of spiritualism, which were also aided by religious fervour and unanimous expectation, a potent formula that does not necessarily imply fraud, even if it may be open to the risk of some element of self deception. As in magical operation, so often reiterated by Dion Fortune, it is necessary to believe implicitly in what one is doing at the time, and reserve critical analysis until afterward.

Phoebe Payne seems also worth consulting. Her informed and sincere book *"Man's Latent Powers"* appeared just before Dion Fortune embarked upon *"The Circuit of Force"*. She states that physical phenomena, which have been so exhaustively pursued in research, will either attract or repel the general enquirer, so apart from being a possible means of convincing a wavering materialist there is not a great deal of point in seeking experience of it.

The simplest form and the easiest to produce is "table turning" but when it comes to receiving messages this method can prove to be laborious and considerably tedious. The practice usually starts with a few friends sitting about a light table and placing their hands upon it in the hope that something may happen. Before long, light tremors in the table may be felt, probably due to involuntary slight muscular spasms in the arms of those involved. This may well appear to beginners to be the beginning of serious phenomena and if they emotionally welcome it their positive response will encourage the start of real phenomena. The slight movements may then increase in volume until there is a very noticeable degree of motion. It is not easy to determine where the subjective physical state ends and genuine psychic phenomena begins. To clairvoyant sight etheric emanations from the sitters' hands will quickly blend into a film covering the whole of the tabletop, and the concentration of interest will cause individual auras to fuse into a unified psychic field.

In the case of a serious group that is well developed through practice together Phoebe Payne reports seeing the build up of a kind of rod or cantilever in etheric matter drawn from all present that stretches from the foot or leg of the medium under the table to assist its tilting. This is very much like the kind of device that in physical terms would be considered fraudulent practice. In more run of the mill groups however, any table movement is the consequence of automatic muscular movements of the sitters, activated through their subjective minds.

At a more advanced level there are various types of manifestation, which might be listed as levitation, apports, precipitation, slate writing, spirit photography, and direct voice phenomena. In Phoebe Payne's view, which includes clairvoyant perception, these invariably require the involvement of skilled and powerful inner helpers of one kind or another working upon the etheric levels.

Levitation

Levitation of the medium is nowadays considered a rarity although the raising of light objects is fairly common. Phoebe Payne reports having had several opportunities to observe such phenomena and found it most readily explainable by the formulation of ectoplasmic hands or other lifting devices, plus possibly an ability to vary the air pressure round a physical object.

Apports

This is the bringing of objects from a distance and is a different phenomenon from levitation and a more complex one. It involves the passage of matter through matter and this can only be achieved by the dematerialization of an object and its subsequent rematerialization elsewhere. In terms of esoteric technicalities this involves dispersing the physical atoms by thought power whilst retaining its etheric counterpart by an act of will on the part of the operator. This is obviously no easy matter despite being almost a commonplace with Madame Blavatsky in her days in India, although the fuss and bother in which it later involved her caused her to wish she had never bothered with this kind of manifestation. It is not as rare as all that however, and in an emergency a close friend of Phoebe Payne had a key apported to her from a drawer at home.

Precipitation

This is another rare skill that is also associated with Madame Blavatsky, and the bulk of the Mahatma Letters, which now repose in the British Museum, were transmitted and received in this manner. Something of the technique is described in the body of the letters which can be read in the published volume of *"The Mahatma Letters to A.P.Sinnett"* that were eventually published in volume form in 1923. Sinnett was a leading figure in the British raj as editor of the main English daily paper *"The*

Pioneer". Techniques that were almost commonplace to Indian holy men were something of a miracle to Sinnett and his friends, and one of the many interesting facets of this correspondence is the difference in attitude it reveals between oriental holy men and colonial westerners of the period - the 1880's.

Sinnett initially wants the mahatmas to apport or precipitate a copy of *"The Pioneer"* newspaper in London on the day of publication, a truly miraculous event in those days before airmail, when the sea passage from India would have taken some weeks. The mahatmas are at some pains to point out that this would not lead to converting the world to their cause but simply bring about heated accusations of fraud, which is very much what happened with other related phenomena. Already swayed by some malevolent false witness, the Society for Psychical Research investigator of the time was in no mood to take it at all seriously. Tibetan thought power has now in any case been rendered obsolete by the modern fax machine but as in the case of animal magnetism, to circumvent a fact of nature is not to prove its non-existence.

Slate writing

Given the ability to manipulate subtle etheric matter it is a small problem to use it to manipulate pieces of chalk in confined spaces.

Psychic photography

This is a similar, but slightly easier process than precipitation, as the medium is a light sensitive negative anyway. The blurring that often occurs may well be due to a lack of definition in the thought image that is projected.

Direct voice

This is the speaking of disembodied voices through light paper trumpets or megaphones. Oddly enough the phenomena is easier to work if there is a background hum of conversation, as if this stimulates the production of sound waves of etheric origin. As with the appearance of etheric forms in ectoplasmic matter, it is possible to interfere with the substance of the message by concentrated thought, which is another reason why trance related communication is such an uncertain business, for thought interference can be unconscious as well as conscious, particularly if impelled by some force of emotion.

We may perhaps best conclude this section by quoting Phoebe Payne's remarks about test conditions for physical phenomena.

"The tests may be either simple or of the most stringent and elaborate kind, but those who undertake them rarely have even an elementary understanding of the power of thought and emotion over the subtle and responsive material with which they are working. They grasp the fact that mediums must be carefully handled and their main conditions accepted, but few realise that the whole subject is governed by a technique as delicate and exact as that of any other scientific experiment. As a scientist may have his research work spoilt by the slightest alteration of temperature or other considerations, so may the bridge of ectoplasmic material be destroyed by numerous factors which the investigator does not recognise as having any bearing upon the experiment. True psychic investigation needs the collaboration of both occultist and scientist."

DANGERS OF
FAULTY DEVELOPMENT

The Circuit of Force Part 9 [January 1940]
Dion Fortune

The devitalising effect of mystical devotion and the unbalancing
effect of psychic development are matters of such common
knowledge and observation that there is no need to produce evidence
of their existence, for every one has seen them. Something, however,
may usefully be said concerning their cause and cure.

The mystic devitalises himself because his mental attitude inhibits
the flow of life force into the physical body, which he regards as an
evil to be overcome. The sensitive etheric double responds to this
attitude; the flow of life force is dammed back; no magnetism is
picked up from the Earth-aura, and the vitality of the physical body,
being cut off from its sources of supply, dries up to a point where
it is no longer adequate to the carrying on of the physiological
processes, and all manner of functional diseases of nervous origin
develop. Of course it is not possible for the average person entirely
to inhibit the flow of all magnetism in its age-old channels, or he
would die out of hand; though this has occurred in cases of eastern
mystics who added a knowledge of mind power to their mysticism;
but even the untrained mind, if single-pointed, is able to close its
channels sufficiently to bring about that curious sickliness and
physical frailness so characteristic of the devout. The wonderful
healings in response to group prayer on their behalf that such persons
experience are due to the influx of vital force they receive from the
people who pray for them. It is also a matter of common knowledge
in such circles that there is nothing so exhausting and devitalising as
personal attendance upon a sickly mystic.

The mental disorganisation is more commonly seen in psychics
than in mystics, though mystics share in it just as psychics also

share in the physical disorganisation; but one is pretty safe in saying that the devout person who has dedicated his life to what he understands by God is more likely to lose his physical health but keep his mental balance than the one who has devoted himself to the development of his own powers. It will generally be found that the psychic who becomes physically sickly and hypersensitive is one who combines devotion with his psychism. God, when worshipped as Spirit and nothing else, is indeed a Moloch who devours his children.

The mental unbalance of the psychic is entirely due to the failure to understand the mechanism of the mind. The mind can, by means of concentration of attention, be divided up into its component parts; be dissected out, as it were, and this is done when the higher modes of consciousness are brought into action. Normal consciousness, with its direction by the will and judgement, can be closed down, and superconsciousness or subconsciousness opened by the appropriate methods; but these are not under the direct control of the will and judgement, and an elaborate technique exists, and has to be carefully learnt, in order that indirect control may be acquired and the integrity of the personality maintained. It is the lack of this knowledge and power that causes the untrained mind to split wider and wider apart when the levels of the mind are disconnected in order to attain extended consciousness, until the point is reached when it can no longer be re-integrated at the end of the psychic trance and is permanently out of control and dissociated.

Control is maintained firstly by the power of concentration which can switch the attention from plane to plane and back again at will; this is greatly aided by the utilisation of the power of associated ideas as developed in the occult symbol systems, without the use of which, in my opinion, psychic work is neither safe nor reliable. The second great factor in maintaining co-ordination and control is a clear understanding of the manner in which the mind works, thus enabling one to realise that psychic visions are subjective representations of other-world things and not direct perception, and that what the mind has made, the mind can unmake. One is not, therefore, hallucinated by one's own subjective mind-pictures, believing them to have an objective existence, when as a matter of fact they are "such stuff as dreams are made of," being symbolic representations of realities of another dimension. Hallucination in these matters is very dangerous, for it can easily lead on to obsession if the symbol-image represents an active potency that is not under proper control. The occultist employs the ceremonial technique of the magic circle and the triangle of art in order to ensure the control of the forces and beings thus evoked and so prevent obsession by them; but the uninitiated psychic, while his spiritualistic technique may, if properly learnt, be quite adequate to control the spirits of the departed, will find it a very different matter should he, by chance, contact the kind of forces with which the occultist is accustomed to work. It is the fact that he does not normally contact these forces because he does not possess the keys to their use that constitutes his protection. But in these days, when the knowledge of not only the occult doctrines but the occult methods is becoming increasingly widespread, psychics who have developed their psychism on spiritualistic lines sometimes try and put into application what they read, and the results are apt to be startling.

The average, undeveloped person can make nothing of these books because he does not possess the necessary basis in a trained mind, but the psychic, his higher centres wide open, has no power either to check or select the influences that enter them if he once leaves the levels he understands, and to which his technique is adapted, and contacts the far higher voltages with which the occultist works. I have seen some pretty startling consequences from such doings, and some pretty disastrous ones as well.

Psychics developed along spiritualistic lines, with years of experience behind them, very often fail to realise that when they touch the occult contacts, they are entering upon an entirely new field to which their previous experience is not an adequate guide. Being accustomed to teach, they are apt to be reluctant to learn. This is, no doubt, a very human and understandable failing, but it is also a very dangerous one, and I would urge all psychics who have not had the initiate's training to refrain from tampering with elemental forces or the Old Gods. I would also point out to them that the initiate gets his training on the physical plane, from other initiates, and that it occupies several years, and is never, in any circumstances, bestowed by means of inner plane experiences received when out of the body. These we call illuminations, and they are never to be confused with the laborious training that constitutes initiation, as can easily be proved when it comes to the exercise of the occult powers and their practical applications.

There is one more point of danger which has to be considered in relation to the development of the higher powers, and it is the failure to realise it which is the cause of many distressing incidents. As I have already pointed out, Kundalini, or personal magnetism, when roused, ascends from the earth, or physical vitality centre, to the Moon or sex centre. It should then, if properly controlled, rise still further to the Sun centre, or solar plexus, and it is from this point that occult work begins. If, however, there is imperfect thought control, or the sex life is inadequately regulated, leakage of force is liable to occur at this level, resulting in a most dangerous stimulus to the passions.

Before such development is undertaken, the power of concentration must have been thoroughly acquired so that the student can rely on being able to banish from his mind all unwanted thoughts. Till this is achieved, no good occult work is possible, let alone safe. Thought control is most carefully taught by a series of graded exercises for several years in the Outer Court of the Fraternity of the Inner Light, and by the end of that course the student should be able to banish any thoughts he does not want. The rousing of the magnetic forces latent in the etheric body can then be safely undertaken, provided there is experienced direction to supervise the work. It is because experienced supervision is essential that our correspondence courses stop with the Outer Court; students, however promising, being taken no further if they cannot work under personal supervision.

Now it is not enough to have such perfect mind control that all sensual thoughts can be completely and permanently banished from consciousness, because, as a certain wise pagan remarked, the more you drive Nature out of the door, the more she will fly in by the window. Sex is a function, not an emotion, and it cannot be treated in such cavalier fashion without disastrous consequences. Its forces rise and fall with well marked periodicity in both men and women, and this periodicity is due to endocrine action. The forces of sex can be controlled and directed, but to attempt to cut them out of life completely is to court disaster, and it is to this fallacious attempt that the great bulk of nervous disorders are due. The problem is not a simple one, and I do not propose to discuss its solution in these pages.

It is a very difficult problem, therefore, to know how to approach the task of developing the magnetic force of persons whom circumstances oblige to deal with their sex life by means of sublimation, for beyond question the rousing of Kundalini is a tremendous sexual stimulus, as is perfectly understood in the east. There is a certain point in occult development when the sex life is stirred up. Once that point has been safely overpassed, the vital forces can be turned to magical purposes and no longer give trouble on the physical plane, magic being the finest and most satisfying form of sublimation there is; but whilst that phase is being passed through, the initiate who has no physical plane outlet in normal sex life that can be used after the manner of a lightning conductor, is in the position of an acrobat who is learning trapeze tricks without the use of a safety-net. If he misses his hold or miscalculates his strength, the subsequent crash is a very serious matter.

People lose their heads badly on these occasions; if they lose their self-control as well, a social crash is probable, and if they maintain it, a mental crash is certain, so they are between the devil and the deep blue sea. To such I would say: unless you have in your life the conditions that make it possible for you to pass through this phase without undue risk, you are unwise to attempt it. For such, the mystic way of sublimation is the better path.

Far be it from me to advise people to outrage their consciences and inflict social injury on others; until the Anglo-Saxon attitude towards sex and its problems changes profoundly we must be content to suffer in order that we may fulfil all righteousness. People without private means cannot afford to outrage convention, and to advise otherwise is to plunge them into misery. Meanwhile, until such time as more hygienic and humane ideals shall rule our social life, people in difficult circumstances have to find such compromises as shall make life endurable. A long step in this direction is achieved when it is realised our moral code is founded on social custom, has changed from reign to reign with the influence of the ruling monarch, that it badly needs revision and that no man or woman need consider themselves sinners on account of their natural feelings.

A very true word was said by Charles Morgan in his preface to the published edition of his play: *"The Flashing Stream"*, admitted on all sides to be one of the great plays of this, or any, age. He says: "The face of the whole world would be changed if the experience of sex were considered to be innocent unless its circumstances made it guilty." I would recommend to the serious consideration of my readers the whole essay, *"On Singleness of Mind"*, which preceds the play in the printed volume. It is a notable exposition of the principles underlying sexual ethics.

SEXUAL ETHICS
IN OCCULTISM

The Circuit of Force Part 10 [February 1940]
Dion Fortune

It is impossible to deal with the subject of magnetic force without relating it to the question of sexual ethics. The basic magnetic force, the energy that manifests in the Muladhara Lotus, turns into sex force at its first transmutation, and it is no use blinking this fact; it is equally true, however, that its next transmutation is into the golden solar force of the subjective Tiphareth. Beyond this come the higher magnetic aspects which we will not concern ourselves with at the moment as they give rise to no controversies.

In considering the question of the transmutation of force from Malkuth to Yesod (the Moon-sex Centre) and from Yesod to Tiphareth, we shall inevitably deal with the force in accordance with our sexual ethics. Of these there are two types - the ascetic and the pagan. It will be observed firstly that I do not contrast the terms Christian – pagan because the ascetic ideal is not solely Christian. Zoroastrianism and Buddhism are both ascetic faiths, and there are ascetic sects in Hinduism and Mohammedanism. It will also be observed that I used the ill-reputed word pagan to represent the contrasting viewpoint to the ascetic. This is because the true meaning of the word refers to Nature worship or pantheism, and means one who remains faithful to the Old Gods.

Unless we can rise above the blinding influence of racial custom and personal habit and seek truth at its source, we shall move in circles, arriving nowhere. We are all too apt to start with certain premises concerning good and evil, right and wrong, moral and immoral, and entirely fail to realise that these as we know them were not handed over by God to man engraved on tablets of stone. They have been formulated out of a mixed mass of superstition and practical experience. In some things practical experience is given a hearing; in others, all is swamped in a morass of superstition. We see this plainly when we observe the social customs of people with cultures that differ so widely from our own that we are free from all association of ideas in judging them; but we are quite unable to see the irrationality in our own social codes, nor the influence that sheer superstition exerts over us.

Our sexual ethics are profoundly influenced by two things – firstly, by certain primitive concepts concerning the magical influences associated with the sexual forces, beliefs which are pure folk-lore and superstition and are but a debased and ignorant echo of the true esoteric teaching on this all-important subject; and secondly, by the old laws concerning the inheritance of property – laws that came to an end in England with the passing of the Married Woman's Property Act. These two influences have played a far greater part than we realise in the moulding of our ideas on the subject of sexual morality.

Finally, we have to consider the third point, the apex of the ethical triangle - the view that the flesh warreth against the spirit and the spirit against the flesh, which is a plain spoken statement of the ascetic viewpoint.

If this viewpoint were taken seriously in all its implications we should settle the conflict promptly and permanently by the only effectual method - suicide. But we do not do this; for though saints have dealt with the flesh in such manner that they were reported to look like roots of trees, most illogically ascetics stop short at suicide and propound a code of compromise.

It is, of course, true, that if the flesh is allowed to get out of hand it will not only war against the spirit but against its own existence by over-indulgence. It is an odd fact that saints live longer than rakes. An asceticism of self-discipline there must be if the flesh is to be kept in working order and the body rendered a tolerable habitation, but that man should take it into his head to remake God's handiwork according to his own ideas is not only blasphemous but impractical. The ascetic methods do not solve the sex problem, they merely disorganise the sex life, and the distorted forces appear in all manner of pathological forms. It is not possible to adventure into the deeper issues of occultism unless one is prepared to recognise that conventional ethics are blind leaders to the blind. To say this is not to abrogate ethics, but to face the fact that conventional ethics need overhauling.

Anybody who regards sex as evil, or is in any way afraid of it or self-conscious about it, had better leave occultism alone; for it is only through a perfectly naturalistic attitude towards the giving of life that life force can be handled. Let it never be forgotten that there is no such thing as sex force per se, but that it is simply the life force on a particular level, and that through this level the force must pass every time it rises and descends on the planes.

This does not mean that every magical act must culminate in orgasm. Far from it. Orgasm is the earthing of the force; its expenditure like a flash of lightning. There is no force available for magic immediately after orgasm, and in magic rightly worked there will be no force available for orgasm either, if all is restored to equilibrium, as it should be, at the end of the operation. A magical rite, properly worked, leaves the operators in the same harmonised state that follows coitus, and magic can be used as a most effectual and satisfying form of sublimation, not because it deteriorates into orgy, but because it rises on the planes. There are rituals in black magic in which the sexual forces are deliberately stimulated through the imagination. There are exponents of unnatural methods, whose names are well known in occult circles, and also, it may be said, to the police. The information I have gathered is, I am afraid, much too startling for publication in these pages. Because I lay the facts of sex in relation to occultism frankly before my readers, it must not be thought that I advocate these practices. Black magic takes place when a knowledge of the magnetic force is deliberately exploited in an unnatural manner. It is exceedingly necessary that anyone who is making a serious study of yoga and magnetic forces, especially if practical experimentation is included in their research - and it is hardly worthy to be considered serious if it is not - should have a thorough understanding of the relationship between magnetism and sex.

In order to perform practical occult work it is necessary to have magnetic force in strong concentration and under perfect control, and the raw material out of which the higher magnetic forces are sublimated is sexual energy. It is for this reason that only persons of vital and dynamic temperament can work magic; but it is equally true that only persons whose sex life, though vigorous, is perfectly controlled and harmonised, can work magic for long without going all to pieces.

There are many ways of harmonising the sex life in addition to the crude methods of repression and promiscuity, which are often considered to be the only alternatives. If the appetite for food were indulged or denied with the same ignorance and caprice as the appetite for sexual satisfaction, the chronic dyspepsia that resulted would soon produce a C3 nation. We need to get at the facts and apply common sense in this matter, and no longer allow our judgement and practice to be directed by clerics who, if the looks of themselves and their wives are anything to go by, are no recommendation for their own theories, "Will I get like you if I do as you advise?" is a very pertinent question to put to the official exponents of moral doctrine. Unless we regard sex as a sacred, but not an unclean thing, we have no business in the Temple of the Mysteries where the esoteric doctrine of sex and polarity is among the secrets of the higher degrees.

It has been my task, at no inconsiderable risk to myself, to give out much of these teachings. I have been attacked by those who would have kept them secret - for what motives save blind adherence to tradition and the advantage to personal prestige I do not know; I have been censured and even calumniated by those whose viewpoint is different from mine. One party says that the teachings, though true and valuable, should be kept secret; the others say that they are untrue and dangerous.

To the former I would say that no one has the right to keep secret what he knows to be true and valuable, and that the leaves of the Tree of Knowledge are for the healing of the nations. To the latter I reply that what is untrue in these matters cannot be dangerous, because if untrue, it is unworkable. Whether it is wicked or not is a matter of opinion, and the only appeal can be to experience "by their fruits ye shall know them." If the fruits are a sane mind in a sound body, it is difficult to believe that the tree that bears them is evil. The experiences of choirboys in the field of Christian morality, of which, by virtue of their office they have a close-up view, make significant reading, but the records have to be sought in the archives of psychopathology and the police courts. Nature, misused, takes a terrible revenge, and the last word in these matters is with Nature, not moral philosophy.

CHANNELS OF SUBLIMATION

The Circuit of Force Part 11 [March 1940]
Dion Fortune

I hope I have made my position in the matter of morality sufficiently clear for anyone to understand it who wishes to understand it. There will always be those who see things differently, but I hope we can agree to disagree and be content to be known by our fruits. There will also, unfortunately, always be those who read books with which they disagree in quest of ammunition for use against the authors; to try to disarm by explanation in this case is like flogging a dead donkey, and I shall not attempt the hopeless task. The interchange of magnetism is an exceedingly important thing, and operates in every aspect of life. For the teacher, the organiser, the group leader, it is the factor which makes the difference between outstanding success and mediocrity; it also plays a part in our daily lives, quite apart from the sex relationship, far greater than is realised, and its lack affects the mental well-being in exactly the same way as a qualitatively deficient diet affects the physical health.

Whatever aspect of character or consciousness is developed and capable of functioning must be permitted to function if a harmonious life-pattern is to be maintained, just as a lactating female animal must nurse its young or suffer general constitutional disturbance and much discomfort. We all, of course, have capacities for which our circumstances make no provision, and the more narrow our circumstances, the more starved are we in this respect. Fortunately for all of us, the full and obvious expression of our capacities on the physical plane is not necessary to maintain our life-pattern.

There is such a thing as sublimation, upon which great stress is laid in books upon psychotherapy and sex advice. Sublimation is a very real thing, and a very important and far-reaching thing, but it has its limits of usefulness, and if pressed beyond them, becomes harmful. In order to understand its right use, it is necessary to understand its real nature, even at the cost of a considerable digression, for it is upon this understanding that the whole question of the control of magnetic force will be found to rest.

The first factor in the case is the principle of the association of ideas, and the fact that these can become associated together quite irrationally if they should be present in the mind in juxtaposition at a moment of emotion. Emotion, if sufficiently strong, colours everything that is in consciousness when it is felt. We have all had experience of this, and know how some place, some odour, some tune, perfectly innocuous in itself, can acquire a significance for us through its emotional associations. This capacity of the mind can be put to many uses, as I have often pointed out when writing of ceremonial and symbolism. When it is to be deliberately utilised in the absence of spontaneous emotion, discernment has to be used in order to choose lines along which ideas will associate spontaneously because of their natural appeal to the imagination. For instance, football is so popular both as a spectacle and as a sport because it appeals to the combative instinct present in all males in varying degrees and permitted little expression in socialised and industrialised life. Music or art would be no adequate substitute for football because they make their appeal to another side of the nature. When a man is past the age for football, which is a young man's game, he will not turn to art as a substitute, but to similar but less strenuous forms of sport, passing from hockey to bowls as his years advance. Music and art satisfy the love of beauty, not the combative instinct, and love of beauty is a vital factor in all sex feeling save the most primitive; indeed, it is difficult to imagine a tribe so unevolved that some women should not be esteemed as more desirable than others on what passes with them for aesthetic grounds, quite apart from their value as beasts of burden.

The two main channels of sublimation of the sex instinct are art and religion. It must be said of art, however, that though it is a means of sublimation in the psychological sense, it would hardly be thus classified by the conventional moralist; for its tendency is to widen the channel that it opens, and consequently to call into action an increased amount of life-force. All great artists in whatever medium have notoriously been great lovers. This is probably due to the fact that the canons of art impose no inhibitions upon conduct. Religion, however, the great rival of art as a channel of sublimation, avails itself of the most rigorous taboos in order to concentrate the whole energy of the life in a single stream. Each has its contribution to make towards the good life. It is not good to call up more and more life-force till the organism is drained and exhausted; the sensualist defeats his own ends. Nor is it good to let sex feeling spread unchecked and break all barriers, for it resembles in its action the stream we have already used as an illustration, and turns life into a muddy morass. But on the other hand, it is not good to dam and canalise any force, regardless of the laws of hydraulics. If the channel is made too narrow for the volume of the stream, it will overflow its banks.

Sublimation must be employed with wisdom, and it never will be so employed if we regard sex as a thing that is evil in itself and to be reduced at all costs to the smallest possible dimensions and entirely suppressed if possible. We must recognise in this great force not only a fundamental, but a legitimate factor in the life pattern, and if it has to be denied its natural expression, must try to supply it with the best compensations we can; nor must we do this in the spirit that regards such substitutes as "a remedy for sin", but with an apology to Nature for the natural rights that circumstances compel us to deny. The best form of civilisation would be that which, while maintaining organised social life, does least violence to the natural instincts.

This is achieved by ample provision for play in the dual forms of sport and art. But however adequate may be the provision made by an enlightened society for these two activities, it is not enough for a man to have an outlet for their energies unless they also have some means of receiving a return flow of magnetism that shall re-charge the battery. We fail to realise that we not only can give out our life-force in a sublimated form, thus by-passing direct sexual activity, but can also receive a return flow of magnetism in a sublimated form, thus satisfying essential emotional and magnetic needs.

Flirtation, friendship, hero-worship, all fulfil this condition, and play an enormous part in the compensation of life's frustrations.

Many a man or woman has been able to make an imperfect marriage workable and life endurable through the vicarious satisfactions obtained in the dance hall or the evening institute, and celibates of both sexes have found in a leader an attraction so great that the lack of a mate was fully compensated.

Such things are very real, and render lives bearable that would otherwise be unbearable; but if left to the untutored guidance of chance, they are not always efficacious. If, however, we apply to them firstly a knowledge of psychology in order to understand the need, and secondly a knowledge of yoga and magic in order to direct and supplement the subtle magnetic forces which are the real key to the problem, we have a really valuable and practical contribution to make to one of the most baffling problems of civilisation.

The ancients had a method of dealing with sex force which has a profound psychological significance and could afford valuable lessons to our modern psychotherapists - they made use of these forces in the temple rites. That force which was not used in human mating was given to the god or goddess. It was done in crude ways that the civilised conscience could not tolerate, but there is a psychological truth underlying the proceeding. Force can be put in circuit cosmically as well as personally, polarising with the Great Isis or primitive Pan as the case may be, and herein is a great esoteric truth for meditation.

Force thus directed does not remain in the aura and decompose, as in the case of sensual fantasising, but is drawn into the stream of the cosmic circuit, and from the Archetypal Being thus constructed a ray of polarising magnetism returns. This is deep teaching but it is also practical truth.

POLARISATION IN PRACTICE

The Circuit of Force Part 12 [April 1940]
Dion Fortune

In the matter of the circuit of force and sublimation we have two problems to solve, not one, as the psychologists believe. We have not merely to find a channel of outlet for unused, and consequently congested force, which is what is usually understood by sublimation, but also a means for the intake of fertilising force, which is so completely unrecognised that it has not even got a name in psychology, and for which we must therefore coin one. Let us call it by its traditional occult name of Magnetism, and the whole process of exchange of force as Polarisation. We must now study the nature of Polarisation as a whole in order that we may the better understand the nature of its dual and complementary aspects. Polarisation, as understood by the occultists, is the exchange of force on any level between any two units. It includes sex as generally understood, but it also includes every reciprocal activity of two different factors. International exchange of raw materials for manufactured goods is an example of polarity.

We must carefully distinguish between true, functional polarity and those one-sided arrangements which bring disaster to nations and individuals. It is a maxim of economics that imports and exports must balance in the budget if sound finance is to be maintained, and so it is in all relations of life. A one-sided existence, all "take" and no "give", or all "give" and no "take" is profoundly unsatisfactory in a reciprocal relationship. A teacher with dull, unwilling pupils finds teaching exhausting to the body and deteriorating to the character; a teacher with eager, intelligent pupils finds it exhilarating. The leader of a divided party feels as if torn to pieces, whereas a united and enthusiastic group of people literally "carry" their leader, inspiring him to greater and greater efforts and realisations. It is also noticeable that successful leaders are always men and women of peculiar physical vitality; this vitality is often not conspicuous during their early struggles, but develops with their success.

Speaking from my own experience in group leadership, I can give instances that are not without significance in this respect. At one time, in the early days of our work, we had afternoon lectures as well as evening ones. At the afternoon lectures we had an audience composed almost exclusively of elderly ladies of no occupation. These lectures I found so depleting and depressing that, although they attracted quite good audiences, I refused to go on with them.

Another interesting fact emerged in connection with many years' experience of group leadership. It might be thought that I would give my best lectures, and receive most inspiration, from my talks to the senior classes of tried and proven workers, highly trained, who have been my familiar associates for several years. Oddly enough, this is not the case unless there is some sort of crisis going on.

I had long ago noticed that after several year's work with the same people, a kind of staleness set in. This may seem gross mutual ingratitude, but nevertheless it was a fact that had to be faced. The remedy was soon realised, however, for as soon as any practical occult work, ritual or meditation, was delegated, freshness returned to the relationship. Students made into teachers were polarised by their own students, and thus re-magnetised, polarised with me again on a higher arc as collaborators instead of pupils.

Curiously enough, my best work is done with a "mixed bag" of Inner Group students of all grades. No strangers being present, we are all of one mind in one place; and at the same time the introduction of "fresh blood" produces a vitality of atmosphere which serves as a magnetic stimulus.

In the practical work this is especially noticeable. It is, of course, impossible to introduce entirely untrained people into a group doing practical work, a framework of experienced people being essential; but if the group is composed entirely of senior members with whom I am long accustomed to associate, we do not get as good results as we do if one or two newcomers are introduced.

It seems as if, when people join a group for occult work, they bring with them a reserve of accumulated magnetism for which life has supplied no outlet. This is probably explained by the fact that the people who take up occultism, or any form of practical religion for that matter, are usually people who are dissatisfied with life, unfulfilled, hungry for emotional satisfaction. Such people need more than anything else an outlet for their unused forces, and they find this par excellence in practical occult work where the first thing that is done is to pool the available magnetism by means of circle-working. These people contribute far more magnetism than those who have made their adjustments and achieved equilibrium, for it must be remembered that an empty life is at the same time a life that is emotionally congested.

In the course of about two years' work, people pass through the phase of pouring out magnetism for others more experienced to work with, and reach a point when, for their further progress, they need in their turn to have a group of juniors to supply them with basic force essential to occult operations. If they are not supplied with what they need, they get very stale and discontented. I attribute the fact that we have never had a schism in the Fraternity of the Inner Light to our practice of providing advanced students with opportunities of group leadership in meditation work and ritual, thus changing students into collaborators. I have also found, however, that unless I keep in personal, individual touch with senior members, they in their turn tend to become de-magnetised.

The question of the sympathetic induction of vibration, which is so important a factor in initiation and occult training, is, of course, another example of the principle of polarisation. To be in contact with a person possessing a high level of consciousness is to have that mode of consciousness awakened in oneself. It was for this reason that we established our guesthouse at Glastonbury, so that students might have an opportunity of personal association with senior members. Unfortunately, however, financial considerations compel us to take others besides members, so conditions are not always as favourable as they might be. Moreover, teachers are apt to come down there tired after a term's work, and further polarisation demands too much of them.

For my own part, I tend increasingly to keep the different levels of consciousness strictly segregated, with somewhat disappointing results for eager students who, when I am working in the garden, approach me with some question arising out of my books, and I look at them quite blankly and don't know what on earth they are talking about. Upon one occasion, in fact, I picked up a brown paper covered book someone had left in the verandah, and began to read it with interest and approval, only to discover, when I had got halfway through, that I had written it myself!

It is not possible, in my experience, at my present level of development at any rate, to have the higher and the lower levels of consciousness open simultaneously. If I am concentrating on organisation on the physical plane, the inner plane contacts are closed down; if these open up, then I lose my grip on practical affairs.

The whole question of the opening and closing of my personal contacts is a very interesting example of polarisation and the circuit of force. I never work alone. I need co-operation of people who are themselves in touch with the plane I wish to work on. Left to myself, I am inert. Realising this fact intuitively, though without understanding the reason, from the earliest days of my work I have always been seeking co-operation, testing and searching until I could find the kind of co-operation I needed. I soon discovered that no single person could give me all the polarisation I required for our many-aspected work, and that I had to find different people to co-operate in the different aspects. Until I understood this, and until my group understood it, I made slow progress.

The capacity to co-operate depends on type, not on personal sympathy or even agreement of viewpoint. Different persons had different capacities and were interested in different aspects of our organisation; when in touch with one or another of them, I, in my turn, became absorbed in that aspect and able to work creatively at it. The people with whom I thus co-operated were never those who sat at my feet, but, on the contrary, those who were critical because they were themselves creative. On the other hand, those who were critical in the "sea lawyer" manner, simply because they enjoyed the sense of power that comes from picking things to pieces, were quite useless to me as a source of stimulus.

The "yes-man" type and the constitutional caviller proving ineffective, I gradually learnt to compound the formula I needed out of the varied human material at my disposal. Work often has to wait to be done till the right type for co-operation comes along. Moreover, after working for a certain time with one person, I then tend to change over and work with someone else, leaving the previous one to stand on his or her own feet and carry on with whatever has been set going. I have found that newcomers generally bring in a fresh rush of magnetism, though I have had too much experience of human nature to trust my weight to a bough until I have assured myself that it will bear me.

From all this I have gradually learned that I depend upon the proper kind of polarisation for my work when any inner plane activities are involved. The polarisation is mental so far as psychic matters are concerned, and magnetic in ritual work. The two kinds of polarisation are quite different, and it is not often that I find the two kinds of capacity combined in one person; nor is it often that the same person can co operate with me for more than one type of work; those who are valuable workers on the nature contacts usually being of no assistance in the Hermetic work, and vice versa.

The whole question is a very curious one, and we can only learn about it by the light of experience. Gradually the Inner Group is accumulating a body of data that is increasingly enabling us to draw conclusions that shed light on the whole intricate subject of individual polarisation and ceremonial sublimation. These results, when fully worked out, should be of great value in psycho-therapy, for so many of the sicknesses of the mind and soul are due to repression in all its aspects and with all its consequences, and repression is but the result of imperfect polarisation.

Modern psychology can diagnose the subtle, subconscious ramifications of mental energies; it can dissect out the soul of an individual and reveal its workings; but, having done so, it has lamentably little to offer by way of remedy.

Commentary D

GATES TO INNER POWER
AND PERCEPTION

Gareth Knight

Spiritual Alchemy

Mrs. Atwood's *"A Suggestive Enquiry into the Hermetic Mystery"*
is a book with a strange history. Its author, Mary Anne South, who
later became Mrs Atwood by marriage, was born in 1817 and her
book was published in 1850, funded by her father.

Her father, Thomas South, was a man of independent means
and an amateur scholar with a very large library devoted to
philosophical and metaphysical subjects. He and his daughter shared
an intense interest into research in these fields and supplemented
their book learning with practical experimentation into subjects
that were then in vogue, such as electricity and magnetism,
(including animal magnetism), mesmerism, spirit communication
and psychophysical phenomena. With their erudition into the
metaphysics of the past they came to the conclusion that many of
these things were simply re-discoveries and new applications of
obscure natural forces that had been described by occult, hermetic
and alchemical philosophers of the past, if only in cryptic terms.

The two of them decided to set out independently to write up
the results of their research. The father, who was approaching his
seventies, decided to cast his version into verse, as befitted so
serious and noble a subject; an attitude by no means eccentric in
those times, when prose was still considered an inferior medium.
His daughter, however, took to prose, finished her task first, and
her father arranged for its publication apparently without reading
it, either in manuscript or in printed proofs. It was only when

the advance copies arrived that he actually did so, and expressed himself horrified. Whether or not this reaction had anything to do with some kind of religious conversion he had at this time is not clear. Anyhow, his alarm induced a similar reaction in his daughter, and with less than a hundred copies sold, and at considerable protest from the embarrassed publisher, they called in the whole edition and burned the books upon the lawn of their house in Gosport, along with Mr. South's verse manuscript.

As Mrs. Atwood privately explained some years later, she and her father felt that they had been on the verge of betraying a most sacred secret; that in their former researches they had inadvertently been trespassing on holy ground.

Old Mr. South died shortly afterwards but throughout her life his daughter never reversed their decision to ban her book, although with the passing of years she did come to a certain ambivalence in that she did not destroy odd copies of the book that later turned up. She even made gifts of one or two copies to friends, and indeed made proof corrections to one. In 1859 she married a clergyman, the Reverend Alban Thomas Atwood, and lived the life of a clergyman's wife until his death in 1883.

In widowhood she remained something of a recluse, although she did show great interest in the formation of the Theosophical Society and gave the bulk of her father's large and valuable library to its president A.P.Sinnett. Eventually however she lost sympathy with the society and the direction in which it appeared to be going. Her esoteric interests remained firmly espoused to the traditions of the west.

She died at the age of 92 in 1910, and her book was eventually published in Belfast in 1918, through the efforts of a friend, Isabelle de Steiger, who had earlier been a student and associate of Madame Blavatsky in her last years in London in the late 1880's. *"The Suggestive Enquiry"* is not an easy book to read and certainly no do-it-yourself guide to the practicalities of alchemy. It is couched in the language of a leisured early Victorian lady, of vast reading and a symbolic turn of mind, who intersperses her observations with a mass of symbolic analogies and long quotations from various alchemists and hermetic philosophers, sometimes in Latin or French, and as the book's title implies, its purpose was to suggest rather than to reveal.

Nonetheless, as Dion Fortune observes, "animal magnetism" and the related phenomena that we have examined in Commentary C, seems close to the heart of Mrs. Atwood's researches. It is evident too that she is referring to an interior discipline of meditation and spiritual aspiration over a period of time, that brings about a form of union between higher and lower nature after some degree of interior turbulence. The invocation of an element of perfection or divine spark seems crucial to this, which, rather after the symbolism of the Eleusinian mysteries, she sees as being like a grain of wheat that enters into the ground and dies, only to sprout forth with new life and manifold growth.

Insofar that yoga techniques control the spiritual and life forces within the body by means of the images of the visual imagination, allied to controlled breathing as might be likened to the draught applied to an alchemical furnace, it is perfectly feasible to envisage the pictorial symbolism of different experimental alchemists as being the equivalent to the symbolism of the chakras to be found in various schools of yoga and in the spheres and paths of the Qabalistic Tree of Life. The athenor or retort of the alchemist consists of the physical and etheric bodies and the subtler levels that they contain, the prime material is the imaginative faculty, and the philosopher's stone the contact with the spirit, the Ain Soph, samedhi, or the buddha fields. Whether in the case of an advanced practitioner this leads to effects in the world of objective phenomena is another matter.

Mrs. Atwood speaks of the discovery of the Causal Nature, which we may take to be that part of nature which is behind the external nature we see. In other words this is the etheric matrix, and Mrs. Atwood had no doubts about its importance. She writes in conclusion to her work, which also gives some indication of her style:

> "...the discovery of Causal Nature is doubtless of all parts of knowledge the worthiest to be sought after, if it be possible to be found; and, as to the possibility, they are computed for ill discoverers that think that there is no land because they discern nothing but sea. Believe it, then, beyond the turbulent sea of sense, there is a haven and signal marks to direct where the Promised Land is to be found."

The aim of alchemy in its fullest sense seems little short of raising the whole of creation from its fallen condition, although one has to start, more modestly, with oneself. This at any rate seems the main burden of Mrs. Atwood's argument, and she cites the works of the Protestant mystic Jacob Boehme (1575-1624) as perhaps being the nearest to which the secrets of alchemy had hitherto been revealed.

Jacob Boehme's writings, like most treatises upon the ways of the inner life, are no easy read, although his English translator, the Anglican divine William Law, has made things easier by an immensely helpful "Clavis" or Key consisting of a series of symbolic diagrams. These at one level show the process of the creation of time and space, and the natural world as we know it, as a fall from grace, together with the means of its restoration to its once pristine spiritual condition. At another level, these universal principles could equally be interpreted in alchemical terms.

In short, whatever the detail of symbolism, the Great Work is carried out within the human organism by means of the creative imagination under spiritual motivation and guidance. As Mrs. Atwood points out, this effectively puts the idly curious, the selfish and materially motivated aspirants out of the running. It also blocks off any likelihood of success by research projects under current rules of objective scientific enquiry.

Eliphas Levi and the Astral Light

Within five years of Mrs. Atwood writing and then suppressing her great work a book appeared in France that might be regarded as being at least complementary to it. This was the work of a French occultist, Alphonse Louis Constant, writing under the pen name of Eliphas Levi. His book *"Dogme de la Haute Magie"* appeared in 1855, and was followed a year later by a companion volume *"Rituel de la Haute Magie"*. These were eventually translated into English by A.E.Waite in a single volume under the title of *"Transcendental Magic"* in 1896. Eliphas Levi's work is important for its dissertation upon what he called the "astral light", and Waite has performed a signal service to English language readers, despite his heavy handed style and the patronising tone of his frequent footnotes, which are quite valuable nonetheless in their reference to relevant sections of Levi's other works, in particular *"La Clef des Mystères"* (1861).

This work, now apparently unobtainable in France, was translated into English by Aleister Crowley, and although he was no doubt up to the task linguistically, one cannot be too sure, without recourse to the original, of how much of his own ideas he may have been tempted to put into his translation.

The Astral Light according to Levi is a universal agent that lies back of the surface appearances of material life. He credits Martines de Pasqually with coining the name "astral light" but says that it is known by various other names. It is the "odic force" of Baron Reichenbach, and was known as "Azoth", "Magnesia" or "Mercury of the Wise" to the alchemists. It is behind the material phenomena of heat, light, electricity and magnetism, and is at the heart of all living beings, not only human and animal, but the planet itself and other celestial bodies. Events that seem miraculous are frequently perfectly natural occurrences brought about as the result of directing this universal occult force.

One branch of its manifestations comes under the aegis of animal magnetism but in Levi's view it is more appropriately described in terms analogous to light. Of interest to modern eyes is a certain ambivalence in describing its qualities that parallels the similar problems found in quantum physics when trying to describe the phenomena of sub-atomic quanta, which may be described in terms either of particles or waves, or indeed of the two states simultaneously. The astral light and its phenomena can similarly be described in terms either of a fluid or a resonance.

In its wider aspects the astral light has been called the Soul of the Earth, or the World Soul, the Anima Mundi, and in this respect it can be regarded as a universal glass of visions and thus the root of prophecy. It is also the bond of sympathies or source of love and all inter-relationships.

It is, moreover, diffused throughout all infinity, and in metaphysical terms is that universal substance which God created before all things when he said "Let there be Light". In the transcendental scheme of things which this deceptively simple creation myth embraces, this light was not the ordinary light of the sun, for the sun, moon and stars had not yet been created, being the work of the fourth, not the first day of creation.

It is on the other hand no far off metaphysical abstraction, for as

Levi describes in *"The Key of the Mysteries "*, the will of intelligent beings acts directly on this light and thereby on all nature. It is in one sense synonymous with what some call the etheric vehicle or etheric matrix of all physical creation, and contains the record of all past forms and actions and the blueprint of that which is yet to come. This is another reason for its being associated with divination and feats of thaumaturgy, that is to say shape shifting, shared illusions, and apports of objects of one place to another, even through solid walls. In physical alchemy the aim was to accumulate and fix the universal fluid in one type of substance so as to transform it into another. In a lesser form of magic, it was simply to change the appearances rather than the inherent underlying form.

It has been known through all ages and is appropriately symbolised by the form of a serpent devouring its own tail, or as the girdle of the goddess Isis, twice folded in a love-knot round two poles. This symbolism emphasises its dual polar nature, the extremes of which in alchemical parlance were the Fixed and the Volatile, which has its reflection in the positive/negative polarities of electro-magnetic phenomena and the host of phenomena symbolised in east and west by the yin and the yang, the ida and pingala, or the dark and bright pillars of the temple.

According to Levi the principle was known to the Gnostics where it was represented as the fiery body of the Holy Spirit. It was also represented by the strange figure of Baphomet in the secret rites of the Templars, as well as the Hermetic Androgyne in alchemical treatises. However, insofar that it is a universal agent it can be used for high or low, for good or for evil purposes. Thus the serpent of wisdom can also be the serpent of temptation in the paradise garden. The dragon power of the earth, like nuclear energy, can be used for any purpose according to the will of he who has control of it.

Levi describes this energy as it manifests upon the Earth as the fourth emanation of the life principle, which derives from the third emanation that is represented by the Sun. The Sun, or "eye of the world" in the language of the ancients is itself an image of the reflection of God. Thus the reflection of God (Chokmah and Binah in Qabalistic terms) and God (Kether and the Ain Soph) may be regarded as first and second emanations. Developing this symbolism Levi describes the Earth as conceiving life by impregnation from the Sun, (the Earth is the Bride of Macroposopos in Qabalistic terms), and the Moon concurs in this impregnation of the Earth by reflecting a solar image during the night. Thus the Hermetic text's description of the universal agent as "the Sun is its father and the Moon its mother". This also has its Qabalistic equivalent in the Moon centre of Yesod, that falls between Tiphareth the Sun centre, and Malkuth the Earth centre, and we may glean from this a hint of why Dion Fortune lays such stress upon moon magic in her esoteric novels. The Moon, or the Yesodic etheric sphere is one of mediation between the solar bridegroom and earth bride, be this in terms of matchmaker, brides-maid, or mid-wife.

In its action the solar or universal agent has two modes of operation, as we have said. One manifests as attraction and is located in the centre of bodies, as the heart of centripetal force. The other manifests as projection and is associated with the periphery or surface of things and centrifugal force. The two forces might also be symbolically represented as spirals or vortices, one tending to roll up and the other to unroll. Every body of manifestation, or form for incarnate life, is a construct of these dual forces locked in equilibrium. The principle is seen in the planets of the solar system, at the same time attracted and repelled by the sun in their expression of orbital movement around their common centre.

It is by this universal agent, made visible by the manifestation of light, but consisting also of other subtle components, that the stars and suns of the universe are inter-related. Men and things are magnetised like the suns by light, and by the subtle magnetic chains of sympathies and antipathies which at the same time are secret, sacred and perfectly natural. Light might be regarded as a carrier wave for more subtle psychic and spiritual forces. These are none the less powerful for being more subtle and refined than gross physical emanations. This is a basis of the immensely complex science of astrology, so complex that it is still regarded as a superstition by those who cannot comprehend its principles, let alone work out its applications.

The means of perceiving and working with the subtle manifestation of the astral light is by means of the imagination.

By this term a trained imagination is intended, and trained in dedication rather than in technicality. To the trained imagination the images that arise are those that pertain or are analogous to truth. To the untrained or undedicated imagination the images will be distorted, erroneous or subjective. They will be mirror images of the interior condition, not clear sight of that which lies objectively beyond. Thus "clair-voyance" or "clear sightedness" in its true sense is a function of the imagination. It is the function of the seer or "SEE-er".

Levi calls this function the "plastic mediator" which, in English at any rate, is not a particularly felicitous term. Alternatively he uses the term "translucid", which is a little better, although we would prefer to use yet another suggestion, the "diaphane". We might also think in terms of a Body of Light, with appropriate sensory powers of the inner light, for as Eliphas Levi says, the diaphane is a portion of the astral light that is particular to each one of us.

Thus everybody has a diaphane, in however crude a state. The term diaphane derives from how inner vision should be – diaphanous – able to see through the veil clearly. The similar faculties in the ordinary crowd are not so much diaphanous as opaque. This is because of the crudity of their organ of inner sight which makes the veil of Isis seem thick and impenetrable. The magic mirror of their consciousness thus reflects their own inner subjective state, (with all its failings and distortions), rather than the world of objective light beyond.

In practice, it has to be said that it is very rare to have a perfectly lucid inner sight. Even Swedenborg, the first of modern clairvoyants, the power of whose visions was sufficient to start a church, was clouded in his visions by various fancies based upon the preconceptions of his upbringing and the cultural environment of his times.

The astral light is also saturated with all kinds of reflections and emanations. The visions of the somnambulistic state are perceived in the astral light. The somnambulist does not actually travel to a distant place but the images of that place are evoked because they are present in the astral light. Errors of sight that can occur in this state may be the result of reading reflections thrown off by the diaphane of others present, and in particular of the magnetiser. Thus a great deal of unconscious suggestion plays a role in trance phenomena.

The astral light as universal fluid is also easily manipulated by the will, which gives grounds for the sceptic, often rightly, to regard visions to be to a great degree subjective. Thus the importance of an imagination trained in dedication. That is to say, undominated by self-centred subjective urges, desires and preconceptions.

On the other hand a trained will and imagination, particularly when working in harmony and concurrence with other wills and imaginations, can direct currents within the astral light. This can, through the natural course of events, produce physical conditions or circumstances. This is not only a matter of ceremonial or other forms of art magic; it happens whenever there is a group of people of one mind and one will and one vision, whether in the field of commerce, sport, politics or the family.

Every intelligent effort of will is a projection of human magnetism or astral light. We all live within a particular environment, and our subtle body absorbs whatever is within that immediate environment and breathes out its own emanations into it. This is what is known as the Respiration of the subtle bodies, an analogy to the way that the air we breathe is taken in and returned to the immediate atmosphere about us. We are constantly interchanging each other's magnetism as we share each other's air. We may be largely unconscious of this but it accounts for spontaneous sympathies and antipathies.

An interaction of the astral light can lead to great friendships or alternatively to strong irrational dislikes. In extreme cases it can lead to infatuation or hero worship. This is what Eliphas Levi calls an intoxication of the glamours of the astral light, and it is for this reason, no doubt, that one of the great animal magnetisers, Deleuze, cautioned the deliberate practice of magnetism between those of opposite sex unless man and wife. It also accounts for Dion Fortune's dictum that magic is best practised by those in stable and satisfactory relationships either in or outside the lodge. Higher magic demands a certain element of impersonality and to indicate the correct approach Eliphas Levi evoked the image from the Book of Revelations of the woman crowned with the sun who has her foot upon the serpent's head, which signifies divine wisdom controlling the dragon forces. To subdue the serpent/ dragon is to govern the cycle of the astral light. That is to say, to place ourselves outside its currents and isolate ourselves from its powers. To avoid unbalanced conditions of the astral light it is not sufficient simply to perform particular banishing formulae; what is required is the tranquillity of mind and heart that only comes from stable outer life relationships and a selfless dedication.

When it comes to directing the astral light then we need to understand its two-fold vibration, which is exemplified in the symbolism of lyre and caduceus as presented in Dion Fortune's *"The Cosmic Doctrine"* that we reproduced in Commentary A.

Eliphas Levi also advocates the Qabalistic senary – that is to say the six dots in the form of an equilateral triangle that represent perfect all-round balance - and which forms part of the Pythagorean tetractys, which is the same principle with the four elements added as four dots below. See Figure D.1. This is an alternative form of pentagram, which likewise designates the control of spirit over the four elements of manifest life.

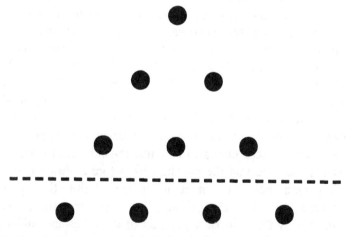

Fig. D1. Pythagoran Senary and Tetractys as summary of number mysticism. The four as elements in another dimension become the basis of a cube, a figure with six faces, and with its central point making up the mystic seven. There are many other extensions, permutations and interpretations possible.

In other terms the astral light is very similar to what is popularly supposed of the astral plane in spiritualist or esoteric circles, or of the collective unconscious in psychological ones. We are all, in our individual conscious personalities, floating like corks in this sea of light, but our corks have a certain porosity. Some personalities may be very sensitive to magnetic conditions whereas others may be almost impervious. Some like a sponge to the astral environment, others like ceramic or hard wood.

Thus we are floating in a sea of images and ideas to which we may be more or less receptive or even vulnerable. Insofar that the astral light ever seeks equilibrium, it will seek to make negative conditions positive and positive conditions negative. Also as in these matters nature abhors a vacuum, the astral light will rush into any space in consciousness where there is a gap or deficiency. It is this that makes emotional moods or instinctive attitudes contagious, and accounts for movements of patriotism or universalism, or social and political attitudes, moral, intellectual or artistic fashions, that swing over time like a pendulum.

In its magnetic aspect the astral light will also attach to or impregnate objects, which is the reason why relics are considered important in certain religious circles. It is also the rationale of talismanic magic and the clairvoyant practice of psychometry.

Our light bodies will also act directly, one upon the other, which in certain conditions can produce contagious hallucinations. Abnormal projections divert the light currents, the perturbation centred in one subject is communicated to the most sensitive in his vicinity, until a circle of illusion is established and a whole crowd affected thereby. Feats such as the famous Indian rope trick come to mind but group religious experiences may also be similarly induced, particularly when it is realised that the worshippers before a shrine may be kneeling with their eyes turned up towards lights, thus giving the classic physiological desiderata for hypnotic trance, aided and abetted by the induced suggestion of the religious ambience along with emotional expectation. In such circumstances even the sun may seem to gyrate in the sky without disturbing the physical equilibrium of the solar system.

Concentration of the astral light is also achieved by means of the "chain" developed by Mesmer and his fellow magnetisers and seekers after spirit phenomena. To form a magical chain is to establish a magnetic current which becomes stronger in proportion to the extent of the chain.

However, this form of chain is a comparatively crude example of a more universal principle, and the greater power is in those subtler chains that are brought about by common devotion to a cause with similar imagery and modes of discipline. A potent example is Ignatius Loyola's Society of Jesus, but the Jesuits that this pious soldier founded are but a latterday manifestation of orders such as the Knights Templar and Hospitaller at the time of the Crusades, which became incredibly powerful agencies and lasting well after the purpose of their foundation was exhausted.

Freemasonry is a less bellicose form of the phenomenon but with similar longevity, even if most of the members no longer understand the symbolism, and the modern institution is more in the nature of a charitable friendly society. It is notable that, like the Jesuits and the Crusading Orders, the Freemasons conjure great and for the most part irrational and paranoid fears about their potential power and possible abuse of it. This again is symptomatic of perturbations of the astral light, which can be "bent" to form centres of gravitational attraction and repulsion after the manner of Einstein's conception of curved space/time.

In Levi's view a part of the astral light coalesces about the soul at the moment of physical conception and is the first envelope for the soul's incarnation, forming the Ethereal Body or Sidereal Phantom of which Paracelsus also speaks. This body is liberated at physical death and attracts, and for a long time preserves, reflections of the past life through sympathetic induction. This is very often the nature of contacts in spiritualist séances rather than the actual spirit of the deceased, which has passed on further into the heavenly realms.

As Levi puts it, nothing can enter heaven save that which came from heaven in the first place, therefore after death the divine spirit leaves two corpses below, one upon earth to be buried or cremated, while the other floats in the astral light to be absorbed gradually by the astral forces which produced it. If a person has lived well then their astral body evaporates like incense and ascends towards the plane of ideals and aspirations but those who have lived dominated by lower appetites and passions may have some difficulty in getting free of this second corpse. When pathological conditions are combined with esoteric knowledge we may have the rare scenario such as Dion Fortune describes in her novel *"The Demon Lover"* and in one or two of *"The Secrets of Dr. Taverner"* stories. Such a combination is very rare but similar principles pertain in the larvae that hang around the polluted astral atmosphere of brothels and other venues associated with sexual perversity, drugs and violence.

Again preoccupation with things of the world, even in a comparatively respectable sense, can result in souls acquisitively hanging around former habitations or sites of concealed valuables. Eventually the stars draw up the materially biased astral forces, which divide naturally into their elements according to the planetary configurations of astrology. With the inevitable dissolution there can be a struggle as the former vices or obsessions rise up and assume monstrous nightmarish shapes that eventually drive off the misdirected soul. This is an aspect of the Dweller on the Threshold, which is a mirror image of the shadow side of the soul. In religious terms it is an aspect of Purgatory.

Thus Eliphas Levi teaches very much the same doctrine as Madame Blavatsky's mahatmas when it comes to trying to contact the souls of the departed. We are, at best, evoking no more than memories which they have left in the astral light in the common reservoir of universal magnetism; or at worst drawing to ourselves astral larvae attached to disintegrating or perishing forms.

It is the power of magnetism that causes tables to tilt, walls to rap and simple musical instruments to play but, according to Levi, Paracelsus had arrived at an understanding of magnetism long before Mesmer, and had taken it into the higher realms of possibility known to the ancients. This is the same level that is hinted at by Mrs. Atwood, of those who understood its universal nature, and did not regard it simply a matter of ectoplasm given off by certain peculiarly constituted individuals known as materialising mediums.

In their letters to A.P.Sinnett the Mahatmas insisted that they did not seek passive minds but on the contrary were seeking those who are most active, who could put two and two together once they are on the right scent. Thus that those who complained of being unable to comprehend the meaning of Eliphas Levi had simply failed to find the key to his way of writing. That it was never the intention of occultists to conceal what they were writing about but rather to present their information in such a way that it was as if in a secure safety box, the key to which is intuition. The degree of diligence and zeal with which the meaning has to be sought is generally the test of how far the sincere student is entitled to possession of the treasure. Students of texts of the nature of Dion Fortune's *"The Cosmic Doctrine"* might do well to bear this in mind, as well as similar challenging works from Blavatsky or the pen of Alice A. Bailey.

Exercises of Light

There are various methods of approaching work positively with the astral light, most of which are form of exercises in the visualisation of light and various symbols which may represent it and contain it.

One example we have already described in the Rainbow Bridge visualisations in Commentary A, which are derived indirectly from the eastern tradition. Many others abound.

"The Armour of Light" is a complete system of exercises revealed to and presented by Olive Pixley, following upon a series of visions she began to have in 1924, whose purpose is the complete reconstruction of the self by drawing from its divine source a new quality of life energy, that might be called the sanctified flow of the astral light into the aura, for onward transmission to other living creatures and the earth itself.

All the exercises consist of the visualisation of light, which she is at pains to point out is an actual force and not a symbol. Just as there are in the world of matter many varieties of substance with different uses, so in the world of the astral light are there many qualities and kinds of light substance, each performing a different function. Some cut away, some suffuse, some absorb impurities, some quicken vital functions. Each is a reality and can play a part in our regeneration.

According to Olive Pixley there is a connection between this light energy and blood. Her standpoint is Christian, and when Christ spoke of the life-giving power of his blood, and the need for us to absorb it, he spoke of this transcendental light, which is the life essence of all blood. In his case it is absolutely perfect and thus is perfect energy mediated to us by the technique.

I have myself used a sequence of light exercises in *"Experience of the Inner Worlds"*, the book upon which I have trained most of my personal students. Here again the principles are expressions of the light in various formulations to tune consciousness to the desired stage of developing consciousness. These in turn were based upon a series of images apparently received on a high angelic contact in Anthony Duncan's *"The Lord of the Dance"*. In brief they consist of a sphere of protective light, a shaft of light coming down from the heights, a rising answering flame from the centre of the earth, then a cup or graal chalice at the heart before becoming aware of a wider sea of light which can then be formulated into more objective formulations such as a table round, an upper room and a winding stairway to a spiritual watchtower. The principles of such image building have been summarised in my most recent little book *"Magical Images and the Magical Imagination"*.

The Hermetic Order of the Golden Dawn also had its various light exercises, which have largely been expounded by Israel Regardie, particularly in regard to the Middle Pillar exercise This consists of building the Tree of Life in the aura and then proceeding with what is called the Fountain Breath for its circulation, within the aura and beyond. It is interesting to note that Israel Regardie, who had quite close links with the New Thought movement, wrote a little book called *"The Art of True Healing"* in which he described the technique in simplest possible terms, almost as an extension of positive thinking and other schools of creating improving circumstances in one's life.

There has always been a certain amount of controversy as to how far such techniques should be used, not as means for spiritual regeneration but almost as spells for changing circumstances. Affecting the material world by psychic means is however, not so simple as it may seem, and requires very much more than knowledge of a few names to chant and coloured symbols to imagine. Personal power comes from deep within and is not dependent upon magical knowledge, as the condition of the most materially successful people in the world should demonstrate. If one has the internal dynamism then spells are an irrelevance. The person bent on money will think of nothing but money and it will come his way. The same goes for any desideratum of human life if we are one-pointed enough. For most of us, however, we only think seriously of food or sex or money when it becomes a problem, which is to say when we feel we are not getting our share. When we find ourselves in that situation then I regret to say that meditational visualisations are really not the best way to remedy the lack. This is simply a way of trying to avoid rendering to Caesar the things that are Caesars. We are here in a physical condition within a physical world and whilst in that state we have to abide by the laws appropriate to it. Our best way forward is to take a long-term view of the situation and to try to reconcile both physical and spiritual elements of our existence and the levels in between them.

How then can we actively turn our eyes and perceptions toward the inner worlds whilst being grounded in the physical manifestation of them? One way of approaching this is to ask if our powers of cognition are lacking, and if so, in what way. Or, in other words, how to cleanse the gateways of perception. If, as a human race, we could see the world as it really is then we might not be so ready to destroy it by technological blundering. We might think in terms of wooing Isis or Gaea, rather than trying to rape her.

Spiritual Science

The eighteenth century writer, philosopher, politician, dramatist, scientist, and man of many parts, Johann Wolfgang von Goethe (1749-1832) saw something of the problem, long before our time, and his approach has been codified by Rudolf Steiner, who as a young academic was first commissioned to edit Goethe's scientific papers, and was so impressed with what he found that he went on to develop his method and to found a movement based upon its application.

Steiner's work, and that of the Anthroposophical movement that he founded, is, of all the occult movements in the twentieth century, the one that has probably come closest to concern with the problems of human life in the world, rather than abandoning them in search of some personal elevation to cosmic heights of consciousness. Not that some degree of personal spiritual development is not a part of the whole endeavour. A world wide network of schools, of homes and residential villages for handicapped children and adults, colleges of organic and biodynamic farming, homeopathic clinics and hospitals, training centres for teachers, agriculture, the arts and social work and research foundations for various projects of "spiritual science" have also been established over the years. With this degree of involvement in an esoteric approach to the physical world it follows that there is a rich vein of knowledge of the etheric world, which is the level with which we are primarily concerned in *"The Circuit of Force"*.

The typical approach of a "spiritual scientist" has been well described by a teacher in one of Steiner's schools, Ernst Lehr, in his book *"Man or Matter"* (1958 & 1985).

We can hardly describe the methodology in detail here, any more than we can describe in detail the disciplines of yoga. It involves a training, or re-training of our powers of perception of the natural world. Thus it might well be termed a "yoga of the west", but it is an outward facing kind of yoga, in keeping with the western temperament.

The aim of the spiritual scientist in his approach to nature is not to tear it apart to see what makes it tick but to seek to co-operate with the intelligent causation behind it. He sees matter as an instrument for the intelligent, form-creating activity of the spirit. This does not involve any diminution of consciousness or mediumistic or trance-like states, but is a fully conscious awareness of the subject under review, with all the sensual faculties operating.

A typical exercise is to start with the contemplation of cloud formation and weather characteristics associated with landscape, and the morphology of growing things.

The aim is not to try to "explain" what is observed by theoretical speculation but to develop a form of contemplation that goes hand in hand with observation until the phenomena reveal their own theory and the archetypal principles behind them.

By this we are led to an awareness of the existence of the Ether, the four-fold subtle condition of matter that lies beyond the three physical states that we know as solid, liquid and gas. We can tabulate these seven states of physical/etheric matter, using the old traditional Elemental titles:

LIFE ETHER	[levity]
CHEMICAL ETHER	[levity]
LIGHT ETHER	[levity]
WARMTH ETHER / ELEMENT OF FIRE	
GASEOUS STATE / ELEMENT OF AIR	[gravity]
LIQUID STATE / ELEMENT OF WATER	[gravity]
SOLID STATE / ELEMENT OF EARTH	[gravity]

Solid, liquid and gas, the three lower states of matter are all subject to gravity, with the possible exception of the two lightest gases, hydrogen and helium whose natural habitat seems to be outer space. (Helium was first discovered on the Sun, by spectrographic analysis, hence its name).

The four higher states, however respond to a polar opposite principle that we may call *levity*, and in order of increasing subtlety they are known as warmth-ether, light-ether, chemical-ether and life-ether.

These ethers have nothing to do with the much-debated ether of physical science, the possible medium of electromagnetic phenomena. They are more in the nature of powers. That is to say, form-creating powers that enable the forms of chemical elements, crystals, plant and animal organisms, human beings, to manifest in terms of the solid, liquid and gaseous states of matter within the physical world. The ethers, that work under the principle of levity, are *creators* of form. The states of matter that work under the principle of gravity, are *expressers* of form.

The warmth-ether or element of fire is a borderland condition between the two domains. It has an alternative title of "chaoticising ether" insofar that it prepares or breaks up lower states so that they may be receptive to new archetypal impressions of form. At one level this may be seen in the plasma at the centre of stars and planets, in particular of the Earth itself. At another level in the way a seed brings forth new life, into a new cycle of form expression.

It is the light ether that brings about the proliferation of forms. The alternate cycle of night and day gives an aspect of weaving. An alternative name is thus the weaving ether. It has an analogue with the image-making thought processes of man, weaving many forms from different strands of fantasy. An interesting analogy is the property of light demonstrated in a camera obscura whereby, with the use of a pinhole of light in a darkened room, a whole external daylight scene can be encapsulated at the single pinhole point. This is like the potential form in a seed. The image expands from the pinpoint to be reproduced on a screen inside the chamber, just as the seed expresses its form in the subsequent growth of a plant.

It is these forms of analogy that interest spiritual scientists in particular branches of mathematics, for instance "projective geometry" wherein transformations and projections of forms are expressed through passing at different angles through a point. One of the pioneers of this form of mathematics was the great 17th century scientist and mystic Blaise Pascal.

Much of the phenomena and properties of electricity have their origin in the light ether, which accounts for the similarity of the observed phenomena of light and electromagnetic waves by "observational" outer science. In esoteric terms it might be said that electricity is light under conditions of gravity.

The chemical ether has the rather unlikely alternative name of sound ether which comes about because all of the chemical elements are distinguished from one another simply by the principle of number. In the Periodic Table their properties depend upon the number of electrons and protons that make up their atomic structure. Number is also the key to sound and the principles of harmony, which of course is part and parcel of Pythagorean mysticism.

The principal of form is not merely a question of a body's external shape, it is an inner quality, and it is from this inner quality, based upon number, that external qualities such as colour, taste, smell, healing or harmful properties depend.

Esoterically speaking there is also a link between the chemical ether and magnetism, which is observable in atomic physics by the "invariants" that prevail in energy jumps from one electron shell to another. Thus magnetic fields are a form of sound ether mastered by gravity.

The most subtle ether, the life ether, is responsible for the manifestation in physical expression of all forms, whether crystalline or organic, in solid physical expression. Its alternative title is the "word ether". This is because of its relationship to the sound ether. If the different chemical elements be regarded as different voices singing forth a note, in accordance with the numerical principles of harmony, their combination into forms may be likened to that formless sound being formed into intelligent and intelligible words. This may be regarded as the great chorus of creation.

The archetypal forms created in the etheric world can be perceived by the trained imagination, sometimes called "the eye of the spirit," or what Rudolf Steiner terms Imaginative perception — or simply Imagination, using this much abused word in its rightful sense.

This method of seeing is to perceive – not the light reflecting object in the corporeal world – but the light itself as it weaves the archetypal image that structures the object. This faculty of perceiving with the eye of the spirit is possessed by all, and although it is generally lost after early childhood, it can be re-acquired by the type of exercises in observation inaugurated by Goethe.

Beyond the acquisition of etheric awareness through "the eye of the spirit" further training can lead on to perception of the astral world beyond the etheric. This entails the development of an intuitive form of perception onto the sevenfold world of extra-terrestrial force fields which play upon the Earth sphere. The seven traditional "planets" – that is to say Saturn, Jupiter, Mars, Sol, Venus, Mercury, and Luna, designate these fields of influence. There is a connection between the sevenfold astral influences and these physical celestial bodies as observed from the Earth but it is not in the nature of a direct connection. Their movements and angular relationships are simply subject to the same higher powers that govern the astral forces within the Earth.

These seven principles or spiritual qualities provide the impulses that stir the etheric and physical forces into action. As the physical/ etheric world was expressed through polar principles of Levity and Gravity, so is the astral world, the polarities being expressed in the traditional alchemical terms of Sulphur and Salt, with a Mercurial mean between them.

LUNA	[sulphurous]	life ether
MERCURY	[sulphurous]	light ether
VENUS	[sulphurous]	chemical ether
SOL	[mercurial]	warmth ether/fire
MARS	[saline]	gaseous/air
JUPITER	[saline]	liquid/water
SATURN	[saline]	solid/earth

This schema validates the old pre-Copernican image of the universe, for the central factor is the viewpoint of perceiving human consciousness on Earth. The extra-Saturnian planets discovered by the telescope are not visible to the naked eye; and it is the appearance of the visible bodies of the solar system as viewed from Earth that is the best gauge of the astral influence associated with them. The Copernican heliocentric system may well be an accurate depiction of the mechanical dynamics of matter, but the viewpoint is an abstract one divorced from human perception and is thus potentially dehumanising. It is arguable that this is one factor in some of the dehumanising aspects of the machine and technological age - the dark Satanic mills of William Blake.

Another way of looking at the apparent role of the planets in Earthly life is in the analogy of the ductless glands in the human body, which although being very small discrete organs are more accurately assessed in regard to the effect of their secretions on the whole human body and attendant psychology. Thus the human body could be regarded as subject to different spheres of behavioural influence that have their reflection in the small discrete ductless glands. In much the same way astral influences within the Earth sphere have a correlation with the discrete celestial spheres of the solar system.

The way to develop astral consciousness is by observation of the world that maintains an appreciation of quality. This has an analogy with the ancient concept of listening to the music of the spheres, and this kind of intuitive consciousness as listening with "the ear of the spirit". The form of training involved is that of seeking to experience the actions of nature, and all that happens to nature, as if they were the deeds and experiences of a beloved friend. This fact alone should point up the difference from the growth of a science and technology which aims to be completely objective, impersonal and to calculate the price and scientific parameters of everything and be careless or ignorant of the value of organic and spiritual life. Modern man has become deaf to the harmony of the spheres but to regain this hearing is the work of gaining Inspiration in addition to Imagination.

It is this perception of quality that differentiates the traditional view of the universe from the modern, which is based fundamentally on quantity, on measurement and abstract calculation. For a philosophical treatment of this divide one can hardly do better than follow through the quest outlined in Robert Persig's famous and memorably entitled "Zen and the Art of Motorcycle Maintenance", and its moral sequel "Lila".

To complete the universal scenario as described by Rudolf Steiner we must proceed to a third stage of conscious awareness. This involves becoming a completely objective observer of our own existence while we are actively functioning within it. Then the world will begin to reveal itself as an arena of activities of spiritual beings, some higher and some lower than man in the scale of things. The opening up of this kind of awareness Rudolf Steiner calls Intuition - again in the fullest and truest sense of the word - "inner tuition." In this we come to realise ourselves in full awareness as spiritual beings acting along with other spiritual beings, human and non-human.

It lies beyond our purpose to elaborate further upon these other spiritual beings, although some may be regarded as overshadowing the group souls of nations. As every human soul may be said to have a holy guardian angel so there are said to be archangels watching over nations and archai or "time spirits" over the spirit of an age. The detail of much of this view of the inner worlds is contained in Rudolf Steiner's "Occult Science - an Outline" (1909) and his other works, many in the form of the pamphlet notes of lectures, until his death in 1923.

Steiner represents an important modern strand in what we might call the Modern Esoteric Tradition, in which he might be regarded as forming a Western Pillar with Blavatsky forming the Eastern Pillar before the Temple of the Mysteries. He takes the line of tradition principally from western sources, through Goethe, the Rosicrucians and the neo-Platonism of Dionysius the Areopogite, complementing Blavatsky's largely oriental sources of inspiration. The combined heritage is a rich one, and we can benefit from it if we are prepared to follow the example of Solomon the King, who in building his temple sent for "gold from Ophir, cedar from Lebanon".

SUBJECTIVE AND OBJECTIVE PRINCIPLES

The Circuit of Force Part 13 [May 1940]
Dion Fortune

The ordinary concept of life regards the human body as a machine for the manufacture of energy from food, and it is only very gradually being realised that the process is not purely mechanical but that the mental attitude affects to a very great degree the amount of energy available. The strength of the maniac is notorious, but the weakness of the unhappy is attributed to any cause except their unhappiness.

The mystics have always felt that they drew on sources of life beyond their own vitality, but they have not always understood the nature of those sources though realising their existence, as appears plainly in their writings. To them, however, these sources formed a reservoir on which they could draw, inexhaustible, it may be, but nevertheless static. To the initiates of the Ancient Wisdom it should be otherwise, for the true concept, albeit a lost secret in the west, is to be sought in the analogy of electricity, and we conceive of life as an alternating current forever flowing in circuit.

Nor is the circuit a simple matter of flow and return, for all the elaboration of electro-magnetics is implicit in the concept and we have to consider problems of induction and changing polarity. Into these elaborations of analogy it would serve no purpose to enter in these pages, even if I were competent to do so, and I am not. It must suffice to indicate the practical working concepts I have arrived at in the course of many years study and experience along these lines, and those who are students of physics will soon be able to find their own analogies.

My approach to the riddles of occultism has always been from the psycho-analytical standpoint owing to early training, and I believe this approach to be the true one, for the principles of the form of psychology that has developed out of the psycho-analytical technique give us a clear explanation of the phenomena presented by psychism and guidance to its principles.

The principle of Polarity, or the Circuit of Force is, in my opinion, one of the lost secrets of western occultism. The essence of this activity lies in reciprocal relationship. Wherever there is physical activity it is recognised that action and reaction are equal and opposite; it is not realised, however, that this is also true of the psychic sphere on all its levels.

The principles of Polarity prevail - the objective and the subjective, and it would probably be correct to say that literally, and not merely metaphorically, the objective arises through magnetic induction from the subjective, and not, as is usually believed, in the reverse order. The subjective experience of an emotion or realisation is what puts us in touch with similar forces on the objective planes, whereas it is popularly believed that it is objective conditions which call forth an emotional response. This concept is not as novel as it may seem to those uninstructed in psychology, for the James-Lange theory of emotion, though not generally accepted, expressed the same concept from a slightly different angle.

This theory, known by the joint names of the two psychologists who, almost simultaneously enunciated it in their separate spheres, William James, the well-known American psychologist, and Lange, the, to English readers, less well-known German psychologist, declares that we do not weep because we feel sad, but feel sad because we weep; that we do not tremble because we feel frightened, but feel frightened because we tremble.

Put in its crude, materialistic form, it had little hope of general acceptance because it is so contrary to common sense; but another, and more profound psychologist had recognised its half-truth and turned it to practical account some centuries earlier. Ignatius Loyola, the founder of the Jesuits, taught that if you assume the posture of prayer, you will soon feel prayerful, however disinclined for spiritual exercises you might have been at the outset. And even he was not the earliest forerunner of James and Lange, for thousands of years earlier the Mystery cults made this principle the basis of sympathetic and ceremonial magic.

It is doubtful if the James-Lange theory in all its materialistic crudity could find supporters at the present day. It is a great half-truth, however, and the half that isn't there, as well as the half that is there, are equally explained by what we now know of auto-suggestion, no adequate concept of which existed in William James' day.

It is exceedingly doubtful if we feel miserable because we weep in the absence of other causes of unhappiness, or else were onion-peelers the most melancholy of mortals. All the same, putting a bold or cheerful face on matters, whatever our inner feelings may be, goes a long way towards alleviating our inner feelings.

These things we know from experience, and so well known are they that we may take them as agreed. If, to this common knowledge, we add esoteric knowledge, we shall now be able to see why it is that subjective conditions may be the causation of objective circuits of force. If, as esoteric science teaches, mind came before matter and spirit before mind, causation is to be sought in the subtler planes of those complexes of events that we call fate, or chance, or the will of God, according to the views we hold. It may then be that the condition of the Higher Self, the immortal spirit, the unit of evolution, may set up what we may aptly call magnetic fields, and put us in touch with various cosmic forces according to type. This, indeed, may be the real explanation of the manner in which astrology works - for by calculating what celestial factors we are in touch with, it becomes possible to deduce the conditions prevailing in the Higher Self, and then, by further calculating the changes in the celestial factors, to deduce the reactions that will result.

Equally, the moods of the personality, and especially its prevailing character, would go far to determine the conditions in which the life would be lived. We all know, however, that by consciously taking thought we can effect as little change in our fate as we can in our stature, but many people have had practical proof that by means of subconscious thought as it is taught by Mrs. Eddy and Coué, that oddly assorted pair of stable-mates, it is possible to produce a complete change of environment.

From all this we may deduce that it is possible, by setting up a subjective circuit of sufficient strength, to induce the corresponding objective circuit to circulate enough through our sphere of sensation. When it is recalled that our sphere of sensation is for us the universe, it will be seen what vital and far-reaching results would proceed from the application of the principle of polarisation above outlined.

COSMIC AND ELEMENTAL CIRCUITS OF FORCE

The Circuit of Force Part 14 [June 1940]
Dion Fortune

Now comes the question of the practical application of all that has gone before. We are dealing at the present moment, it must be borne in mind, with the relationship between the Higher Self and the Cosmic Forces. The relationship between the Lower Self and the Elemental Forces is quite another matter which we will consider presently.

The Higher Self, or Individuality, is the unit of evolution, the immortal spirit that never dies and that is the basis and background of the successive personalities it projects downwards into incarnation. It is beyond the range of normal consciousness and uninfluenced by the brain consciousness, our only approach to it being in those states in which the brain consciousness is eliminated, producing unconsciousness, which we call the higher trance conditions.

The personality in its normal state never touches these planes of existence, though in certain abnormal or supernormal states the Higher Self takes control of the Lower Self in the same way that a hypnotist controls his patient. Therefore, so long as we are functioning in the personality we can only experience and control the higher states of consciousness by indirect means.

It may be thought strange that I should speak of the control of the higher states of consciousness by the lower, but this is quite correct. So long as consciousness is focused on the physical plane it is in abeyance on the higher planes; consequently, if it is intended to change the focus from the lower to the higher, the initiative must come from the personality into whose hands it passes at the moment of incarnation. The higher consciousness cannot force its way through, as we know to our cost; it can only enter when the personality opens a way for it.

This interaction of the Individuality and the Personality is a true and very important example of polarisation. The Lower Self can be polarised by the Higher Self, and unless this circuit is working we are liable to certain dangers and aberrations when we try to avail ourselves of the practical implications.

The Lower Self and the Higher Self should work together as a self-contained circuit of polarisation, serving as a kind of storage battery to keep things going when we are temporarily out of touch with one or another cosmic force. Unless we have such reserves of magnetism as are afforded us by this self-polarisation, our condition is very unstable, for we can hardly exist for an hour without somebody or something to lean on and supply us with the self-confidence and vital force that is lacking to us. It is this power of self-polarisation that enables us to stand alone and resist an unsympathetic environment. It is not mere self-will, which is a quality of the Lower Self and which tends to cut us off from cosmic currents, but essentially a function of the Higher Self, and in fact the first aspect of it that makes itself felt through the Personality when consciousness begins to extend its scope beyond the personal desires. It appears to us as an impulse to regulate our conduct with regard to principles instead of expediency and desire; and it is this, and this alone, that enables a man to maintain his inner poise and peace in face of adverse circumstances. Self-polarisation is the basis of all deliberate induction and control of the Circuit of Force. We must be able to guide our steps by the Inner Light when all around is darkness, and to live on our reserves of magnetism as the camel lives on its hump during the desert journeys that are the inevitable experience of all wayfaring souls.

Nevertheless, we cannot live on our psychic reserves indefinitely, any more than the camel can exist forever on his hump. If we make, or are forced to make, the attempt, we are reduced to that state of vital and spiritual aridity that characterises the recluse, for a person who is forced to insulate himself from an unsympathetic environment is just as much a recluse in the midst of a crowd as any hermit in the wilderness. Books, to a great extent, alleviate the mental isolation, but they cannot supply that semi-physical magnetism of elemental force that is derived from the normal human relationships.

Occult knowledge can, however, do a great deal to supplement and direct the magnetic circuits that are so essential to our well being on all planes, but it can only do it for persons whose minds are sufficiently trained to enable them to carry out the instructions and whose Personalities are sufficiently developed to enable them to make contact with their Higher Selves.

It must always be remembered that man is a complex being, and all the aspects of his nature must receive their appropriate nutriment, just as his body must have a balanced diet. For practical purposes we divide the two aspects of his nature into the Higher and Lower Selves, the Individuality and Personality, the pair of terms being synonymous. His Higher Self polarises with cosmic forces by means of meditation and realisation, and the centre through which this contact is made is represented upon the Tree of Life by the Sephirah Daath.

The primary circuit, which is the cause of manifested existence, consists of a flow of force from the Unmanifest, where "our spirits ever behold the face of the Father" - a state beyond human realisation - down the Middle Pillar and through Malkuth to the Earth-soul, and it is, as always, an alternating current.

The polarity between the Higher and Lower Selves is secondary to this, and dependent on it; it is, in fact, a case of magnetic induction. Both these circuits are purely subjective in that they depend on no external contacts, save the relationship with the Immortal Spark in the Unmanifest at one pole and with the Earth-soul at the other, and they are as automatic and innate as the beating of the heart; but just as there are means of altering the speed and rhythm of the heart, so there are means of increasing or checking the voltage of these currents.

These means depend upon the power of mind-control we possess, and are studied in the science of yoga. There are various types of yoga; Hatha Yoga develops the current that originates in the Earth-soul; Raja Yoga develops the current that originates in the Divine Spark. In my opinion, the true line of development is to be found in the recognition that in the principle of the alternating current alone is full development to be found.

As we have already noted, the Higher Self obtains its cosmic polarisation through meditation upon and realisation of the Cosmic Principles. This is its normal method of nutrition, as it were. We know that in sleep nutrition can be reduced to a minimum, and so it is when a man's Higher Self is asleep while his life is focused on the personal level. But as soon as the Higher Self wakes up, it needs nutriment; consequently the first sign of the awaking of the Higher Self consists in a stirring and reaching out of the religious feelings, because it is by means of religion that we come into touch with the Cosmic Forces, relationship with which we establish by adoration and develop by meditation.

The Lower Self, on the other hand, makes contact with Elemental Forces which have their sphere in the Earth-soul and Solar System. To these we should not offer adoration, as they are less highly evolved than we are, and to do so would be to lower ourselves in the scale of evolution. Neither can we meditate upon them without due precaution lest the same disaster should happen. When handling the Elemental Forces, though they are in no sense evil or malignant, precautions must be taken lest they spread beyond their proper sphere in our psycho-spiritual organism, and the lower swamps the higher.

When dealing with these forces, we bring them through carefully constructed channels, banked, as it were, with impervious concrete, and controlled by sluice-gates at each level, just like an irrigation system, which, in fact, the whole process of elemental contacts so closely resembles. By this means we obtain the benefit of their fertilising flow while avoiding the dangers to which we should be subject if they got out of control; these dangers are exactly analogous to the problems provided by water out of control - the danger of acute damage by flood or the chronic detriment of water-logging.

The channels and sluice gates by means of which the Elemental Forces are controlled are constructed in the aura by means of yoga practices. These enable us to polarise and fertilise our own natures; but for large-scale operations, magical or ceremonial methods are used. By means of these we can handle forces of far greater potency than by the solitary yoga methods, and we can also enable others to share in the experience of these forces. But such operations can only be undertaken successfully by persons who already have the necessary channels developed in their auras —and this is another of the lost secrets of western occultism.

In our imperfect civilisation, some persons, in the name of purity, cut themselves off from the earth contacts, which they consider low and bestial because they operate through the instincts and senses; these persons invariably present that dried-up, arid appearance we have already referred to; if they are sufficiently dried-up, they are content with their half-lives just as the bound feet of the Chinese lady were painless when growth ceased; but if the desiccating process is incomplete, if elemental life stirs in them, they suffer as the Chinese child suffered before the growth of the bones of the foot were finally checked. Others, owing to the imperfect presentation of religion so prevalent in the present day, never realise their cosmic contacts and so suffer another kind of deprivation, as unwholesome and crippling as the first. Both these pathologies can be obviated by the teaching of a true philosophy of life, and even when established, can be alleviated by methods known to occultists.

TECHNIQUES OF RITUAL

The Circuit of Force Part 15 [July 1940]
Dion Fortune

If the principle of the circuit of force has been clearly grasped, a further application of it can be made. The practice of ceremonial, so powerful, yet so uncertain in its workings, is yet another example of this all-important factor. Unless the principle of the circuit of force is applied, ritual is uncertain in its practice and incomprehensible in its theory.

As I have pointed out in a previous chapter, Hatha Yoga and spiritualism between them reveal the lost secrets of western occultism. Hatha Yoga is concerned with the subjective aspect of the circuit of force, functioning in the form of magnetic circuits in the etheric double; the spiritualistic method of sitting in a circle for development and manifestation supplies us with a further clue, and the traditional practice of ceremonial, blind though it is, furnishes the rest of the data. Once again we see an example of the triune nature of all manifestation. Each factor by itself is incomprehensible; taken together, they mutually explain each other. Taken together, equally, they form a functional whole.

Let us consider them in their functional aspect. Hatha Yoga develops the magnetism of the etheric double and teaches its directed use; spiritualism in its circle-working practises the use of human electric batteries in series; occultism in its ceremonial uses high power individuals, developed by initiation and linked in series by means of the ceremonial pattern of its rites. I have dealt in detail elsewhere with the nature of ceremonial, and will not repeat myself in these pages, but, having given the above clues to the lost secrets, leave the reader to discern as much as he is entitled to receive of this teaching, which is as much as he is able to perceive. Equally, he will find that he is able to discern only as much as he is entitled to receive.

Let us now consider the purposes for which ritual is used, apart, of course, from spurious and superstitious practices. It is used for selecting and concentrating force, and there are many different kinds of force which can be isolated and concentrated by means of ceremonial and many different purposes to which they can be applied. Many of the magical operations of which one reads in books are perfectly futile and impractical, the formulae being copied from one author to another after the manner of those untested recipes to be found on the ladies' pages of daily papers. All the methods of promoting thunderstorms and discovering buried treasure may safely be eliminated from the canon of occult tradition without any diminution of its value. The real aim of ritual is to increase the potency of the individual in certain definite ways; all attempts to work on external nature are futile.

Nevertheless, when the potency of an individual has been raised, not merely in general, but in a specific and specialised manner, it then becomes possible for him to do very remarkable things with external nature if, through understanding, he is able to contact it in its specialised aspects; for here again a generalised contact, like a generalised potency, is ineffective until concentrated into a specialised channel, because here, as elsewhere, the principle of the pairs of opposites governs manifestation. All modes of generalised force contain opposing factors which cancel each other out and produce equilibrium and consequently inertia. Therefore, for active working, it is necessary to pick out a single factor of a pair and employ it in a purified form, free from all discordant elements.

Apart from initiation ceremonies, which aim at awaking the higher levels of consciousness, ritual can be classified under the different planetary and elemental influences, so that a given ceremony is described as an operation of this or that planet or element. This is a sound method of classification because the planets and elements correspond to the psychological factors in the soul of man. Consequently, the performance of an operation of a particular type puts that aspect of the mind in touch with the corresponding aspect of the cosmos, thus reinforcing its activity along that particular line.

We can analyse the instincts and factors in the human soul and tabulate them in relation to the planets and elements; and we can take the mythical divine beings in any given pantheon and use them as connecting links between the subjective and the objective. A mythical divine being is a projection of the subjective and a symbolisation of the objective. In them, subjective and objective meet and unite. They are the projection of our desires and the representation of the factors in the cosmic life of which our desires are the subjective experience.

Those who are familiar with occult ceremonial will recall that there is always a personification of the force or forces employed. They are never dealt with in the abstract, but represented by an angel or elemental according to the circumstance of the working and the grade of the operator. By this means, subjective and objective are united and the connection made with the cosmic forces.

Thus we have in ritual a threefold example of the circuit of force - first of all within the individual, for without raised magnetic potency, ritual is a feeble affair; secondly, by the establishment of a circuit of force among the celebrants after the manner of a spiritualist circle the magnetic potency available for the ceremony is rendered far greater than the sum of their individual contributions, because each stimulates the others; thirdly, and most important of all, a circuit of force is established with the chosen cosmic centre of force, the mythical divine being forming the link.

The process has been dealt with in principle elsewhere in my writings, and its practical details must be withheld from the uninitiated, but enough has been said to give understanding to those who already have the essential knowledge but lack the necessary keys, which are the lost secrets.

By means of a given factor in ourselves, picked out and made single-pointed and pure in the chemical sense, we touch the corresponding cosmic factor through the traditional symbolism. Generalised efforts are as useless as diffused daylight for lighting fires, yet when sunlight is concentrated as if through the lens of a burning-glass, fire is obtained.

Care must be taken, however, to maintain the equilibrium of the nature and ensure its even development. An operation of one type must always be balanced by an operation of the opposite type. It is for this reason that initiates follow the phases of the solar cycle and vary their work accordingly.

THE PAIRS OF OPPOSITES IN ACTION

The Circuit of Force Part 15 - Conclusion [August 1940]
Dion Fortune

In the foregoing pages I have tried to show the practical implications of the doctrine of Manifestation by means of the Pairs of Opposites, which is one of the most fundamental and far-reaching tenets of the esoteric tradition. Much of what I have had to say is so profoundly esoteric and so immediately practical that I have been obliged to adhere to the ancient method of myth and metaphor. These things are not for the profane, who would either misunderstand them or abuse them. Those who have eyes to see can read between the lines.

In this concluding chapter I will try to sum up the principles involved and bring the whole concept to a single focus; yet even so, such is its inherent nature, as in fact the nature of all manifestation, that my argument must needs move in a circuit, returning whence it started for its final explanation and application.

Manifestation takes place when the One divides into Two that act and re-act on each other. Manifestation ends when Multiplicity is resolved or absorbed back into Unity. The transition from plane to plane of manifestation takes place in the same manner. In order that any thing or factor shall be brought down from a higher to a lower plane, it is necessary to analyse it into the contradictory factors that are held in equilibrium in its nature. To do this, one imagines the opposite extremes of which it is capable and expresses them separately while retaining in consciousness their essential unity when in equilibrium.

Equally, if it is desired to raise any factor from a lower to a higher plane, one conceives its opposite and reconciles the pair in imagination and realisation.

Any pair of factors, divided for the sake of manifestation, act and re-act upon each other, alternately struggling to unite and, in the act of uniting, exchanging magnetism, and then, their magnetism having been exchanged, repelling each other and striving to draw apart, thus re-establishing their separate individuality; then, this established and a fresh charge of magnetism having been generated, once again they yearn towards each other in order to exchange magnetism, the more potent giving off, and the less potent receiving, the charge. It must never be forgotten in this respect that relative potency is not a fixed thing, depending on mechanism or form, but a variable thing, depending upon voltage or vitality. Moreover, the charge passes backwards and forwards as an alternating current, never with a permanent one-way flow.

These are fundamentals of concept, and they have their application to every aspect of existence. Ignorance of them, and our inveterate tendency to try and maintain the status quo whenever and wherever it is established, causes endless sterility, as needless as it is destructive and wasteful, and whose cause is utterly unsuspected.

An illustration will serve to show the far-reaching ramifications of the influence of this principle. Apply these concepts to the relationship of initiator and candidate, of leader and follower, of man and woman; then, having so applied them, re-read these pages and see if you can then see what is written between the lines.

But not only is there a flow of magnetism between the Pairs of Opposites, but there is a circulation of force between parts and the whole. Man is a perfect Microcosm of the Macrocosm; none other creature, so it is taught, shares this development. To the angels, the lower aspects are lacking; to the elementals, the higher. In consequence of his manifold nature, man is in magnetic relationship with the cosmos as a whole, not merely with a limited or selected presentation of it. There is a flow and return between every aspect of our beings and characters and the corresponding aspect in the cosmos. Just as the chemical elements in our dense body are derived from and returned to the general fund of matter, so by the processes of metabolism, the psychic factors in our subtler bodies are neither static nor exclusive, but are maintained by a perpetual flow and return like a hot water circuit which flows from boiler to storage tank and back again by virtue of its own physical properties. If we are for any reason cut off form this free flow of natural force, some aspect of our nature atrophies and dies. Or if the flow is checked without being blocked, some aspect suffers starvation. There is a characteristic deadness when this occurs, readily recognisable in all the relations of life when once its nature is realised.

If the initiator is not in contact with spiritual forces, he cannot pass them on to the candidate and so "fails to initiate". If the candidate brings no real depth of feeling to his initiation, he gives out no magnetism; and as magnetism can only be poured into a person who is giving it out - a little understood, but far-reaching truth - that candidate receives no down-pouring of power and the initiation is ineffective. If a leader has no great principles to guide him but is a mere opportunist, his inspiration to his followers will consist in no more than a hope for a share of the spoils. If a man and a woman are not each in touch with Nature, they will have little to give each other that is of any vital value and so will soon part - on the inner planes, even if convention holds them together on the outer plane.

The operation of magnetic interchange in all its aspects can be cultivated and developed. In its subjective aspect it is developed by certain Hatha Yoga practices, which, though definitely dangerous if done incorrectly, are very valuable if done correctly. Without this development of the subjective magnetism and the acquirement of skill in its direction and control, it is impossible to operate either safely or satisfactorily the contacts with the corresponding reservoirs of magnetic force in the cosmos; but once some degree of development and skill has been attained, it is a waste of time to persevere with exclusively subjective methods.

Contacts with cosmic forces, however, are not things to be made at random, any more than contact with a lightning flash; therefore formulae are used to enable the mind first to contact and secondly to control the chosen cosmic force. These formulae can, in the case of experienced operators, thoroughly skilled in the art, be purely mental and consist of images in the imagination representative of the force in question. But only very highly developed people can obtain results by purely mental means, and for less developed people, the co-operation of others in group working is necessary. Solitary working soon becomes arid, wearisome, and unproductive of results, as every student of occultism can testify.

Nevertheless, unless there is solitary working, the operator becomes de-magnetised. Consequently we must accustom ourselves to the idea of a perpetual change of state, and alternation between subjective solitary working and objective group working. Not otherwise can we hope to maintain the sense of zest which tells us that the forces are flowing freely.

These things are the secret not only of magical power but of life itself in all its relationships. They are things of which even the most enlightened exoteric thought is entirely ignorant, and they are the real keys to practical occult work. They are the lost secrets of the Mysteries, secrets which were lost when an ascetic religion, though a valuable corrective to excess, destroyed the polarising opposite truth which alone could maintain it in equilibrium. It is the great fault of our ethic that it is incapable of realising that one can have too much of a good thing.

When, in order to concentrate exclusively on God, we cut ourselves off from nature, we destroy our own roots. There must be in us a circuit between heaven and earth, not a one-way flow, draining us of all vitality. It is not enough that we draw up the *Kundalini* from the base of the spine; we must also draw down the divine light through the *Thousand-Petalled Lotus.* Equally, it is not enough for our mental health and spiritual development that we draw down the Divine Light, we must also draw up the earth forces. Only too often mental health is sacrificed to spiritual development through ignorance of, or denial of, this fact. Nature is God made manifest, and we blaspheme Her at our peril.

Commentary E

THE CIRCUIT OF FORCE IN THE NOVELS OF DION FORTUNE

Gareth Knight

Dion Fortune wrote six works of occult fiction. A series of short stories, *"The Secrets of Dr. Taverner"* (1926), and five novels: *"The Demon Lover"* (1927); *"The Winged Bull"* (1935); *"The Goat-foot God"* (1936); *"The Sea Priestess"* (1938) and *"Moon Magic"* (1956). The dates given are those of publication so the actual time of writing would have been during the previous year or so. However, some at any rate of the Dr Taverner stories had been previously published in *"The Royal Magazine"* and so would have had a somewhat longer lead-time. Her last novel, *"Moon Magic"* did not see publication until ten years after her death, and as with this book she experienced some teething problems, going through half a dozen false starts, its writing may have been spread over some time between 1938 and 1945. The order and dating of her fiction is of some importance because, as with her non-fiction, it demonstrates the evolution of her teaching and thought.

Just prior to the publication of *"The Goat-Foot God"* in 1936, Dion Fortune announced a new aim in her fiction writing. *"The Secrets of Dr. Taverner"* and *"The Demon Lover"* she says "stand as early work, written a dozen years ago" when she had been concerned with "interpreting occultism in the light of psychology". She now announced that she was about to change tack, and write a series of books in which she intended "to interpret psychology in the light of occultism."

At the time of writing this article she had a trilogy in mind, although if the books were successful she envisaged writing as many as ten, each with a theme based upon one of the ten Sephiroth of the Tree of Life. This Qabalistic schema is by no means obvious but can be discerned as the sun magic of the Sephirah Tiphareth for *"The Winged Bull"*, (it is prefaced by an invocation to Apollo); the earth magic of the Sephirah Malkuth for *"The Goatfoot God"* (with its invocations to Pan); followed by the moon magic of the Sephirah Yesod for *"The Sea Priestess"*. *"Moon Magic"* might well be regarded as a Sephirothic sequel to *"The Sea Priestess"* although in the higher levels that it aspires to at the end, it could arguably be allocated to Daath.

This Sephirothic scheme dates from the time when she had completed writing her major textbook on the Tree of Life, *"The Mystical Qabalah"*. This important work was at first serialised in her mimeographed *"Inner Light Magazine"* but was given the dignity of print and published in volume form by Williams & Norgate in 1935, who also began publishing her new sequence of novels, which were intended to represent the practical side of the occult teaching that was theoretically expounded in *"The Mystical Qabalah"*.

This occult textbook, as good occult textbooks tend to do, has remained in print ever since. However, truly occult novels (as opposed to occult blood and thunders by professional writers) never have such a clear run of popular demand, whatever their esoteric merits. Indeed Williams & Norgate declined to publish the third one *"The Sea Priestess"*, so Dion Fortune published it herself. The outbreak of war and paper rationing prevented any further ventures of this nature, and so the final novel *"Moon Magic"* had to wait some years before it saw the light of day.

We will find that much of the subject matter of *"The Circuit of Force"* is exemplified by situations in the novels, and her writing this series of articles might well be regarded as an attempt to hint at some of the practicalities of *"The Mystical Qabalah"* that had perhaps been too well concealed in the novels.

With this in mind we will examine some of the detail of the novels in the light of the subject matter of *"The Circuit of Force"* which, as we have seen, includes ancient Greek magic, western forms of yoga, etheric polarity, animal magnetism, induced auto-suggestion, reflections in the astral light and so on.

In any such analysis we need not only to examine the polar relationship between the characters but also the locations, for each of these also has its "magnetic" significance, being as often as not a symbolic "composition of place" in which the characters, and the archetypal forces that they may embody or evoke, play out their parts.

In a novel of high symbolic significance nothing within it is likely to be arbitrary. Everything is there for a reason, even if that reason is beyond the normal level of functioning of the analytical concrete mind. There is also frequently an ambiguity about the experiences that are undergone, which is just how such things are experienced in occultism in real life. It is this that marks out Dion Fortune's occult fiction as superior to most other works in the genre. It is based upon first hand knowledge and experience, with excellent descriptions of the subjective states involved and the way interior conditions are perceived in magical ritual. This however can militate against the conventions of writing successful popular fiction.

Another problem, if the novels are judged for their value as esoteric tuition, is that the reader can very easily be led astray by the surface events of the story and some of the more colourful superficies. On the one hand these may be akin to the genre of the occult thriller, the esoteric fictional equivalent of cops and robbers. On the other hand they may give the appearance of a somewhat offbeat "Mills and Boon" romance.

Dion Fortune's earlier fiction, *"The Demon Lover"* and *"The Secrets of Dr. Taverner"*, (as also to a degree *"The Winged Bull"*), incline to the first category, with a scenario of black magicians and various dirty deeds and derring do. The later novels, and including *"The Winged Bull"*, (which in this respect is something of a hybrid), concentrate on the love interest, on the general theme of a priestess bringing inner fulfilment to a male companion who has been badly dealt with by life.

It is important that we do not mistake this fictional scaffolding for the real teaching behind it, for there is far more to occultism than being a metaphysical dog fight on the one hand or a psychic dating agency on the other.

When we look at the underlying structure of the novels we will find a basic triangle of characters:

a) an initiating priestess, who in the earlier novels may not at first be aware of her role;

b) a male who has not been able to come to terms adequately with life and who is aided in this by means of an initiating or redemptive process at the hands of the priestess;

c) a male figure in the background who provides deeper occult wisdom and guidance.

This conforms to a pattern that derives from the metaphysical principles laid down in *"The Cosmic Doctrine"* of two complementary polar principles guided or reconciled on a higher level by a unitary third.

In the earlier novel *"The Demon Lover"* this is spelled out categorically at the end of the story when the adept who oversees the dénouement says to the hero with regard to his attempt to bring a fresh impulse into the mystery tradition:

"Yes, my son,...you were right, it needed a fresh impulse, but you were not able to do it single-handed. Three are required for that, in order to work the sacred triangle. A positive force, a negative force, and the reconciler between them."

Which is the positive and which the negative force will vary, depending upon the plane which is being worked. This is the lesson of the lyre and caduceus upon which we have remarked in Commentary A. Upon the outer levels the male will more often than not play a positive role but upon the magical levels the positive role will tend to be played by the female. There is, however, or should be, a balancing out of the partners by their alternating polarity on the various levels, until we reach the ideal state of the equilibrated caduceus, enabled to fly.

Let us examine how some of these dynamics are worked out in each of the later novels.

The Winged Bull

The priestess role in this novel is played by Ursula Brangwyn. She, however, is initially suffering from several problems, having taken part in a system of magical training that has gone rather badly wrong. She has been working closely with a young man, Frank Fouldes, whose impatience at making progress has led him into the undesirable company of a very seedy occult character, Hugo Astley, who offers a somewhat more rapid and highly coloured progress to occult power. A strong magnetic relationship having been built up by their work together, Ursula finds it exceedingly difficult to break away from Fouldes' influence, particularly when aided and abetted by the more powerful and unscrupulous Astley, who sees in Ursula a highly suitable recruit for his particular brand of sex magic.

The adept in the background is Colonel Brangwyn, Ursula's guardian and considerably elder half-brother. He comes to the conclusion that the only chance to enable Ursula to break this link is to find a more attractive substitute for the smooth Frank Fouldes. This is easier said than done, but by a sequence of coincidences, he comes upon Ted Murchison, a young man who had served under him as a junior officer in the war, who is now down on his luck, and despite the fact that he has no magical knowledge or training, Brangwyn selects him as the only available chance.

Things do not run smoothly. The rough and ready Ted, a bluff and somewhat scruffy Yorkshireman, is a polar opposite in many ways to the socially sophisticated and convent educated Ursula Brangwyn. He sees her as a spoilt and stuck up prig, and she sees him as a scruffy and uncouth failure. Nor, understandably, do either of them fancy the role that seems cast for him, which in crudest terms would seem to be that of hired gigolo with aspirations to becoming a pensioned stud.

The action of the novel comprises the gradual coming together of Ursula and Ted and the resolution of their differences until eventually they achieve a mutual understanding and magnetic sympathy, so that in the end all is set for their marriage and the dirty grey magicians who have spiced the story with enforced hypnosis, telepathic projections and downright bribery and corruption, retire to the stews where they belong.

The Sephirah on the Tree of Life that Dion Fortune has in mind for this novel is the Sun sphere of Tiphareth. This is quite clearly signalled in the poetic fragment from William Watson in the front of the book, which is an evocation to the mating of Sun and Earth.

> For of old the Sun, our sire,
> Came wooing the mother of men,
> Earth, that was virginal then,
> Vestal fire to his fire,
> Silent her bosom and coy,
> But the strong god sued and pressed;
> And born of their starry nuptial joy
> Are all that drink of her breast.

At first sight Ted Murcheson seems somewhat more of a Martian or Geburic hero. He is an old soldier and man of action and his means of dealing with the magical chicanery of Fouldes and Astley is initially to throw them downstairs, and later to beat Fouldes into a state of broken ribs and concussion by hurling him against a temple pillar. Fields has asked for it, it has to be said, in his attempts to hypnotise Ursula against her will, and Astley for his general combination of physical and magical skulduggery.

However, in a preliminary ritual that is laid on by Colonel Brangwyn for the purpose of bringing Ted and Ursula closer together in magical sympathy, Ted is given the part of a priest of Apollo, while Ursula is cast as an Earth priestess, which with the poem of William Watson in mind can lead eventually to only one thing. The ritual itself is decorous enough however and in stark contrast to Hugo Astley's brand of magic. Ted also gets involved in one of Astley's rituals in a last ditch attempt to save Ursula from Fouldes' clutches, and here again although Astley's use of symbolism is in the tradition of a blasphemous travesty of spiritual values, Ted likewise finds himself cast in a Solar role, as Saviour of the World bound to a cross, a primary magical image of the Sephirah Tiphareth.

The whole theme of the book therefore is that of fructifying the virgin Earth and at the same time redeeming Ursula from the fallen occultist Fouldes and his dark master, a role which is performed by Ted under the watchful eye of his old commanding officer and her guardian/half-brother Alick Brangwyn. There is thus a cosmic parallel to the drama of human personalities played out in the story line of the novel.

However, on the personal level, Ted is going through a considerable process of self-realisation and initiation. The down and out mis-fit at the beginning of the book, hen pecked by his sister in law, a shrew of a suburban vicar's wife, is at the end a fitting husband for the socially sophisticated half-sister of his old commanding officer.

This development is played out against a framework of specific instances of the interplay of etheric magnetism, or the astral light, not only between characters but in relation to specific locations.

This is signalled in the very opening scene of the book which is in the evocatively symbolic location of the forecourt of the British Museum, in a thick fog, before the high temple-like portico that resembles a Greek temple or even a religious edifice of yet more ancient times. Ted, at the end of his tether, having just been turned down for a job, wanders through the different galleries of the museum, wraithed in mist, his psychic faculties opened up by the various exhibits, especially the great sculptures of the Egyptian galleries but most particularly with one of the giant Assyrian winged bulls, with which he forms a kind of instinctive rapport. Leaving the museum he experiences a surge of desperate emotion and stands in the darkness crying "Io Pan!", an invoking cry of the ancient Mysteries.

Unknown to either of them, his old war-time commanding officer, Colonel Brangwyn, has been in the reading room of the British Museum, pondering how he can possibly get Ursula out of the fix which she is in, and for which he bears some responsibility, through his lack of discretion and discrimination in taking on Frank Fouldes as a student. As he leaves the building, still vexed by this question, he hears Ted's cry. They meet up as a result, recognise each other as old comrades, and the colonel leads Ted out of the darkness into the adventures which come eventually, through initiatory experiences, to a happy ending.

The symbol of the winged bull plays an important role in the magnetic relationship that is built up between Ursula and Ted, but of more immediate import is the way that coincidence has brought about the two men's meeting, for this is no coincidence in the form of a crude fictional device for a less than expert novelist but a demonstration of the way that coincidences do happen in the process of magical working, particularly when emotions are aroused in highly magnetic atmospheres.

Later in the novel there is an interesting sequence describing a process of magnetisation where Ursula rejuvenates Ted after he has fallen into an exhausted condition after a particularly demanding encounter with the telepathic powers of the black magicians, which has temporarily drained him of vitality. This starts with an aborted effort wherein the magnetisation cannot happen because of the initial embarrassment and lack of immediate sympathy between the two of them, not helped by Colonel Brangwyn's somewhat insensitive initial prompting.

"Go on, Ursula, you little vamp, charge him up again."
Ursula flushed scarlet, and flashed an angry look at her brother.
"I'm afraid I can't," she said. "I don't feel like it."
"Go on, my child. It's the least you can do. He's run himself out for you."
The girl rose reluctantly and advanced towards the embarrassed Murchison, who wondered what in the world was going to be done to him.
"Put the palms of your hands against hers and enter into it imaginatively. Take what she is going to give you," commanded Brangwyn.
Murchison, looking about as receptive as a shying horse, did as he was bid. He felt a pair of small, cold palms pressing against his. Nothing happened. Ursula Brangwyn looked so cross and uncomfortable that he forgot his own embarrassment in feeling sorry for her. He thought he felt a faint tingling warmth coming into the palms, but before he could be sure it was not his imagination, she withdrew them.
"It's no good, I can't do it. My hands are cold," she said, and walked out of the room.

A little later however, when the two are alone, and she has had time to reflect upon what he has done for her, in absorbing an occult attack that was intended for her, she relents and feels a wave of sympathy for him. She is then able to go on with the process of re-magnetising him.

> She looked at him in silence.
> "Alick is perfectly right, there is only one thing to do for you, and there is only one thing to do for me. Hold out your hands. No, like that, fingers up. Now press your palms against mine."
> He did as he was bid. There was no need to bid him enter into the experiment imaginatively now. The girl's feelings were evidently deeply stirred, strive as she would to hide them, and her emotion infected him. He felt her hands trembling as she pressed her palms hard against his, but they were no longer cold, but burnt with a kind of dry, electric heat that pricked and tingled against his flesh as if an electric current were coming through them.
> He felt himself take a deep breath involuntarily, and then everything faded out except the girl's face, with its great dark eyes fixed on his.
> He was aware of nothing save the tingling in his palms and a sense of glowing warmth that was spreading slowly all over him. It was like taking an anaesthetic. How long it lasted, he never knew, but at length the girl stepped back, panting, withdrawing her palms from his, and the spell was broken. He found himself standing in the roof garden in the pale winter sunlight facing a girl whose cheeks were flushed and her eyes bright and starry, and a curious smile on her lips. Something had been done to him; something very definite had been done to him, but he did not know what.
> But whatever it was, it had restored him to normal. He no longer felt that terrible drained sensation, as if he had had a bad haemorrhage.

Reading between the lines in this sequence we may see some cause for the concern that Deleuze felt about magnetic interchange being practised indiscriminately by members of the opposite sex.

This description seems almost like a sexual encounter without any physical union but a confrontation of hands, although one thing could obviously soon lead to another. Yet while this process is all part of the romantic plot of *"The Winged Bull"* and *"The Goat-foot God"* we shall find the magnetic process being completely chaste on a physical level in the more "advanced" priestess figure who appears in *"The Sea Priestess"* and *"Moon Magic"*.

The esoteric courtship of Ted and Ursula represents a union of opposites in many different senses, which Dion Fortune drew attention to in an article she later wrote about the symbolism contained in *"The Winged Bull"*. Apart from their difference in social graces, upon which we have already remarked, the couple come from different bloodlines in the British Isles. He is of blond Nordic stock, from an old Yorkshire family, whilst she is a dark and olive skinned Celt. This difference is pointed up in the locations of the story. She has a hermitage high up on the flanks of Snowdon whilst he finds his natural location in a cottage between the Yorkshire moors and the North Sea. As Dion Fortune explains in her article:

"If a line is drawn from St. Alban's Head in Dorset to Lindisfarne off the coast of Northumberland, all the Keltic contacts are found on one side of it, and all the Norse contacts on the other. The Keltic Ursula is contrasted with the Norse Murchison, and on this turns much of the inner magic of the book, as will be appreciated by advanced students of these subjects.

Consequently: Up on the flanks of Snowdon, Murchison is at a disadvantage; he is not contacted with the native magnetism of the place; Brangwyn knows this, and when he wants to find a place in which Ursula and Muchison shall do the work he intends them to do, and make a magical marriage, he chooses the spot where Murchison, the less experienced of the two, shall have the advantage of the site, because he needs the extra force to bring him up to the necessary magnetic voltage and enable him to balance Ursula; she, being highly trained, will be able to adapt herself to the conditions. Consequently Brangwyn made an excuse to get rid of the Keltic hermitage and send Murchison off in search of a Nordic hermitage that would aid him in getting onto his own particular contacts. It will be remembered ... that as soon as Murchison crossed the Humber when bringing the car from Wales, he felt as if he had 'come into his own'. The whole book, in fact, is full of such touches as this, not put in deliberately, but coming out unconsciously, because I am not merely creating the world of the story, but living in it, and thus do those live and work who go after the deep things of occultism."

In like manner, the other locations in the story, different parts of London, are chosen for the type of magnetism they contain.

"Anyone who is at all sensitive knows that places have very definite psychic characteristics, and these characteristics are exploited to the full in this story."

Thus the main movement of the plot takes place in Bloomsbury, which to Dion Fortune's mind is a peculiarly potent spot psychically, although she feels at a loss to say why this should be so. Whatever the reason, she claims

"Bloomsbury is a district in which it is easy to do magic, and so is Chelsea; whereas in the neighbouring Fulham it is very up-hill work."

It would seem that she speaks from first hand experience even if she declines to vouchsafe the details! In like manner she describes how

"Astley's noisome abode is laid in north-east London because there are some very sinister spots round about that district."

There is also a magnetism associated with the location within buildings of the places set apart for magical working.

Both Astley's and Brangwyn's temples were in the basements of their respective houses; those who are familiar with the history of the Mysteries will know that crypts and caves were always used for initiation ceremonies. Anyone who has had experience of underground working is well aware of the manner in which a cave or cellar will hold the magnetism as compared with a structure that is above ground. He will also know that a heavy, stone-built structure is much to be preferred to a flimsy one for magical purposes.

However, whereas in the world of fiction Dion Fortune's magicians are blessed with sufficient private means to indulge themselves in this fashion, she is sufficiently realistic to observe that in real life occultism is not a wealthy movement and most groups have to work without ideal conditions. However, this is a challenge that the trained magician should be able to meet, even if a burden on those who are starting in on the game.

The Goat-Foot God

As in the previous novel we have a situation where a young man and a young woman of very diverse qualities and uncongenial life circumstances come together and find fulfilment aided by magical means.

Hugh Paston is a weak character in a high society set who only value him for his money. When the story opens he has just received a devastating blow in finding out that his wife has been having a long-term affair with his best friend, a deception he only discovers when both are killed in a road accident together.

On the verge of a complete breakdown he happens upon and is psychologically helped by Jelkes, a second-hand bookseller with a leaning towards metaphysical philosophies. Jelkes plays the function of overseeing adept in this story, but although he is much read in occultism he has never actually practised it, and so is largely a theoretical adviser in the magical adventures that follow.

Hugh Paston decides that in order to catch up with all that has been missing in life he needs to plunge into occult experimentation. Jelkes gently guides him away from some of the more lurid manifestations of it but by an odd combination of circumstances Hugh discovers some old farm buildings that once formed part of a monastery and decides to make this the focus for his new life. Possibly as a result of his innate psychism being awakened by his recent emotional upheaval he starts to become identified with the medieval prior of this place, who was walled up there, with a number of his monks, for performing heretical rites. This identification with Brother Ambrosius, who is an altogether stronger character than Hugh Paston's modern personality, is somewhat ambivalent. We are never quite sure whether it is a ghost which haunts the place, whether it is a secondary personality that is breaking through into Hugh's conscious waking life, or whether it is a memory of a previous incarnation of Hugh's – or it could possibly be a combination of any two of these or even all three.

The role of priestess is taken on by Mona Freeman, with whom Jelkes has a long-standing kind of avuncular relationship. She is dowdy and under-nourished, struggling to make her way as a freelance designer in whatever jobs on the fringe of the art world that present themselves. By Jelkes' intervention she is brought in to do the interior decoration for the refurbishment of the old abbey farmhouse. However, she becomes more and more involved in Hugh's personality problems and advised by an increasingly nervous Jelkes, they find a magical dimension to their relationship which involves celebrating a Rite of Pan. This is at the same time an acknowledgement of the nature forces that have been repressed in Hugh's life, as well as in the life of the medieval monk. In the end they successfully perform the rite which leads to what promises to be a happy marriage despite their opposing backgrounds and characters.

In terms of Dion Fortune's Sephirothic schema this book is concerned with the Sephirah Malkuth, that of nature forces of the Earth, and a fragment from a Rite of Pan is quoted at the beginning of the book.

The characters discuss what they think they mean by Pan, and as might be expected in a novel based upon the Earth Sephirah, the geographical location and the buildings upon it are magnetically very important in what is to follow. They have been used for nature rites before, in both buildings and grounds, and what is more are situated upon chalk, enhanced by ley lines. Talking of the old place, Monk's Farm, Hugh remarks to Mona:

"So you have fallen in love with it too, have you? So have I. There is a queer fascination about it, isn't there? One would expect it to be gloomy and sinister from its history, but I don't get that, somehow. It seems as if all that were superficial, and the real thing there, that's coming to the surface now, is what Ambrosius set out to do. Have you tumbled to what that is?"

"No, what is it?"

"The same thing we're going to do – invoke Pan. And the house knows it. That's why we feel welcome there. It was awfully pleased to see us. That house was no more cut out for a monastery than Ambrosius was cut out for a monk. I bet you anything that all these centuries Pan has been waiting to keep that appointment the Pope's visitor interrupted."

"That explains a good deal," said Mona thoughtfully. "I have been addling my brains to discover why an invocation of Pan landed you in a monastery. It seemed the most unlikely spot one could possibly imagine. But it is coming clear now. The same path leads to both Pan and Ambrosius."

At mention of the local pub being called The Green Man in the nearby village of Thorley, Mona draws attention to the significance of this, as well as to their differing bloodlines, a theme that also featured in the situation of Ursula and Ted:

"I suppose you know who the Green Man is? He's Pan.... He's Jack-in-the-green, the wood-spirit - the fairy man who runs after the maidens at mid-summer eve - What's that but Pan? The British Pan? And do you know the meaning of the name of the village – Thorley? It's Thor's ley, or field. You're in the thick of the Old Gods there; the Scandinavian old gods, because it's towards the east side of England. In the west it's the old gods of the Kelts you get. But you will like the Norse gods best because you're fair. Now I'm dark. I belong to the Kelts. But it's all one, you know – the same thing with different names. Pan is the same everywhere. He's elemental force – that's all he is. He comes up from the earth under your feet, just as spiritual force, the sun-force, comes down from the sky over your head."

The problem facing Mona is much the same problem that faced Ted Murchison in *"The Winged Bull"*, and which will be a recurrent theme in the two books that follow. How far can one work powerful magnetic magic without it spilling over into a sexual liaison that might not be in the best interests of either party, to say nothing of any existing relationships or responsibilities?

In *"The Winged Bull"* and *"The Goat-Foot God"* this turns out not to be a problem in the end, for both pairs find circumstances open up for them to embark upon a financially secure and socially unencumbered life together. Until this occurs though, all parties concerned find themselves involved in considerable heart searching, and something of the issues involved occur in Mona's reflections shortly after the above conversation.

> He liked her as a friend, she felt. But is that relationship possible between a man and a woman to any great degree without the sex factor entering into it? Only, she knew, if both were adequately mated elsewhere. Old Jelkes had taught her a good deal of the secret knowledge on the subject of sex that is so important a part of the Mystery Tradition – one of its secret keys in fact. He had steered her round a very difficult corner by means of his knowledge, and what she had learnt was standing her in good stead now.

The secret knowledge thus referred to by Jelkes might well have been culled by him from an earlier little book by Dion Fortune entitled *"The Esoteric Philosophy of Love and Marriage"* and Chapter 18, entitled *"The Nature of the Ties Between Souls"*, could well have been written for the protagonists of these later novels. The following paragraph is of particular relevance:

> ...for the use of the greater potencies and the operations of the higher occultism, it is necessary to have a pair working in polarity; only so can the great cosmic voltages be carried without danger of 'earthing', so well known to all practical occultists. The pair, working thus, open a channel for the Divine forces which flow through them with astounding power, and magnetise not only themselves but their immediate neighbourhood. By this means the powers of each are tremendously augmented, and the whole nature is vivified and brought to the highest perfection of its capacities.

In a sequence from *"The Goat-foot God"* where Mona performs her moon dance we see how a magical operation can induce psychic perception in a sympathetic observer, in this case Jelkes. To a sceptic of course all this could be interpreted as fanciful imagination on Jelkes' part, and Mona's dance as an arch and even ridiculous form of flirtation. However, there is more to it than this. The purpose of the dance is not sexual arousal but a particular form of magnetic therapeutics to draw a secondary personality or reincarnationary memory, (whichever rational explanation one prefers), out of the repressed Hugh. This is the stuff of Dr.Taverner's casebook, of the meeting ground between abnormal psychology and occultism that was of perennial interest to Dion Fortune.

In Mona's moon dance we have a considerable advance in the proto-sexual dynamics of animal magnetism than was demonstrated by Ursula Brangwyn's hand to hand recharging of Ted Murchison. Also, in what follows, Mona is trying to draw magnetism out, not put magnetism in to her partner in magnetic interchange.

Mona stood erect in the moonlight on the short grass of the barren pasture; the pallid light taking all colour from grass and gown and face so that she looked like a wraith. Hugh, tall and gaunt in his black cowled robe, stood a dozen yards away...

Then Mona began her dance. It was not so much a dance as a series of mime-gestures, for she never moved more than a few steps forward and back. A low rhythmical humming that hardly seemed to come from human lips at all was her accompaniment, and to its rise and fall she swayed and gestured. Jelkes, knowing the symbol-language of the ancient faiths, was able to read her meaning, and with his heart sinking within him, wondered how much of it Hugh was picking up subconsciously.

...he knew that Mona's dance was perfectly decorous and unexceptionable; and yet he knew that she was deliberately drawing magnetism out of the man with her weaving hands. It was all make-believe, he told himself over and over again. Mona and Hugh were simply play-acting, and knew it. There was no more in it than if they had taken part in amateur theatricals together. It was perfectly decorous, and he was there to play propriety – and yet there was a vivid kind of reality about it.

...Jelkes knew in his heart, and felt that Hugh knew also, that what was going on was very far from make-believe. Jelkes was no psychic; he had never seen anything in his life; but he could picture Mona's electric hands going out and touching Hugh and drawing him to her, for he knew that that was what she was doing in her imagination.

He pictured to himself the weaving hands drawing lines of light upon the air, and then reaching right out, like tenuous silvery tentacles, and stroking Hugh. He could see Mona's hands on Hugh's shoulders, although she was a dozen yards away. And then he saw what he never expected to see – he saw a grey, shadowy replica of Hugh standing a yard or so in front of himself, so that there were two Hughs, one black and one silvery grey. Jelkes gasped, feeling as if the universe were turning round on him. He had only been picturing in his imagination what he knew Mona was picturing, being familiar with the technique of that operation; he had never visualised Hugh moving out of his physical body – then why had he seen it? True, he had only seen it in his mind's eye, but nevertheless, he had seen it, and he certainly had not formulated it. The picture had risen spontaneously without any volition on his part, and it set Jelkes thinking.

This is obviously quite hot stuff, and the type of problems that can arise in this type of approach are explained in *"The Esoteric Philosophy of Love and Marriage"*.

If the greater cosmic forces should be called down by an individual who is not working in conjunction with another who is a suitable channel of return, they will be very apt to make a path of returning for themselves through any conductile vehicle that approaches sufficiently close, leaping the gap like an electric spark; and if the individual who receives the force be of insufficient calibre to carry the voltage, her emotional nature will, metaphorically speaking, fuse, and there will be an open circuit of cosmic forces which will also fuse the positive or male vehicle, burn all in their immediate neighbourhood, and break the contact with the Divine forces. Anyone who is familiar with those circles that are interested in occult studies must have seen this happen, for it is a very common occurrence among those who, while only partially instructed, seek to operate the unseen forces. How often does some man, who as a teacher and initiator is doing fine work, suddenly cast all aside for the sake of a woman who, utterly unworthy of him...

This can happen in various ways it should be said, for any blowing of fuses can also easily result in uncontrolled antagonism, of which there is ample evidence in the history of many short-lived occult groups who contact powers that some of their members are incapable of handling. Schism and mutual recrimination are also common enough in the history of all religious movements, and various schools of thought, particularly in psychology and the arts, in fact wherever creative forces are involved, indicating that the problem is not confined to occultism alone.

To revert to Dion Fortune's text, however, we may see how the problem occurs in particular relation to occultism:

> [These forces] will, in fact, go to whatever part of our nature we direct our attention, and if we have not trained ourselves sufficiently in thought-control to be sure of keeping our minds off any particular subject for a certain period, we are running grave risks if we open the channels of our nature to more force than it is normally constructed to deal with. The risky enlargement of receptiveness is effected by certain forms of breathing, meditation, or ritual magic, and the risk lies in the fact that if a sensual thought intrude into consciousness at a time when the channels are open and the forces are flowing, those forces will immediately follow the focus of attention, and the result will be an outbreak of passion and sensuality. It is by concentration of thought that these powers are held to their work.

It should be said however, that the pair working in isolation, as occurs in the Dion Fortune novels, is a somewhat unstable situation, even with the guidance of a higher third. The advantage of this situation in the novels is that it exemplifies magical dynamics in simplest terms but it is not one that should be emulated in real life without some caution.

The bulk of responsible magical work of high potential is worked not by lone pairs but by formal groups of highly trained people. There is thus a pooling and distribution of magnetic resources and participants working in polar relationship will do so only in their function as officers mediating forces, not as personalities looking for emotional fulfilment. There is a fundamental and important difference here, but one of the problems of trying to teach occultism via the novel is that the fictional genre demands that motivation be expressed in terms of personality relationships. This has been the case with the two novels considered so far, and also with the earlier novel *"The Demon Lover"*. In all three cases the magic is largely on the level of mutual psychotherapeutics, mostly by protagonists who are not too sure what they are doing, and who are fortunate to find that the end result is the state of matrimony. In the two novels that follow however we see something of the formidable "impersonality" that can characterise the true adept.

The Sea Priestess

The priestess figure in this next novel is certainly well aware of her function right from the start. There is little psychological development in the character of Vivien Le Fay Morgan. She appears mysteriously, gets on with her job and then as mysteriously disappears, closely reflecting the role of an ancient goddess. Any development that takes place as far as she goes is concerned is in regard to her magical work, which in practical terms requires the preparation of a sea temple in an appropriate spot, along with the training of a male assistant to help her.

She may also undergo less personal development because, in contrast to the previous priestess figures, all of whom were in their twenties, Vivien would seem to be a very well preserved senior citizen, not that she is incapable of casting a spell of glamour over Wilfred Maxwell.

He, hen pecked into asthma by a dominating sister and an ailing mother is not the most prepossessing of heroes. Nonetheless he proves to be an admirable general factotum as far as the Miss

Morgan is concerned. Not only does he perform the function of estate agent but also architect, clerk of works, removal man, interior designer, decorator, symbolic artist and magical apprentice.

The relationship between them can hardly be called one of magnetic interchange in the sense of Ursula and Ted or Mona and Hugh in the earlier novels. Miss Morgan undoubtedly wears the trousers, so to speak, in her relationship with Wilfred, and they are armour plated. There is certainly a magnetic interplay but it is hardly one of level exchange. Wilfred is pushed into the love of an unattainable ideal where there is no question of any physical sexual relationship entering into things, despite her apparent nobility.

This brings to mind an explanation in *"The Esoteric Philosophy of Love and Marriage"* regarding the possible achievement of an inner self-polarisation by means of an interchange between the personality and the higher self.

> If an individual is sufficiently evolved to have any of the levels of his individuality in function and fully correlated with his consciousness, he can cause the flow and return of cosmic force to take place within his own organism, and thereby attain a considerable degree of power and enlightenment. For instance, the spiritual ideals and aims, and the abstract perceptions of principles belonging to the fifth and sixth vehicles can be used to illumine and inspire the activities of the personality,

This is somewhat abstractly stated, but in practical terms implies that this aim can be assisted by focussing upon an ideal personal figure who embodies the intuitive and spiritual wisdom of the individual's own higher self. It may take the form of communing with an inner daemon, muse, guardian angel, god or goddess, master or saint or other spiritually exalted being. This may well turn out to be a real unseen companion of the heart, but can also prove to be an element of one's own higher consciousness. This is a higher analogue of the magic mirror of the astral light when images are allowed to rise in the course of imaginal magical work. It also means that much "channelled" communication may have its source in the individuals own higher consciousness rather than from an objective higher plane being. However, the quality need be none the worse for that.

What the Sea Priestess is doing is a variation on this kind of individual work whereby she provides a vividly present but unattainable ideal in the form of the contra-sexual image wherein her admirer may find reflected something of his own higher consciousness. This is a similar dynamic to that employed by some of the medieval troubadours in the tradition of courtly love, where an actual human woman was placed upon a pedestal and all but worshipped.

The subject is a complex one with diverse developments and applications. In one form of medieval expression it definitely led to a physical sexual liaison, whereas in other cases it became abstracted into the cult of the Blessed Virgin. It seems to have originated in Arabic mysticism and to have infiltrated Christian Europe from Moslem Spain and via the Crusader Kingdoms of the Near East.

Another development from it is in certain aspects of the alchemical tradition, as Dion Fortune acknowledges in her Introduction to *"The Esoteric Philosophy of Love and Marriage"* where she quotes Blavatsky's *"The Secret Doctrine"* in support:

"For the production of alchemical results such as the Elixir of Life and the Philosopher's Stone...the spiritual help of the woman was needed by the male Alchemist. But woe to the Alchemist who should take this in the dead-letter sense of physical union."

Wilfred Maxwell receives the fruits of his labours in service to the Sea Priestess after she has departed from the scene. Circumstances and his own realisations then conspire, (and these two factors are ever mirror images of each other), to bring him freedom from his family, marriage to a local girl whom he has overlooked all these years, and eventually the blossoming of this marriage into a fruitful magnetic and magical partnership such as he had desired of the unattainable Sea Priestess.

The level of magical working within this novel is also revealed to be on a higher level in that the third element in the polar equation, the supervising adept, is now an inner plane being, referred to as the Priest of the Moon.

In Sephirothic terms the novel is of the sphere of Yesod, the sphere of the great moon and etheric tides of the inner earth. The magnetic significance of place is also important, for the temple working is on a headland with ancient associations that is one of the few places on the English coast that faces the deep Atlantic, without Ireland or the Cornish peninsula getting in the way.

The locality is embroidered somewhat by Dion Fortune to make it an even more magical place but nonetheless the actual location does carry a strong magnetic aura that is perhaps even enhanced for those familiar with Dion Fortune's novel. The bell shaped hill in the story is Brent Knoll in Somerset and the rocky headland Brean Down, and although Brent Knoll has survived the laying down of the M5 motorway which now bends round it rather than going through it as originally planned, it is perhaps doubtful how long Brean Down will survive the steady encroachment of caravan parks and proposed theme park and leisure centre. At least the Sea Priestess timed her coming and her going well, when these were still wild and untamed shores.

Another interesting factor is that Vivien le Fay Morgan seems capable of casting a certain spell over the reader as well as the hero of the tale. She did so over her author too, for Dion Fortune felt compelled to write a sequel allowing the character her head to reveal other aspects of her strange wisdom.

In some respects she deliberately represents in her personal behaviour the figure of the goddess Isis, who is traditionally veiled, and this is why she effects large brimmed hats and turned up collars at the expense, as she admits, of appearing something of a poseur. Some adepts have indeed been colourful figures but others, such as those of the 17th century Rosicrucian brotherhood, sought anonymity and adopted the ordinary dress and customs of the country in which they happened to reside.

Dion Fortune's depiction of adepts follows certain characteristics, one of which is a taste for epicurianism. Both Miss Vivien Le Fay Morgan and Alick Brangwyn live very individual life styles, selecting choice foods that they may have specially imported from small producers the world over. They also have private financial means to live in secluded places furnished exquisitely according to their taste, concealed behind grubby commonplace exteriors, and served by admirable discrete and dedicated retainers. There is a certain unrealistic idealism in all of this although perhaps it reflects a certain utopian ideal of gracious living to which we all should aspire.

However, all, as children of their time, have a penchant for tobacco which seems a little incongruous nowadays, particularly as one of Alick Brangwyn's justifications for his life style is healthy living, which however does not seem to take much account of pulmonary carcinoma. But we speak with the wisdom of hindsight.

The depiction of adepts or masters has always been a thorny question but on the whole Dion Fortune has a very down to earth sensibility in this matter. As she trenchantly observed in her article on *"The Winged Bull"*

> ...alas, human nature is not altogether estimable, and whatever my characters may or may not be, they are at least human beings. Brangwyn, who ought, being represented as an adept, to be likewise a plaster saint – according to my critics, anyway, which shows how much they know about adepts – is represented as a man, who, although he has great knowledge, is not perfect in wisdom. This, they say, is a weakness in the book, overlooking the fact that if Brangwyn had been perfect in wisdom, there would have been no plot, because he would have nipped Fouldes in the bud and Ursula would never have got involved with him.
>
> Is this true to the psychology of an adept? I only know that it is true to my psychology; and the psychology of Mme. Blavatsky and Mrs. Besant, though whether any or all of us are adepts is a matter of taste.

Moon Magic

In this final novel the Sea Priestess turns up in London and her magic is of a more advanced kind, although she use much the same dynamics. She is paired this time with a considerably more high powered male protagonist than Wilfred, the Somerset estate agent. This time her partner is an eminent neurologist with an international reputation, Dr Rupert Malcolm. He too has his psychological and domestic problems however, as his wife is a permanent invalid and so he is another male lacking sexual or magnetic polarisation on any level.

This again is exactly the type of magical collaborator that Lilith Le Fay, as she now calls herself, is looking for. In a sense she is a pretty ruthless operator and if judged in normal human terms could be accused of the worst kind of emotional domination of a vulnerable partner, who is already pretty sorely tried by his less esoteric womenfolk.

One might indeed expect a 120-year-old priestess aiming to work at this level to seek out a priest of her own age and calibre rather than pick on some complete beginner who is not even remotely interested in the magical arts in the first place. However, this would not give much pabulum for a story and here we have what is in effect an advanced magical textbook passing off as a novel.

In this respect we have to say that it is hardly the type of text that can readily be used by a beginner starting to learn the ropes, even if Dr. Malcolm has to make his way in similar circumstances. Nonetheless its descriptive passages of inner experience are valid and give a fair idea of the kind of thing that is to be expected within the higher grades of the western esoteric tradition. It is of course one thing to dress up in magical robes and go through the motions of a ritual script and another to have developed the interior ability to raise awareness to the higher levels of consciousness so that these dynamics may be mediated down the planes in the process of a ceremonial rite.

Insofar that Dr Malcolm is very much a beginner in the occult way we can be shown all the problems of such a disparate magical pairing, which in truth is rather like an experienced mountaineer taking a beginner up the north face of the Eiger – not likely to be a comfortable experience for either party. He is all the time looking at things through the eyes, and with the feelings and speculations, of the personality, while she is working at an impersonal level of higher consciousness. It is a highly artificial situation but in the context of the novel provides dramatic tension to sustain the purposes of fiction, with a sub-plot of reincarnationary memories and the cliff hanging suspense as to whether or not he will stand the emotional strain she puts him through without raping or strangling her.

She might well be accused of a high handed ruthlessness that amounts to the vivisection of human emotions - and she is sufficiently aware of the issues involved to use this comparison herself. Nonetheless Dr Malcolm, as Wilfred Maxwell before him, gets his reward. Maxwell is led to a happy married life of more than normal fulfilment with a suitable spouse. Malcolm on the other hand is vouchsafed an experience on a high spiritual level that might be regarded as the equivalent of samedhi in a western equivalent of tantrik yoga.

This passage might also be seen as the ultimate stage in a type of magnetic interchange that has been foreshadowed in Ursula's recharging of Ted Murchison and in Mona's moon dance before Hugh Paston. The preliminaries in this case are not quite so simple, involving mirror working and a species of somnambulistic trance, but the effects are correspondingly startling.

He could feel the beginnings of the gathering of power. The magic was starting to work. He was in the place of the priest, and whatever this unknown force might be, it meant to work through him. He steadied himself and waited. Let it work! It was the only way. He needn't do anything. It was a natural force, and it would use him, its natural channel; all he had to do was let it use him.

He concentrated on the idea of passivity, of presenting an open channel to that which would come to him from behind, and through him to her. Great Nature was drawing near; the tide was rising along the appointed channel.

Then, for the first time, he knew himself as part of Nature. Such a thing had never entered his head before, for all his study of comparative anatomy. He knew that, deep in him, was a level that had never been separated from the earth soul, just as the image of the primordial woman in the Black Temple had never been cut away from the living rock but was united to it along her back-bone, and he knew that he too, at the spinal level, belonged to Nature, and that through the channel of that hollow rod Nature would use him, and he gave himself to that power.

Then in a flash he felt the levels coalesce; that which he had previously known as purely physical he felt to be spiritual as well. The force was rising from the spinal to the cerebral level and passing out of the province of physiology.

Then he felt it lift level again, and pass out of the province of psychology into that which lies beyond. A vision of starry spheres seemed around him. The room had faded. Lilith had changed into Isis and he himself was the Nature-force rising up from primordial deeps to fertilise her! He was not a man, he was a force. He was part of the earth-life, and Nature was manifesting through him; and she, Lilith, was not a person either; she was the goal of the force – that was all. It was quite simple. The force had taken charge. There was no thought, no feeling, save the terrific pressure of force that used his organism as a channel of manifestation. The less of personality there was in this the better – let the force do its own work!

It was like being struck by lightning. The power came, and passed, and as its reverberations went rolling away into space, he saw as the clouds parted before his eyes the face of Lilith le Fay, but made young and lovely, and he gazed at her as Adam must have gazed at the newly-created Eve when he awoke from his deep sleep and found her beside him.

The straight run-through of power had blown clear all the obstructions and blockings and tangles in his nature just as a choked channel is cleared by a force pump. From level to level the power had risen, and cleared the channel as it went. He was a man utterly re-made. How, and by what, he could not say, He only knew that, exhausted and at peace, he was ready to sing with the morning stars as soon as his strength came back to him, and that his mind had the crystal lucidity of sunlit space.

This sequence illustrates some of the parallels with yoga that we have been examining in *"The Circuit of Force"*. The purpose of it all was not simply the experience of some kind of cosmic orgasm even if this is how it may have felt at the time to Dr. Malcolm. Rather was it part of Lilith Le Fay's magical aim of freeing the constraints of society, bending the bars of the over crowded monkey house, bringing clean air to the emotional cholera pit, by means of working upon her chosen priest whom she had trained and who had himself grievously suffered from these very constraints, and which probably gave him the necessary power to function in this way and to have been selected for the work in the first place. A strange intermeshing of karma and destiny.

And who is to tell if the magic of Lilith Le Fay did not have some contribution to the breaking of the chains that were later to occur in the free-wheeling nineteen sixties? After which nothing was quite the same again.

INDEX

Other titles available from Thoth Publications

AN INTRODUCTION TO RITUAL MAGIC
By Dion Fortune & Gareth Knight

At the time this was something of a unique event in esoteric
publishing - a new book by the legendary Dion Fortune. Especially
with its teachings on the theory and practice of ritual or ceremonial
magic, by one who, like the heroine of two of her other novels,
was undoubtedly "a mistress of that art".
In this work Dion Fortune deals in successive chapters with Types
of Mind Working; Mind Training; The Use of Ritual; Psychic
Perception; Ritual Initiation; The Reality of the Subtle Planes;
Focusing the Magic Mirror; Channelling the Forces; The Form of
the Ceremony; and The Purpose of Magic - with appendices on
Talisman Magic and Astral Forms.
Each chapter is supplemented and expanded by a companion
chapter on the same subject by Gareth Knight. In Dion Fortune's
day the conventions of occult secrecy prevented her from being
too explicit on the practical details of magic, except in works
of fiction. These veils of secrecy having now been drawn back,
Gareth Knight has taken the opportunity to fill in much practical
information that Dion Fortune might well have included had she
been writing today.
In short, in this unique collaboration of two magical practitioners
and teachers, we are presented with a valuable and up-to-date text
on the practice of ritual or ceremonial magic "as it is". 'That is to
say, as a practical, spiritual, and psychic discipline, far removed
from the lurid superstition and speculation that are the hall mark
of its treatment in sensational journalism and channels of popular
entertainment.

ISBN 978-1-870450-31-0 Deluxe Hardback Limited edition
ISBN 978-1-870450-26-4 Soft cover edition

THE STORY OF DION FORTUNE
As told to Charles Fielding and Carr Collins.

Dion Fortune and Aleister Crowley stand as the twentieth century's most influential leaders of the Western Esoteric Tradition. They were very different in their backgrounds, scholarship and style.

But, for many, Dion Fortune is the chosen exemplar of the Tradition - with no drugs, no homosexuality and no kinks. This book tells of her formative years and of her development.

At the end, she remains a complex and enigmatic figure, who can only be understood in the light of the system she evolved and worked to great effect.

There can be no definitive "Story of Dion Fortune". This book must remain incompete and full of errors. However, readers may find themselves led into an experience of initiation as envisaged by this fearless and dedicated woman.

ISBN 978-1-870450-33-1

*   *   *   *   *

PRACTICAL TECHNIQUES OF MODERN MAGIC
By Marian Green

What is the essence of ritual magic?
How are the symbols used to create change?
Can I safely take steps in ritual on my own?
How does magic fit into the pattern of life in the modern world?
Will I be able to master the basic arts?
All these questions and many more are answered within the pages of this book.

ISBN 978-1-870450-14-0

ENTRANCE TO THE MAGICAL QABALAH
By Melita Denning & Osborne Phillips.

In this significant new work, Denning and Phillips set forth the essential traditions and teachings of the treasury of mystical and arcane learning which is known as the Qabalah.

Everything that is, ourselves included, is seen by the Qabalah as existing in some or all of four "Worlds" or levels of being.

These Worlds supply the whole fabric of our existence, and we in turn are integral parts of them. It is from this primal unity of person and kosmos that our great aspirations spring: our longing to know and to experience the reality, not only of that mystery which encompasses us, but also of that mystery of selfhood which is within us. For each of these mysteries reflects the other.

This very fact of the reflected likeness gives us a key to both mysteries, a key to mystical and to psychological understanding, It is this fact which makes magic possible. It is this same fact which makes the Qabalah a coherent system in which the aspirant does not follow blindly but with a comprehension ever increasing, and without ever losing that uplifting sense of wonder and of adventure which are rightfully a part of life itself.

With clarity and insight, the authors explore the origins and spirit of this system, its relationship to the Hermetic writings and the Zohar, its great patterns of thought and method, its spiritual sources of power and its tremendous creative potential. The question of evil is addressed in a study of the Qlipphoth and unbalanced force. Here also, among many other vital topics, are considered the role of the Supernal Mother in the cosmic scheme, the structure and functions of the psyche, spiritual realms, the destiny of the soul after death, the nature of the Gods, the way of magical attainment and the crossing of the Abyss.

ISBN 978-1-870450-35-5

PRACTICAL MAGIC AND THE WESTERN MYSTERY TRADITION
Unpublished Essays and Articles by W. E. Butler.

W. E. Butler, a devoted friend and colleague of the celebrated occultist Dion Fortune, was among those who helped build the Society of the Inner Light into the foremost Mystery School of its day. He then went on to found his own school, the Servants of the Light, which still continues under the guidance of Dolores Ashcroft-Nowicki, herself an occultist and author of note and the editor and compiler of this volume.

PRACTICAL MAGIC AND THE WESTERN TRADITION is a collection of previously unpublished articles, training papers, and lectures covering many aspects of practical magic in the context of western occultism that show W. E. Butler not only as a leading figure in the magical tradition of the West, but also as one of its greatest teachers.

Subjects covered include:

What makes an Occultist
Ritual Training
Inner Plane Contacts and Rays
The With Cult
Keys in Practical Magic
Telesmatic Images
Words of Power
An Explanation of Some Psychic Phenomena

ISBN 978-1-870450-32-4